MIAMI

METROPOLITAN PORTRAITS

Metropolitan Portraits explores the contemporary metropolis in its

diverse blend of past and present. Each volume describes a North

American urban region in terms of historical experience, spatial

configuration, culture, and contemporary issues. Books in the

series are intended to promote discussion and understanding of

metropolitan North America at the start of the twenty-first century.

JUDITH A. MARTIN, SERIES EDITOR

MIAMI

Mistress of the Americas

JAN NIJMAN

University of Pennsylvania Press
Philadelphia

Published by
University of Pennsylvania Press
Philadelphia, Pennsylvania 19104-4112
www.upenn.edu/pennpress

Printed in the United States of America on acid-free paper

10 9 8 7 6 5 4 3 2 1

Library of Congress Cataloging-in-Publication Data
Nijman, Jan.
    Miami : mistress of the Americas / Jan Nijman.
        p. cm. — (Metropolitan portraits)
    Includes bibliographical references and index.
    ISBN 978-0-8122-4298-0 (hbk. : alk. paper)
    1. Urbanization—Florida—Miami—History.   2. Miami (Fla.)—History.   I. Title.
    HT384.U62F645   2010
    307.7609759'381—dc22

                                        2010025223

CONTENTS

PREFACE

Once viewed from the North as a peripheral place or a city on the edge, Miami has in past decades moved to the center of a bigger, hemispheric stage. Its story is of a remarkable urban transformation, timed to perfection to coincide with the surging forces of globalization. Miami is the "mistress of the Americas" in terms of her cultural influence and economic dominance at the nexus of north and south. The city has unparalleled hemispheric connections, a strong hold on transnational communities, unique hybrid qualities, and a powerful, if subtle, role in the shaping of inter-American perceptions.

At the same time, Miami has developed an intriguing urban persona through the years. This subtropical city, so congenitally adept at stirring the imaginations of strangers, has always lured visitors and migrants. During its first half-century they came primarily from the American north, then from the Latin south, and eventually its magnetic pull extended across the hemisphere and beyond. If the city's seductive appeal is one half of that story, the other half is that few ever ended up staying permanently. Home was, and is, usually somewhere else. In that sense, too, the city invokes the mistress metaphor. By many measures, this is the most transient of all major metropolitan areas in America.

Transience, one might say, is Miami's *genius loci*. It has been the city's defining characteristic from the beginning to the present day. Transience is the underlying current in different historical episodes and geographical parts: from the real estate bonanza of the 1920s to the cocaine cowboys of the 1980s; or from the migrant labor camps in south Miami-Dade to the affluent gated communities along Biscayne Bay.

Understanding Miami requires an integrated perspective of the ways in which economic, political, and cultural developments have combined against an unusual historical and geographical backdrop. Miami's location, inside the United States but protruding deeply into the South, always seemed to destine the city for a special future. Miami was in the right place, at the right time, to emerge as a leading "world city" in the Americas in the early 1980s, a sort of a hyper-node, or massive urban router, connecting business flows between north and south. Its rise owed much to the cross-cultural affinities of Miami's ethnically hybrid workforce, many of whom originated elsewhere.

South Florida has always been the décor to population shifts yet there are major differences in the identity of its residents. Locals, born and raised in the area, make up only one-fifth of the population. This may be "their" city but many are struggling to get by and seem frozen in place in a city that is permanently in flux. Exiles are those who have come to Miami of political or economic necessity. To them, Miami is a temporary haven and their mind-set is expressly focused on a return (real or illusory) to the homeland. Mobiles are the kinetic elite who reside in Miami by choice. They are generally affluent, well educated, and live in the city's most prized neighborhoods. The duration of their stay is usually unpredictable.

This biography of Miami is about the city's international position but also about its local character, each shaping the other. It engages matters of political economy but also probes the city's social fabric and argues why the city feels the way it does. Over the years, Miami has assumed an ever closer resemblance to a social laboratory, raising critical questions about identity, attachment to place, citizenship, transnationalism, rights to the city, and cosmopolitanism. The book neither chastises nor celebrates Miami—it provides a careful and revealing dissection of one of the most intriguing cities of our time, one that offers a window into the global urban future.

I am grateful to the John Simon Guggenheim Memorial Foundation for a Guggenheim Fellowship that allowed me to embark on this project; to Alvah Chapman (who died in 2009) and Maurice Ferré for graciously allowing me interviews about some crucial moments in the city's history; to Chris Hanson for creating the maps and graphics; to Robin Bachin, Harm de Blij, Mazen el-Labban, Richard Grant, Miguel Kanai, Jean-Francois Lejeune, Peter Muller, Elizabeth Plater-Zyberk, Alejandro Portes, and Allan Shulman for interesting discussions and helpful comments along the way; to Daniel Pals, Associate Dean for Interdisciplinary Programs in the College of Arts & Sciences of the University of Miami, for financial support; to the publishers of the *Annals of the American Academy of Political and Social Science*, the *Annals of the Association of American Geographers*, the *Journal for Economic and Social Geography*, and *Urban Geography* for permission to use some ideas that originally appeared in the pages of those journals; to AP/ Wide World Photos, the State of Florida Archives, the Miami Herald Media Company, the University of Miami Libraries, the U.S. Coast Guard, Robert Kloosterman, Dewi Nijman, and Soraya Nijman for permission to reproduce photographs; and, for editorial support, to Judith Martin and Robert Lockhart of the University of Pennsylvania Press.

Early Liaisons

The Miami Circle sits on Biscayne Bay at the mouth of the river, on the south bank. It is a perfect circle with a diameter of thirty-eight feet. Along the perimeter are twenty-four equidistant and identical holes cut in the limestone bedrock. The holes were probably cut for the base of the wooden pillars of a round building. Other finds at this archaeological site included bones, human teeth, shell tools, stone axe-heads, and charcoal deposits.[1]

Radiocarbon dating of the charcoal indicated that the structure is about nineteen hundred years old, making it the oldest known human-made structure in South Florida. Most archaeologists agree that it was built and used by the Tequesta, a branch of the larger Native American Glades tribe that inhabited the coastal areas of central and southern Florida since about ten thousand years ago. There is no clear evidence what the building was used for, but most likely it had some ceremonial purpose and it must have been surrounded by other structures and dwellings.

It is an unusual site because it is the only one in the entire United States with this kind of structural foundation and it pre-dates other known permanent settlements on the East Coast. It is so unusual, indeed, that in the wake of its discovery there was considerable skepticism. Some argued that it was not a Tequesta site at all but the remains of an early twentieth-century septic tank installation (this view still has not gone away entirely). Others speculated about the role of Mayans, given the circular and apparent celestial orientation of the building. And then there were those, inevitably, who attributed the structure to the cosmic design of aliens.

The circle is of great importance because it provides an unprecedented window on the area's prehistory, even if it all remains rather mysterious—and we will stick with the view that it was indeed a Tequesta site. It is also significant because, after a long struggle, it was saved from the hands of real estate developers and added to the National Register of Historic Places in 2002.

The circle was discovered only in July 1998 after the demolition of a 1940s apartment complex. The prime real estate site was bought by a developer for $8.5 million, with plans for a luxury condominium tower of the sort that have sprung up all over downtown Miami in the past decade. A routine archaeological survey by the Miami-Dade Historic Preservation Division stumbled upon the remains and put a temporary halt to the development process. What followed was an intense struggle involving the developer, archaeologists, the City of Miami, the State of Florida, Miami-Dade County, Native American groups, various public organizations, and stables of lawyers.

In 1999, it almost came to the point that the circle was excavated and moved to another location for preservation—this was, after, all, a highly desirable residential location. The idea was supported by the developer and by Joe Carollo, then the mayor of Miami, whose mind must have been on the prospect of future property taxes. It was a foolish notion even in development-crazed Miami and it ran into opposition. The stonemason hired for the job, Joshua Billig, publicly quit and briefly became something of a local hero. In the end, the developer handed the site to the State of Florida for the sum of $27 million.

But modern-day Miami is constantly in flux and its attention span regarding public matters is notoriously short. There is little time for history in this city. For nearly twelve years after its discovery, the Miami Circle was a neglected, abandoned, and inaccessible grassy lot adjacent to some busy high-rise construction sites. A groundbreaking ceremony in August 2009 to turn the site into a park was based on tentative budget agreements between the city and the state, but few seem to care. The circle stands as a lonely reminder of a distant and disconnected past.

The Tequesta, their name so recorded by Spanish explorers in the sixteenth century, were the first inhabitants of coastal southeast Florida for which we have a historical record.[2] They descended from Paleo-Indians who came from the north and they were probably in contact with other so-called Glades tribes to the west and north in Florida such as the Calusa. It was a sparse population of several thousands, with small settlements mainly on top of parts of the Atlantic Ridge that rose slightly above the Everglades and that were free from flooding. The area around the circle was one of those small settlements, probably counting about three hundred people. Their word "Miami" meant "sweet water," referring to the fresh water coming down the river. The inland environment was harsh and the Tequesta had chosen a prime location. Being at once on the river and on the bay gave them maximum mobility and they were close to their main food sources. The sea breezes and ocean views must have been as soothing and serene as they are today. Extensive mangroves provided a protective barrier to stormy seas and an ideal spawning environment for many fish. Multiple generations lived what was mostly a tranquil and sustainable existence, supported by fishing, hunting, and gathering. It was probably the most stable human occupation that South Florida would ever know, but it was not to last.

The first European encounter was in 1513, when Juan Ponce de Leon set foot on the shores of Biscayne Bay. He had accompanied

Columbus on his second voyage to the New World and was now the Spanish Crown's first appointed governor of Puerto Rico. Ponce de Leon called the peninsula La Florida—it is not clear if this was in reference to the area's flowery appearance or because the landing occurred at the time of Easter, in Spanish "Pascua Florida." Popular legend has it that Ponce de Leon was in search of the Fountain of Youth (old Spanish sources mention his lack of virility) but more likely he was looking for gold, as were most Spanish explorers of the era. Either way, he did not get lucky. During an expedition to Florida's west coast in 1521 his forces were caught in skirmishes with Calusa Indians. A poisoned spear was thrust in his shoulder; it killed him shortly after he made his escape to Cuba. Ponce de Leon's visits to Florida seem to have been largely inconsequential in their own right but they did, of course, open the door for subsequent Spanish incursions, which were usually staged from Cuba. Most of these were confined to the much more accessible northern parts of Florida. In 1565, Pedro Menendez de Aviles founded St. Augustine, fortified the place, brought in Jesuit priests, and oversaw the construction of the first church. This was four decades before the foundation of Jamestown, and so St. Augustine can be considered the first permanent European settlement in North America.

Menendez also established a small mission on Biscayne Bay. He brought a Tequesta Indian back to Havana to immerse him in Spanish Catholic ways, intending to return him to Miami a few years later. But the mission appears to have been largely ineffective; by 1570 it was abandoned. Hence, while faraway northern Florida experienced notable change in the second half of the sixteenth century, things remained quietly the same on Biscayne Bay. Much of this must be attributed to the inaccessible nature of the place: the treacherous reefs deterred ships, the heat and mosquitoes were hard to endure by any visitors, and the lack of navigable rivers precluded easy reconnaissance and mobility. The

Miami River, it should be noted, led only a few miles inland where it transitioned into the Everglades.

The historical record on seventeenth-century South Florida is even thinner, with nothing more than some scant reports on small and usually ill-fated Spanish missions that operated from Cuba. In the early 1700s, the Spanish intensified efforts at conversion and brought ever larger numbers of Tequesta to Cuba and some even to Spain. Most did not survive. The lack of resistance to European pathogens, fatal to so many Native American populations in general, had caused a steady decline of the Tequesta. The Spanish Empire in Florida lasted about two hundred years, from 1565 to 1763. The settlements of St. Augustine and Pensacola in the north were the main accomplishments. In South Florida, the Spanish had not come to stay and they did not leave a single artifact of historical significance. But they did bring diseases that virtually wiped out the Tequesta. In 1763, when Spain ceded Florida to Great Britain, the last Tequesta left with the Spanish for Havana. Southeast Florida was deserted.

Great Britain's rule in Florida lasted only two decades and as far as South Florida was concerned, it was a non-event. Britain divided Florida in two separate colonies with West Florida ruled from Pensacola and East Florida administered from St. Augustine. They did manage to attract more settlers to these parts with newly designed land grant schemes but South Florida was mostly beyond their horizon. British rule came to an abrupt end with the American War of Independence. Ironically, since Spain had sided with the patriots against the British, the Treaty of Paris of 1783, which ended the war, stipulated that Florida return to Spanish hands.

The second Spanish period witnessed sustained arrivals into northern Florida of British colonists, Native Americans, and former black slaves who were seeking economic opportunity or refuge from the newly formed United States. The Spanish referred to the Creek Indians as *cimmarones* (renegades), which later became "Seminoles." Spanish rule was weak: English colonists in western Florida proclaimed allegiance to the British Crown, and Seminoles supported the Creek wars with the United States across the border in Georgia. Incursions of U.S. troops into northern Florida culminated in the First Seminole War of 1817, and Spain was effectively reduced to the role of spectator. By 1821, the United States and Spain agreed to a deal in which the United States acquired Florida by renouncing any claims to Texas. With Florida's accession to the United States, the Seminoles spread out into the central and southern parts of the state, with U.S. troops on their heels.

During the first half of the nineteenth century, tension between the U.S. government and Native Americans in Florida continued to build. Seminole defiance of U.S. reservation policies led to the Second Seminole War from 1835 to 1842, which took place mostly in central Florida. It was a bloody conflict that took the lives of fifteen hundred U.S. troops (as a result of disease, mainly) and many more Native Americans—nobody bothered to keep track. One of the earliest victims on the U.S. side was Virginia-born Major Francis Dade, killed with his entire company by Seminoles in 1835 on a campaign near Ocala, an event that became known as the Dade Massacre. Dade County was named after him in 1836, even though he probably never set foot near Biscayne Bay. When it was first created, Dade County was much bigger than now and included present-day Broward and Palm Beach counties.

As time went on, the war spread southward and reached the area around Biscayne Bay. There were a small number of white settlers who would sometimes seek refuge in Key West, which had grown into a respectable town where many made a living as ship wreckers. One of the main incidents in newly founded Dade County involved the lighthouse at Cape Florida, at the southern tip of Key Biscayne just across the bay from Miami. The light-house was built by the U.S. government in 1825 to bring an end to the large number of shipwrecks caused by the reefs (the government constructed the first lighthouse in Key West as well, at the same time). In 1836, Seminoles protesting harassment by U.S. troops attacked the Cape Florida lighthouse and set it on fire. The lighthouse keeper made it out alive and joined his family in Key West, but his assistant was killed. The lighthouse was rebuilt in 1855 and is still there, the earliest modern landmark of Greater Miami.

During and after the Seminole wars some groups of Native Americans moved into South Florida, and some settled in the less accessible Everglades to be safe from U.S. troops. One of these groups was the Miccosukee. They were closely associated with Seminoles but maintained a distinct language and identity. Since the mid-nineteenth century, they have carved out an existence on the tiny islands in the Everglades, living off fish, duck, deer, and small crops and getting around by canoe. Their exact where-abouts were not documented until the introduction of airboats after World War II. It took until 1962 for the Miccosukee to be officially recognized by the State of Florida, and to acquire sovereign nation status within the United States. When discovered, they were the only surviving Native American tribe of the Great Creek Confederacy east of the Mississippi River. With a population count of about 550, they are presently the longest continuous population group of Greater Miami.

For white North American and European settlers, South Florida was hardly an appealing place during the Seminole wars. The official population of Dade County actually declined between 1840 and 1860, from 446 to 83 persons. Most whites in Dade County at this time were soldiers stationed at Fort Dallas, the military post established in 1836 on the north bank of the Miami River, near present day Lummus Park. Fort Dallas was not a real fort but

Figure 1. The Florida lighthouse, undated photograph. Originally built in 1825 and reconstructed in 1855. State Archives of Florida.

merely a collection of barracks built on land owned by Richard Fitzpatrick, who was born in South Carolina but lived in Key West. He owned about two thousand acres and tried to operate a plantation, but business was not good. In 1842, he sold the property to his nephew, William English, and he moved to Texas. It was William English who platted the "Village of Miami," but people kept referring to the area around the bay as "Fort Dallas." About ten years later English, too, packed his bags. He sold the property in different parcels and joined Fitzpatrick to try his luck in the California gold rush. Fort Dallas continued as a military post through the Civil War and was then abandoned.

South Florida was one of the most remote, inaccessible, and "empty" parts of the country. In much of the rest of the nation, and many parts of the world, the Industrial Revolution, hand in hand with urbanization, was transforming human society. In 1880, a number of major cities had formed in the United States, along with many smaller ones. The New York urban region, the largest of all, had almost reached a population of 2 million. Philadelphia was approaching 1 million and Chicago half a million. Cities like Boston, Baltimore, New Orleans, and St. Louis each housed over 300,000 people. San Francisco, all the way on America's West Coast, had almost a quarter of a million. The main cities nearest to Miami were in Georgia: Atlanta and Savannah each had over 30,000 inhabitants. In that same year, 1880, the entire area of Dade County had an official count of 257 persons.[3]

The last decade of the nineteenth century witnessed a growing number of farmers and homesteaders as well as the arrival of some enterprising individuals whose investment in the area proved crucial to its future development. What is interesting about Miami's beginnings is not just that it happened so late, but that so many key players were established outsiders who came and went, without planting any roots. Foremost among these early pioneers were Julia Tuttle and Henry Flagler.

Tuttle, a widow from Cleveland, Ohio, arrived with her two children in 1891, at the age of fifty-one. She had inherited some 40 acres of land north of the Miami River from her father and she used the money from her deceased husband's business to purchase another 640 acres of orange groves along the northern banks of the river. This land included the old Fort Dallas and she had one of the main buildings converted into a home. That build-

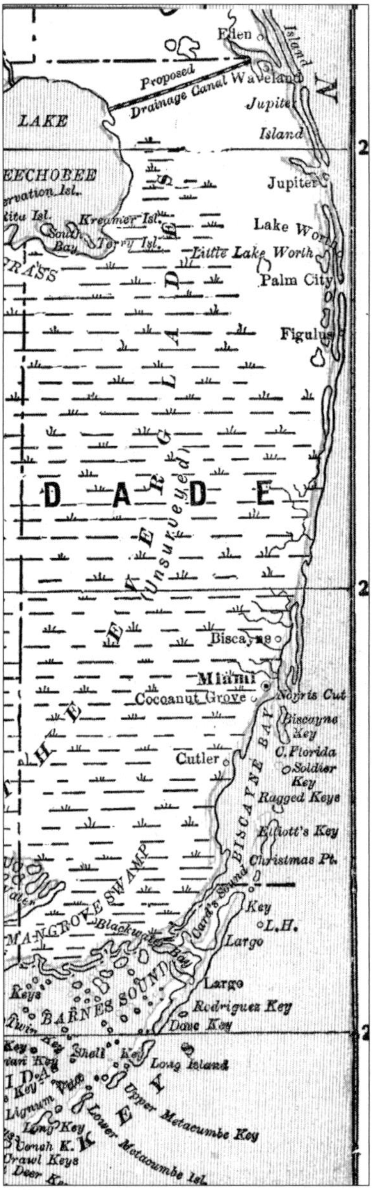

Figure 2. Southeast Florida, covered by the Everglades, 1893. © Florida Center for Instructional Technology, University of South Florida.

ing has survived to this day and sits in present-day Lummus Park in downtown Miami.

Tuttle seemed to be on a mission to turn Miami's wilderness into a real town and she realized this required better connections to the rest of the country. Her most important contribution was to persuade Henry Flagler to extend his railways down south. Her idealism must have exceeded her business instincts, and the opposite was probably true for Flagler. Tuttle lived in Miami for only nine years and when she died, on September 14, 1898, she left a considerable debt as a result of her land grants to Flagler. Her son and daughter, who were already in their twenties when they migrated with their mother to Miami, did not share her enthusiasm for South Florida's frontier. They sold the rest of the land to pay off the debts. One moved to New York, the other to Cleveland. Julia Tuttle was one of the first people interred in the City of Miami Cemetery.

Henry Flagler was perhaps the most indispensable of all the characters involved in Miami's beginning. He was the one who built the railway, first to Miami and later all the way down to Key West. It was vital because it allowed agricultural produce to be transported north. It provided a powerful injection into South Florida's agricultural sector, which in turn attracted growing numbers of farmers and laborers. According to popular legend, Julia Tuttle persuaded Flagler by sending him a box of fresh oranges from her grove in 1894, the year that the entire Florida harvest some sixty miles north of Miami had been destroyed by frost. At the time, Flagler's railway was not supposed to go south of West Palm Beach. Tuttle added to her plea by offering him parts of her land.

The first train pulled into the Miami station on April 13, 1896. Flagler was a seasoned businessman whose partnership with John D. Rockefeller in Standard Oil had already made him a multimillionaire. Most likely, he had estimated the profitability of a southern extension well beyond the citrus industry that was promoted by Tuttle. In addition to constructing the railway, he acquired large tracts of land and drew up the grid for Miami's street pattern. Present-day Flagler Street is the center of Miami's grid pattern, dividing the city into northern and southern halves. He was instrumental in creating the town's basic infrastructure with roads and water and electricity systems, and he designated a separate residential area for black workers. He also financed the first newspaper, which carried the somewhat grandiose title *Miami Metropolis*.

Perhaps most of all, Flagler had his eye on South Florida's potential as a magnet for tourists. In 1897, he opened the exclusive Royal Palm Hotel on the north bank of the river. It was a grand five-story building fully equipped with four hundred rooms, electricity, elevators, and a swimming pool. The Royal Palm soon became a place to be seen for the nation's elite. Among the guests were John D. Rockefeller, Andrew Carnegie, and the Vanderbilts. When the city was incorporated in 1896, some of Flagler's supporters proposed to name it after him, but he is said to have declined the honor. Instead, it was decided to stick with "Miami," the name used half a century earlier by William English and first recorded by the Spanish after their encounter with the Tequesta.

Henry Flagler became known as the Father of Miami but he was a distant father at best. Born in New York in 1830, he was in his sixties when he came down to work in South Florida. He was already independently wealthy. Between 1895 and 1900 he spent part of his time in Dade County, some of it in the Keys, New York, and elsewhere, and most of it in Palm Beach, where he had his primary residence. From 1901 to his death in 1913 he lived in his Whitehall estate in Palm Beach and he was buried in St. Augustine. Flagler never called Miami home.

It is estimated that in the last five years of the nineteenth century the population of Dade County tripled to 4,995 persons. The rapid increase was due to the railway. A town was arising on both sides

Figure 3. The Royal Palm Hotel on the north bank of the river, 1917. State Archives of Florida.

Figure 4. Teeing off at the Royal Palm, 1899. State Archives of Florida.

Figure 5. Workers digging the foundation of the Royal Palm Hotel, 1896. State Archives of Florida.

of the Miami River, stimulated with the construction of the first bridge. At the center of the town was a retail district along today's Miami Avenue and the Royal Palm Hotel, both north of the river. The town was supported by agriculture, construction, and incipient tourism. It attracted an unusual mix of people from various walks of life. The material and social inequalities were enormous.

For some, like James Deering, South Florida offered an opportunity to live a fantasy. Born in 1859, he was the son of William Deering, a well-known industrialist and the inventor of the harvester machine. Based in Chicago, the Deerings were one of the wealthiest families in the United States. James Deering set himself the task of building "the finest private house ever built in America" right on Biscayne Bay about a mile south of the river. The Villa Vizcaya, as it was named, was inspired by Renaissance-style Italian mansions from the sixteenth and seventeenth centuries. Construction started in 1912 and the house itself was finished in 1916—work on the gardens continued. Many of the materials were shipped from the Mediterranean. No less than one thousand workers were involved, including craftsmen from Europe and the Caribbean, this at a time when the city of Miami counted about ten thousand people. Set on 180 acres, the estate had meticulously kept gardens and was designed to be self-sufficient with livestock, horticulture fields, and wells.

Vizcaya represented the apex of the American renaissance movement. Deering traveled most summers to Europe with his general art supervisor and close friend, Paul Chalfin, to buy materials, furniture, antiques, and art for decoration. The villa had lavishly designed renaissance, baroque, rococo, and neoclassical rooms. Deering spent the winters here from 1916 to his death in 1926. Presently, Vizcaya is a museum of sixteenth- through nineteenth-century European decorative arts and most of the interior is in its original state.

Why James Deering embarked on the Vizcaya project remains a mystery. One might say he was in Miami not to work but to play and he did not associate much with local business circles. His unmarried status, frequent travels with Chalfin, apparent affection for the male nude statues displayed on the estate, and the rococo decorative overkill made it all seem rather queer—but this was half a century before such things were even talked about in public in South Florida. Deering died on board a steamship en route to the United States and was buried in the family grave in Chicago. The beneficiaries of his philanthropic legacy were mainly up north and included several Chicago hospitals and the Art Institute of Chicago. Vizcaya came into the hands of family members up north as well, but they donated it to Dade County in 1952, to turn it into a museum.

To the large majority of the population at the time, Deering's life must have seemed a fairy tale. Most were poor laborers living in harsh conditions. The clearing of most of southeast Florida's dense mangrove vegetation was done manually with machetes; it

Figure 6. Colored Town, 1906 (later renamed Overtown). © Florida Photograph Collection, Special Collections, University of Miami Libraries.

took tremendous efforts and caused a fair number of casualties. The building of the railway and the expansion of farms required hard labor as well. Many workers were recruited from the southern states and from the Bahamas. By 1910, more than 40 percent of the city's residents were black, most of them laborers. About half of them came from the Bahamas.[4] Little is known about the personal histories of these working people and even of black business leaders like Dana A. Dorsey,[5] in sharp contrast to that of white pioneers.

The Sewell brothers "worked Negroes as their specialty. With hundreds of them, they accomplished wonders in clearing land so that buildings could be erected."[6] John Sewell arrived from West Palm Beach to work for Flagler in 1896. To make sure his personal history would not be lost to humanity, the immodest Sewell published his own memoirs in 1933.[7] He was a shrewd entrepreneur and political operator for Flagler. People would speak of Sewell's "black artillery" in reference to the groups of black workers he commandeered around town, carrying shovels on their shoulders like rifles. He was known for his manipulation of these workers' votes whenever needed in local elections. In 1905 Sewell himself was elected the mayor of Miami. His self-aggrandizing memoirs place him at the center of Miami's growth: "I have decided to have the history published as my point of view is different from the others. My data are from the inside of the ring and absolute facts." In an appendix on the assassination attempt on the president-elect, Franklin Roosevelt, in Miami in February 1933[8] he wrote: "Myself and my wife were within 25 feet of Governor Roosevelt and 40 feet from the assassin, which shows after 37 years I am still on the inside of the ring."

There is a pertinacious quality to stories about Miami's early pioneers. Although they were portrayed as adventurous and persevering heroes who beat the odds and became self-made men on Miami's frontier, in reality most of them were millionaires and savvy businessmen even before they arrived in South Florida. This was another investment opportunity and a spectacular one at that. They risked their fortunes, sometimes, but rarely their lives. Most of them dealt cleverly in South Florida's wilderness and became wealthier still. During the long, hot, humid summers many of them left for their homes up north. In some ways, these pioneers were Miami's first wave of mobiles. They appropriated South Florida's earth, and they appropriated its history.

South Florida is a flat, porous, limestone plain without major rivers or streams and with a shallow soil cover. A few feet below it is a massive aquifer that covers about 3,000 square miles, evenly dived between present-day Broward and Miami-Dade counties. Its depth ranges from 20 to 140 feet and its bottom consists of impermeable rock called marl. At times of heavy rain, the aquifer would fill to capacity and surplus water would slowly flow south through the Everglades. Hence, most of the area was subject to recurrent flooding. Hundreds of years ago the Tequesta chose to live on the elevated coastal ridge, at the mouth of the Miami River, precisely for that reason. The "river of grass," as Marjorie Stoneman Douglas famously called the Everglades in later years, was about 40 miles wide and flowed at the tranquil speed of about a mile per day.[9] From Lake Okeechobee in the north all the way south toward the mangrove swamps on the Florida Bay, it created a unique American ecosystem and wildlife habitat. It was one of the world's great wetlands.

But that is not how people looked at it. When Napoleon Bonaparte Broward was elected governor of Florida in 1905, his campaign promise was to create an "Empire of the Everglades" by draining it.[10] The chief purpose was the creation of agricultural land and Broward's plans received enthusiastic support[11]—protests in the legislature were timid and mainly limited to concerns that the plans would first "drain" the state's budget. The Everglades Drainage District was created in 1907, opening the door to massive digging of canals and the construction of levees. One of the new waterways intended to control water levels and transport surplus water rapidly and directly out to the ocean was the Miami Canal (1909), connecting Lake Okeechobee directly with the Miami River. The drainage projects started to gradually dry out the Everglades, and hardly anybody was paying attention.[12]

Around the turn of the century the city of Miami itself received a good number of *temporary* visitors.[13] The drainage of the Everglades and the building of the railroad brought many construction workers. It was hard work and there were quite a few deserters. Most of the railroad workers kept moving down south with the track construction. The Spanish-American War involving Cuba led to the establishment of Camp Miami and brought an estimated seven thousand soldiers, most of whom left within months without having experienced battle. But they had seen South Florida and took the images and stories of Miami's beckoning frontier back home.

Some decided to stay. Between 1900 and 1920, the county's population increased to 42,753. This was without the county's northern portions, which became Palm Beach County in 1909 and Broward County in 1915. By 1920, the population of Palm Beach County was 18,654 and that of Broward was 5,135. Southeast Florida had 9 percent of the total population of Florida in 1920, a small but rapidly increasing share. New population clusters sprang up around the area and several new cities were incorporated. They usually counted no more than a few hundred inhabitants. In the south, Homestead became a city in 1913 and Florida City followed in 1915—the latter with a large African American population. These were quiet agricultural towns that lacked the metropolitan aspirations of Miami, as they still do today. Homestead is located about thirty-five miles southwest of the center of Miami, up against the Everglades. Florida City borders Homestead to the south, the last stop before leaving the mainland for the Keys. These parts first attracted settlers in the 1890s when the so-called Homesteaders Trail opened up. After the railway arrived in 1904 population growth accelerated.

Up north, in present-day Broward and Palm Beach counties, some towns were incorporated as well and they too were mainly farming communities: Dania in 1904, Pompano in 1908, and Fort Lauderdale in 1911. Prior to the railroad, these coastal towns had been connected by a main road for several years. Fort Lauderdale was named after a U.S. military post built near the mouth of the New River during the Second Seminole War in 1838. After the wars the area was abandoned and it took until the early 1890s before it was settled again. By 1920, Fort Lauderdale counted a little more than 2,000 people.

Between 1900 and 1920 the city of Miami itself grew from 1,681 to nearly 30,000 persons. It was the most central and by far the largest town in a region that did not yet deserve the label "urban." Several U.S. metropolitan areas had surpassed 1 million people by this time and New York had more than 5 million. Miami was only a small, and still quite insignificant, dot on a big map. This was also true in comparison to South America, where, for example, Buenos Aires already had more than 1.5 million inhabitants and boasted the continent's first subway system. But in relative terms, Miami's growth was considerable and it was clear that this time around its development would not be cut short or reversed. The city expanded to the north, west, and south and the downtown area grew denser. In 1912, a Burdines department store opened in a new five-story building, the city's first skyscraper. It was an event, city leaders said, that heralded the arrival of new times.

The most impressive changes in the first few decades of the twentieth century were eastward and had to do with the "billion dollar sandbar" that would become Miami Beach. Situated a couple of miles across the bay, it was an elongated island only about a thousand feet wide filled with swamp, mangroves, and mosquitoes. One of the first major infrastructure projects in South Florida, in 1905, was Government Cut, an east-west harbor channel that cut through the southern part of Miami Beach. In previous times, all ships headed for Miami had to sail the treacherous waters around Cape Florida, the southern tip of Key Biscayne where the first lighthouse was built. The new channel created a small landmass to the south, later named Fisher Island. To the north of Government Cut is the southernmost point of what is now Miami Beach.

John Collins, a successful fifty-nine-year-old farmer and land owner in New Jersey, moved to South Florida in 1896 and bought up large tracts of land on Miami Beach. In 1911, he formed the

Miami Beach Improvement Company and embarked on a mega-project: the building of the first bridge across the intracoastal waterway. It was finished in 1913; at 2.4 miles in length, it was the longest wooden structure of its kind in the world. The island's development took off and in 1915 the City of Miami Beach was incorporated. More and better connections to the mainland followed suit: the County Causeway (later renamed the MacArthur Causeway) was completed in 1918 and the Collins Bridge was replaced with the Venetian Causeway in 1925.

The state-funded large-scale Everglades drainage projects, combined with the development of Miami Beach and growing tourism, led to the birth of a feverish real estate industry. "Speculators purchased millions of acres of reclaimed land from the State of Florida, then marketed it aggressively in many parts of the nation. The unsavory sales tactics of promoters who sold unwitting investors land that was underwater earned for Miami an enduring reputation for marketing 'land by the gallon.'"[14] By 1920, Miami had become a city where "the pioneers were mostly fast-talking real estate sharks."[15] Nonetheless, South Florida was now in the national spotlight and appealed to many, whether investors, tourists, job seekers, or adventurers. Money was pouring in. The city was ready for takeoff.

CHAPTER 2

Shades of a City

The 1920s in Greater Miami "roared" like nowhere else. The first
half of the decade witnessed one of the greatest urban real estate
booms in history, far beyond the already hot market of the preceding years.[1] It was accompanied by what seemed an unprecedented urban culture that combined advertising, spectacle, and
the promotion of leisure and pleasure—especially for the rich. The
Miami Herald in those days was said to be the heaviest newspaper in the nation because of its extensive land advertisement sec-
tion. Miami earned the label "magic city" partly for its rapid
emergence but also because it was a place where fantasies could
turn real. It was a playground for developers and architects. They
designed from scratch while living off, catering to, and encourag-
ing the indulgence of affluent newcomers.

This was a formative stage in Miami's development as a city of
leisure. Where other U.S. cities owed their emergence to a good
port (for example, Boston) or proximity to raw materials (Pittsburgh) or political circumstances (Washington, D.C.), Miami's development was mainly based on a new demand for upper-class
vacationing, winter homes, and the enjoyment of spectacles. For
wealthy northeasterners, a trip to places like Atlantic City came
to be seen as lowbrow. They wanted something new-fashioned,
more distinctive, and, indeed, something more expensive and out

of the reach of America's growing middle class. Across the nation there was a new subculture that revolved around leisure and lifestyles, sightseeing and being seen.[2] In this context Miami became a citadel of fantastical consumption. Miami created an image of "popular engagement with leisure that lingered for decades and functioned as an important component in defining modern consumer culture."[3] No one person embodied this culture more than Carl Fisher:

To millions of Americans by the early 1920's, Fisher had successfully associated Miami Beach with speeding cars and motorboats, spectacular stunts, grandiose hotels, mansions, lavish parties, polo matches, bathing casinos, and crowds of sunbathers. His personal relationship with nationally known celebrities and wealthy auto magnates became a powerful engine in selling land and attracting winter tourists to the area. Sleeping under pictures of Lincoln and Napoleon, he was thoroughly enamored with self-made men—like himself.[4]

Fisher hailed from Indiana and was a nationally known entrepreneur in the automobile industry and in civil engineering. He created the Indianapolis Speedway, developed and manufactured electrical car parts, and was involved in the construction of the Dixie Highway. He came to Miami in 1913, a wealthy man in his late thirties with a passion for speed and spectacles. He and John Collins became the two most influential developers of Miami Beach in the early years—it was Fisher's money that completed Collins's bridge. They recruited large numbers of black workers from Mississippi, Alabama, Georgia, and the Bahamas to reclaim the island from the mangroves and to build roads. The two men ended up owning large parts of the Beach. Today's Collins Avenue is the island's main north-south artery. Fisher's name is still attached to the small island south of Government Cut—according to the most recent U.S. census it is the richest community in the entire United States. Fisher's personal admiration for Abraham Lincoln was expressed in the naming of various landmarks: Lincoln Road, the Lincoln Hotel, and the Lincoln Theatre among them.

Miami Beach proved a magnet to affluent northerners who desired a second home in the subtropics. Among them were Lindsay Hopkins Jr. of Coca-Cola, the publisher W. C. Blakey, Russell Stover of candy company fame, and Everett P. Larsh of Master Electrical Company.[5] On Brickell Avenue, just south of downtown Miami, arose "millionaire's row," a string of mansions for out-of-towners of comparable stature. One of them was William Jennings Bryan, the three-time populist presidential candidate. When not preaching the gospel and debating evolutionists, he lent his oratory skills to promote the development plans of George Merrick.[6] Like most others on millionaire's row, Jennings Bryan never really considered Miami his home. He died in Tennessee and was buried in Washington, D.C.

Miami's developers since 1920 have sought to exploit the aesthetics of the South Florida landscape. More often than not, it was a mission born of sheer opportunism. The most important exception was perhaps George Merrick, whose name is inextricably bound to the city of Coral Gables. Merrick wanted more than tourism, spectacle, and leisure. He wanted Coral Gables to be a "real" place where people enjoyed their environment but also worked and lived year-round. He dreamed of "a modern tropical economy that would attract the new population that would establish the city as a permanent place and bring science, theatre, art, institutes of literature, a symphony orchestra, adult education, and forums."[7]

Arriving with his family at the age of twelve, Merrick became one of the few whose passion for the place exceeded the urge to make a profit. His ambition was nothing less than to create a whole new town, the so-called city beautiful. Coral Gables, incor-

Figure 7. Aerial view of the construction of the Venetian Causeway, replacing Collins's original wooden bridge to Miami Beach, 1925. State Archives of Florida.

porated in 1925, was one of the first suburban towns designed around the automobile. Mediterranean style houses and mansions were set in lush subtropical vegetation. The gently winding roads, aptly named after iconic Spanish and Italian places, were ideal for leisurely Sunday afternoon drives. Landmarks included the commanding Biltmore Hotel, inspired by the Cathedral of Seville (1926), the elegant Venetian Pool (1924), the Coral Gables Country Club, which served to entertain visiting real estate clients (1922), and many more. Merrick also planned the University of Miami (1925), which, despite its name, is located centrally in the Gables. The development of Coral Gables was (and is) based on very strict zoning and building codes and one could argue that it was overplanned, lacking spontaneity and vivaciousness. But few would disagree that it is a beautiful area in its own right, of a design that respected the natural environment and that has withstood the test of time.

That is more than one could say of Opa Locka, another devel-

Figure 8. The newly constructed Biltmore Hotel, 1926. State Archives of Florida.

oper's fantasy design of the early 1920s. Glenn Curtiss, a widely known aviation pioneer and showman who made a fortune selling motorcycles and airplanes, arrived in Miami in 1916. His first development projects in South Florida were in the emerging city of Hialeah, northwest of downtown Miami. They included a new racehorse track that acquired national fame, a jai alai arena with athletes imported from Spain and Cuba, and next to the racetrack a landscaped lake with two hundred imported flamingoes. Curtiss was one of Miami's premier publicity hounds, for whom image prevailed over substance and quality and who had no regard for authenticity.

 Opa Locka was meant to be the "Baghdad of Florida," a page out of "Arabian Nights" and the greatest collection of Moorish architecture in the Western Hemisphere. The name of the area came from the Native American word "Opatishawockalocka," a tongue twister that had to be shortened and simplified to suit potential buyers. By 1926, Curtis had constructed over a hundred buildings with an array of domes, minarets, and other Moorish features. The streets bore names like Sinbad, Caliph, and Aladdin. The main road through town was (and is) Alibaba Avenue. Even for South Florida, it was too much. The area did not entice many wealthy buyers. These were drawn, instead, to more appealing and prestigious residential environs that would leave less doubt about their taste. The quality of construction in Opa Locka was poor and much of the area was destroyed or damaged in the hurricane of 1926. It soon became a low-income neighborhood, a painful contrast to nearby Coral Gables.

The boom of the 1920s was accompanied by fast population growth. Between 1920 and 1930, Dade County's population increased from 43,000 to 143,000 and Broward's from 5,000 to 20,000. Many cities were incorporated in both counties: Coral Gables, Hialeah, Miami Springs, Opa Locka, North Miami, South Miami, North Miami Beach, Golden Beach, Davie, Deerfield Beach, Hallandale, Hollywood, Lauderdale by the Sea, and Oakland Park. The most spectacular growth was in Miami Beach: between 1920 and 1930 its population increased by 1,000 percent from 644 to 6,500. These numbers did not include the winter population on the Beach, which was estimated at 40,000 in 1925.[8] In the same year the number of hotels on Miami Beach had increased to 234. South Florida, and especially the Beach, became an important destination for seasonal migrants and snowbirds from the north. Most of the hotels opened in the winter only. The present-day Wolfsonian Museum on Collins Avenue (1927) was originally built as a summer storage facility for the winter visitors.

Land prices on Miami Beach went up 1,800 percent between 1916 and 1925. So much money was poured into South Florida that it drained a couple of Massachusetts banks and caused them to fail. Seven banks in Ohio joined forces to launch an advertising campaign blasting Florida.[9] A very large percentage of investment was speculative and sometimes land would change hands several times a day. It was only a matter of time before the bubble would burst.

Figure 9. Biscayne Boulevard, downtown Miami, around 1930. State Archives of Florida.

By August 1925, the market started to stagnate and prices moved downward for about twelve months. Then, on September 18, 1926, a devastating category-4 hurricane struck Miami head-on. The number of dead was estimated at 350 and the material damage was enormous. On Miami Beach, one in four houses was destroyed and the area east of Washington Avenue was almost completely flattened. On the mainland, too, the storm wreaked havoc. It caused irreparable damage to Flagler's Royal Palm Hotel, which had to be taken down. Thousands of investors pulled out, the market collapsed, and many left the area.

Miami went into a depression a few years before the rest of the nation did with the stock market crash of 1929. Those fortunes not already wiped out by the hurricane were destroyed by the stock market crash. Merrick went broke and spent his last years as Miami's U.S. postmaster. Glenn Curtiss died in debt in New York in 1930. Carl Fisher lost almost everything, moved into a modest cottage on Miami Beach, and drank himself to death in 1939. Looking back at his adventures in South Florida, he said,

Figure 10. Aerial view of downtown Miami, 1939. State Archives of Florida.

"It wasn't any goddamned dream at all. I could just as easily have started a cattle ranch."[10]

Miami was anything but a cohesive community. There must have been a high turnover of residents, many did not stay during the summer months, and class differences were huge. In addition, the population was divided along racial and ethnic lines, and blatant discrimination was commonplace. Miami's elite was an exclusive WASP community. Southern racists dominated much of the police force, and anti-Semitic northerners kept Jews from buying land or registering at many hotels.[11]

Along with the rising demand for labor, the black population kept growing. An area north of the town center and west of the railroad was designated for blacks and in 1911 a "color line" was drawn to restrict its expansion. This area would be named Colored Town, later renamed Overtown. By 1915 it housed some five thousand people. Another dense pocket of black settlers was the so-called McFarlane subdivision in west Coconut Grove, where Bahamian immigrants built their homes. White protests against black expansion into adjacent neighborhoods were fierce and usually effective—the black areas were among the most densely populated. There was no question where the major newspapers stood on this matter: a 1911 *Miami Herald* article stated that "the advance of the Negro population is like a plague and carries devastation with it to all surrounding property."[12]

In 1917, a group of whites bombed the Odd Fellows Hall, the black community center on Charles Avenue in Coconut Grove. The guilty parties were never arrested. A few years later the Ku Klux Klan established a Miami branch; by 1925 it claimed to have fifteen hundred members.[13] In 1921, the Klan kidnapped the black minister H. H. Higgs from Coconut Grove in response to his message aimed at racial equality. He was released after promising to return to the Bahamas. The Klan was known to be closely associated with members of the police force and the force itself was notorious for its rough treatment of blacks.[14] An early postcard from the 1920s shows a festive image of the KKK float in a parade on Flagler Street—the American Legion decided to give the Klan the award for best float of the year.[15] In the summer of 1926, the Ku Klux Klan opened a new headquarters in downtown Miami at S.W. 4th Street and 8th Avenue. It was destroyed a few months later in the hurricane of September 1926—what some must have considered divine intervention. But open racism and discrimination would continue for many more years, with repeated efforts by city leaders (including, for example, George Merrick) to resettle blacks in completely segregated communities further from the city center.[16]

The exclusion of blacks from Miami's designs in this era became painfully evident with the discovery of a historic cemetery in April 2009. The site, at N.W. 71st Street and 4th Avenue, dates

Figure 11. Woman at a sign for South Florida's only beach for colored people on Virginia Key; the sign was blown down by a storm in 1950. State Archives of Florida.

to around 1920. Located outside the emerging towns of the time, it served as the final resting place of black Bahamian immigrants, most of whom were construction workers. But its existence was subsequently erased from the records and the site was not marked on any known maps—until ninety years later when a construction crew working on a housing project stumbled upon human bones.[17]

Blacks were not the only targets of bigotry. Jews were shunned and systematically excluded from buying real estate. Flagler, for example, was known to refuse to deal with Jewish clients. The situation in Miami Beach was particularly harsh. When Collins and Fisher developed Miami Beach, part of the design was to keep the area "exclusive." They marketed their real estate sales mainly to wealthy midwesterners. The Lummus brothers, who owned the Miami Beach area south of 5th Street, started to assume a more liberal posture in the early 1920s, selling property to middle-class Jews from New Jersey and New York. Among them was one Joe Weiss, who bought himself a small lunch stand and later turned it into a restaurant named Joe's Stonecrabs—one of the best-known restaurants to this day.

The first synagogue in Miami was built in 1913 and the event marked the assertion of the Jewish community in Dade County. By 1926, there were about thirteen hundred Jews in the city of Miami. In Miami Beach, there were no more than a few hundred, and the first synagogue was not built until 1927, on the corner of 3rd Street and Washington Avenue. It is said that almost every Jew who was a permanent resident of Miami Beach between 1927 and 1932 was a member of and a financial contributor to the synagogue.[18] The central and northern parts of Miami Beach continued as the domain of wealthy gentiles, and some hotels even posted signs indicating that Jews were not welcome until such signs were banned in 1949.

The way Miami's urban society evolved seemed to set a pattern that, with some variation, is still with us today. A strong sense of community was forged among some of the less powerful segments of South Florida's population, particularly blacks and Jews. These communities had a strong ethnic base, lived in highly segregated neighborhoods, and developed a sense of local identity.[19] The business elite, in contrast, seemed to have a more loose association with Miami. They viewed it as a business opportunity, rather than a place to live, and they usually held on to homes elsewhere. Their prosperity fostered individualism; their mobility withheld local community membership.

And then there was Miami's flourishing underworld. Like most frontier towns, Miami around the turn of the century was an environment conducive to lawlessness and crime. In the 1920s, Prohibition and the real estate boom combined to turn crime into organized business. Miami became a major port of entry for alcohol smuggling, mainly from the Bahamas, as well as an ideal area for local moonshine distilleries. With its yacht clubs, regattas, glamorous hotels, racehorse track, and gambling parlors, Miami was obviously a thirsty and lucrative market as well. That market got even bigger when the real estate boom lured large numbers of investors to town.

Miami blatantly ignored Prohibition and some of Miami's "best citizens" were engaged in rum running.[20] It was common knowledge, for example, that in Flagler's Royal Palm Hotel you could have any drink money could buy. Carl Fisher, who himself became a heavy drinker during Prohibition, threw extravagant parties with abundant refreshments for out-of-town clients and friends. Alcohol was routinely delivered to the wealthy on their yachts. According to one account, "Limousines [were] lined up at the wharfs to welcome the boats laden with bootleg liquor that came in from Havana, Bimini, Nassau, and people drove off with their 'fish' neatly wrapped in brown paper. At other times, that 'fish' was shipped north in refrigerated railroad cars, under cover of grapefruit, tomatoes or avocados."[21]

The mob was well represented among the new groups of snowbirds arriving in the 1920s. Al Capone drew Miami into his Chicago-based crime network and made millions. In 1928 he bought a mansion on Palm Island, his winter home until he could no longer avoid prison in 1932. The mob engaged mainly in smuggling, gambling, and prostitution, but it also infiltrated legitimate business, including real estate, construction, hotels, and nightclubs. Members of the mob were said to be working quite comfortably with the sheriffs from Dade and Broward counties.[22] From the mid- to late 1920s, the murder rate for South Florida was greater than at any time since the State of Florida began keeping records and it was much higher than the U.S. average. "It would appear that there was a . . . culture that promoted violence. . . . This culture was fueled by the stress created by the boom and the bust and by the large numbers of transients who had no permanent roots in the community."[23] From the ethnic schisms and pervasive bigotry to its criminal underbelly, it appears that Miami's social fabric in the 1920s was as fragmented as it was fragile.

South Florida entered the Great Depression before the rest of the country and it recovered sooner as well—even if it did not return to the high-rolling times of the 1920s. Tourism picked up again in the early 1930s. For those who could afford it, Miami continued to have a special appeal. In addition, the real estate bust of the late 1920s now allowed people to buy land at cheaper rates. Population turnover continued to be very high: in 1940, about one-third of the resident population had arrived only since 1935.[24]

Once again, some of the most eye-catching developments took place in Miami Beach. The need for new large-scale construction in eastern Miami Beach after the hurricane of 1926 coincided with the arrival of a new type of design and architecture. Stylish modernism originated in France and was highly influential in the 1920s and 1930s. By the time it reached Miami Beach it had evolved into streamline moderne, with simpler structures and machine-inspired, industrial forms. Later, in the 1960s, this style became popularly known as art deco. The deco district in south Miami Beach, about eight hundred buildings in one square mile, was put up in less than ten years. It includes well-known hotels such as the Tides (1936), the Beacon (1936), Essex House (1938), the Breakwater (1939), and the Avalon (1941). The most exquisite art deco building is probably the U.S. Post Office building (1937) on Washington Avenue and 13th Street. The district also included many apartments and served mainly tourists, as it does today.

Among the newcomers to Miami Beach were many Jews who settled mainly in the southern parts of the island but soon started moving farther north as well. The Jewish population on the Beach went from about 300 in the mid-1920s to 3,300 in 1935. The main push occurred between 1945 and 1950 when their numbers tripled in only five years. The Jewish population in Dade County as a whole increased from 8,273 in 1940 to almost 55,000 in 1950.

Miami Beach's early and vigorous recovery was reflected in the fact that its total population quadrupled in the course of the 1930s. In 1940 the number stood at 28,000 and by 1950 it would reach 46,000. On the mainland, population growth and urban expansion continued steadily. During World War II, Dade County housed several air and naval bases, with a total of 80,000 soldiers stationed in Miami and in Miami Beach. A popular saying went that many had "felt the sand in their shoes" and returned to live there after the war. The overall population of Dade County roughly doubled during the 1930s, again during the 1940s, and once more during the 1950s. Broward's population doubled as well in the 1930s and 1940s, and then quadrupled in the 1950s to reach 334,000 in 1960. The introduction of air conditioning in many middle- and upper-class homes since the late 1940s (and central air since the mid-1950s) played a part in this growth just as it did in other cities in the U.S. Sun Belt.

The South Florida urban region grew more dense and expanded south, north, and west. Fifteen new cities were incorporated and hundreds of new subdivisions emerged in the two-county area during this period. But Miami and Fort Lauderdale remained dominant within their counties and had by far the largest population concentrations. Major infrastructure developments included the creation of Miami International Airport[25] in 1949, the expansion of the port of Miami through the annexation of Dodge Island in 1956, the beginning of construction of interstate highways across South Florida in the late 1950s, and the opening of Fort Lauderdale-Hollywood International Airport in 1959.

But while South Florida grew rapidly in the postwar years, the essence of Miami did not really change. It continued to function as a sort of appendage to the nation but it had not (yet) acquired most of the traits typical of major cities elsewhere:

Miami's postwar decades, bracketed by the return of the GIs beginning in 1944 and the Republican Convention of 1968, witnessed a dramatic demographic increase and a radical mutation from seasonal resort to year-round metropolitan environment. Yet, unlike Los Angeles, Miami continued to be defined in relation to other places (more as a playground for escapees, transient or not, from the industrial northern and mid-western cities) than as a city in its own right. This perception shaped Miami's status as a commodified "city of leisure." . . . [Further, the city's] infantile and innocent character was exacerbated by the body culture, tropical weather, beaches, golf courses and other amenities. [Miami was a] city of recreation versus a city of culture, a city of attractions versus a city of institutions.[26]

The environmental transformation of South Florida that began at the beginning of the twentieth century continued apace. Drainage of the Everglades accelerated after the major flooding caused by the hurricane of 1926. The construction of the Tamiami Trail in 1928 was probably the single most environmentally destructive project in South Florida's history. It must have seemed like a good idea at the time. The 112-mile long canal helped transport "surplus" water east to the Atlantic and west to the Gulf of Mexico. The dike protected urban areas against flooding, and the road on the dike was the first major east-west connection between Miami and Tampa.

The Tamiami Trail also (very) effectively blocked the "river of grass" from flowing south. It dried out much of the Everglades and killed a variety of plants, birds, fish, mammals, amphibians, and reptiles. The growing agriculture sector compounded the problem with the polluting emission of phosphorous, mercury, and nitrogen. More engineering projects followed in subsequent decades. As it became apparent that overdrainage was a problem

Figure 12. Governor John W. Martin meeting a Seminole Indian at the construction of the Tamiami Trail, 1927. State Archives of Florida.

during dry periods, water-storage efforts were made and the system grew ever more complex. By 1970, there were "720 miles of levees, 1000 miles of canals, 200 gates, and water control structures, and 16 pumping stations."[27]

Widespread public awareness of environmental decline did not emerge until later in the twentieth century. The prevailing mind-set at the time is pungently expressed in the film *Sunshine State*: a sly developer points to the meticulously landscaped surroundings of an exclusive South Florida golf resort and declares in an imperious and self-indulgent manner to his golfing partners, "We created this nature on a leash." Still, some important early voices helped to stave off even greater disaster. The first ideas to create a protected park in the Everglades took shape in the 1920s. In those days, environmental consciousness of politicians and business leaders in South Florida and in Tallahassee lagged considerably behind that of some federal agencies. The pioneers behind the initial local environmental efforts consisted of a small group of individuals with influence in Washington, D.C. They included Stephen T. Mather, the first director of the National Park Service, Ernest F. Coe, a Miami local and a landscape architect who was educated at Yale, and David Fairchild, a famous tropical botanist.[28] The latter was the first president of the Tropical Everglades Park Association, established in 1928.

After a visit to the area in 1929, an investigative committee authorized by Congress issued a report that revealed the changing appreciation of the South Florida wetlands: "We are compelled to admit that in a good deal of the Everglades region, especially in those parts now readily accessible by road, the quality of the scenery is to the casual observer under most conditions somewhat confused and monotonous. Its beauty in the large is akin to that of the other great plain: perhaps rather subtle for the average observer in search of the spectacular; though sometimes very grand, especially when seen in solitude and at rest instead of from a hurrying automobile."[29]

Congress authorized the creation of the Everglades National Park in 1934 and President Truman dedicated it in 1947. It covers almost one-third of Miami-Dade County. The same year saw the publication of Marjorie Stoneman Douglas' classic *Everglades: The River of Grass*.[30] It was a milestone in South Florida's historiography because it expressed a view of nature that had been completely overshadowed by the mantra of development. It struck a chord with some segments of the public, but most locals remained remarkably disinterested in the ecological environs of their city.

In 1949 *Life* contained a feature article on Miami Beach, referring to the island as the "crown jewel" of South Florida. To be sure, the 1950s once again belonged to the Beach. The island became immensely popular as one of the nation's hottest vacation spots, especially for the rich. The 1950s saw a return of the glitz and glamour reminiscent of the roaring 1920s. Yet again a new style of architecture emerged, mainly in the central and northern parts of Miami Beach. Art deco was already passé and considered gaudy. In MiMo, short for Miami modern, the square structures with rounded corners and symmetrical ornamentation of art deco made way for a whimsical tropical style that was curvaceous, asymmetric, and daring. The best example of MiMo is the Fontainebleau Hotel, at Collins and 44th Street.

The Fontainebleau was designed and built in 1953 by Morris Lapidus, whose adage "Too much is never enough"[31] fit perfectly with the hedonistic disposition of the Beach's wealthy pleasure seekers. Many critics considered the building a monstrosity and despised its flamboyant style. It became a symbol. With five hundred rooms, the Fontainebleau was double the size of any existing hotel on the Beach. Indeed, it caused problems for a number of smaller hotels in the deco district. Such is the backdrop to *Hole in the Head*, a movie from the 1950s in which Frank Sinatra plays a struggling small hotel owner on Ocean Boulevard who tries to connect with the tycoons who hang out in the Fontainebleau. Lapidus also designed one of the first outdoor pedestrian malls in the country: Lincoln Road was converted from a heavy-traffic artery into a shopping way for pedestrians in 1960 and promoted as the "Fifth Avenue of the South."

In the course of the 1940s and 1950s, Miami Beach's clientele started to diversify. Besides its customary niche for the rich leisure classes from up north, it began to attract middle-income residents and tourists, northern retirees of more modest means, and Cuban visitors. For a growing number of upper-middle-class Cubans, a vacation in South Florida became a yearly event; for the wealthy, daily shopping trips to Miami were not uncommon. Many of the new residents settled in South Beach, the area roughly equivalent with the deco district. Despite the gradual introduction of air conditioning in the 1950s, the large majority of wintertime people on the Beach were snowbirds. In 1952, for example, the winter population of Miami Beach swelled to about 200,000 while the summer population stood at 45,541 residents.[32] The growing Jewish population on the Beach maintained a seasonal character well into the 1950s: "The constant influx of a great number of visitors gave a special character to local Jewish institutions. The synagogues have the highest rate of 'out-of-town' attendance in the nation."[33]

South Florida, and particularly Miami Beach, also continued to be a magnet to organized crime. By the late 1940s, the area was firmly embedded in Mafia networks centered in Chicago and New York, making it the "winter gangster capital of the world."[34] In 1947, FBI director J. Edgar Hoover remarked, "If you put a dragnet around Twenty-third and Collins, and slapped every mobster you caught into jail for life, you'd end organized crime in America."[35] Big mob names from this era include Hymie "Loudmouth" Levin and Jack "Greasy Thumb" Guzik. Miami's appeal consisted of the weather, beaches, wealthy patrons, lots of entertainment, the absence of state taxes, and relaxed policing.

Since the end of Prohibition, the main focus of organized crime was on gambling. Some of it was legal, as at the Hialeah racetrack, but most of it was not—there was also much irregular gambling at Hialeah Park and at the dog races. Lottery games, such as Cuban *bolitas*, targeted people with lower incomes. Miami, Hialeah, Fort Lauderdale, and Hollywood had well-known gambling parlors, but most of the action was on the Beach. Much of the racketeering money was spent lavishly on alcohol, food, women, cars, and entertainment. The Mafia also used its financial prowess to influence elections and public opinion, and to bribe officials. Considerable funds were plowed back into real estate, hotels, industries, and sports.[36] Miami Beach hotels owned or controlled by the Mafia around this time included the Wofford, the Boulevard, the Roney, the Grand, and the Sands.

In 1950, the U.S. Senate appointed the Greater Miami Crime Commission, chaired by Senator Estes Kefauver, to investigate the escalation of organized crime in Greater Miami. The committee conducted hearings in Dade and Broward counties and reported in detail on key figures, places, practices, and networks. Kefauver branded Miami as a "plunder-ground . . . for America's most vicious criminals."[37] The committee's work received lots of publicity but it did not stop the Mafia from extending its activities.

One of the leading figures during the 1950s was Meyer Lansky. Born in Russia, he migrated to New York as a child and grew up with the mob. He first visited Miami in 1936 and brought the New York Jewish Mafia along with him. Lansky was known as the chairman of the board of the National Crime Syndicate, one of the biggest criminal organizations of the 1940s and 1950s. The syndicate had close ties to the Cosa Nostra and maintained operations in New York, Las Vegas, Miami, and Havana.[38] Lansky set up gambling halls across South Florida but especially in Fort Lauderdale, where the competition was less. Many big hotels on the Beach, such as the Fontainebleau and the Singapore, were owned or controlled by the Minneapolis Group, one of Lansky's corporate fronts. Lansky was one of the most successful mobsters ever. He brilliantly mixed illegal earnings with legal activities and lived a quiet private life. Lansky's name is inscribed as a benefactor in one of the stained-glass windows of the Synagogue on Third Street. He died at the age of eight-one, in 1983, and never went to jail.

To add to the mix, in the 1950s Miami was "the underground capital-in-exile for the plotters of revolution in the Caribbean and throughout Latin America" with gunrunning as a major industry.[39] In the slightly hyperbolic words of the mob expert and author

Hank Messick, Miami was "very much like Casablanca in the for-ties—a city full of stateless men and women, soldiers of fortune, spies and secret agents, con men of all persuasions, and even a few patriots."[40] The most important group of "plotters" was the Cuban exile community that opposed the Batista regime. The Ca-ribbean island, only ninety miles across the southern waters, was about to resume its historical role in the shaping of Miami, and it would do so in dramatic fashion.

CHAPTER 3

Extreme Makeover

A *Time* magazine article in 1958 reported that "gaudy, gritty Greater Miami" had become "the revolutionary headquarters of the Americas."[1] The area was referred to as a "plotters' play-ground" for Dominicans, Haitians, and especially Cubans who were aiming at the demise of the governments in their home countries. South Florida was the ideal location because it was close by, it had various big and small airports and seaports, and its coastline was like a maze with innumerable winding water-ways. In addition, the city's transient atmosphere and crime net-works made it relatively easy to engage in subversive activities.

It was not the first time that Cubans had used South Florida as a backstage for their political struggles. Ever since the begin-nings of armed resistance against Spain in the 1860s, they would at times seek refuge in Key West. From the 1920s onward, Miami was the haven of choice. Since the establishment of the Republic of Cuba in 1902, politics had been erratic and unstable. The island witnessed several irregular transfers of power and occasionally politics turned violent.

When President Gerardo Machado's rule took a dictatorial turn in the late 1920s, it caused a flow of refugees to Miami. In 1933, the president was pushed aside in a military coup: his opponents returned home and celebrated while disillusioned *machadistas* took their place in Miami. Machado himself fled to the Bahamas before settling in Miami. It was a pattern to be repeated several times. Almost two decades later, in 1952, the democratically elected president, Carlos Prio, was unseated in a coup d'état led by General Batista, resulting in the largest number of refugees yet to arrive in South Florida, Prio himself among them. There were about twenty thousand Cubans in South Florida then. For some upper-class Cubans, Miami was familiar terrain as it had been a popular vacation and shopping destination since the 1940s.

Batista's government in the 1950s was characterized by corruption and nepotism. Poverty was widespread and the gap between rich and poor was enormous. Havana, with its casinos and famous nightlife, was an important place in American organized crime networks and the Mafia provided political support for Batista. So did the U.S. government, best illustrated by the infamous remark of a State Department official in 1956 that "Batista is considered by many a son of a bitch . . . but at least he is *our* son of a bitch."[2] It was a reference to Batista's warm treatment of U.S. multinationals and his fervent anti-communist rhetoric.

Prio dedicated himself to the overthrow of Batista and provided financial support to various militant groups. Fidel Castro stopped by in Miami in 1955 to accept a hefty financial contribution and went on to Mexico to organize and train his military forces. In December 1956, Castro's troops invaded Cuba and for the next three years fought the Batista regime from their base in the Sierra Maestra Mountains. Batista fled to Brazil on December 31, 1959 and later settled in Coral Gables. Castro's triumph, or at least Batista's downfall, was a cause for celebration among the large majority of exiles. "The familiar changing of the guard took place, with exultant *fidelistas* leaving, to be replaced by defeated *batistianos*. Scuffles broke out in the Miami airport between passengers arriving from and departing for Havana, causing local police reinforcements to be sent in."[3]

It took another two years for Castro to proclaim his communist sympathies openly and for the United States to break off diplomatic relations. During 1959 and 1960, many Cubans saw the clouds gather and turned away from the revolution in disillusionment.[4] At first, the return of exiles to Cuba exceeded the arrival of new refugees in Miami—the Cuban population in South Florida most likely dropped around this time. But as Castro's revolution revealed its true colors, a growing number of Cubans packed their bags. On December 26, 1960, operation Pedro Pan commenced, in which desperate Cuban parents sent more than fourteen thousand children on their own to the United States, to be cared for by relatives, friends, and foster parents.

Between 1959 and 1961, about 50,000 exiles reached Miami.[5] The first waves of refugees contained a large number of wealthy business people who had been able to hang on to their possessions and get out in time to bring their wealth to Miami. They were soon followed by other elite Cubans who had waited too long and had seen their properties confiscated. They, in turn, were succeeded by smaller business owners and professionals from the middle classes. The exodus accelerated in 1962. Between June and August, an estimated 1,800 Cubans arrived in Miami every week and by October of that year there were a total of 155,000 registered refugees. Leaving Cuba became harder after the failed Bay of Pigs invasion of April 1961, and even more difficult after the missile crisis of 1962.[6] Still, by 1965 the number of exiles had climbed to 210,000.

In the national news in the United States, most attention was on Cuba, not South Florida. The CBS evening news on December 1, 1966 reported that "to a great extent these people represent the professional and business class of Cuba; the able, the educated, the successful. . . . Cuba has been gutted. This exodus is the biggest brain drain the Western Hemisphere has known."[7] The federal government's preoccupation with Cuba was expressed in the immense resources dedicated to gathering intelligence on Castro's government, Cuban politics, and counter-revolutionary movements in Miami. During the 1960s, there were three hundred to four hundred CIA agents in South Florida, making it the largest CIA "station" after Langley headquarters in Virginia.

The majority of refugees remained in Miami. They stayed with relatives and acquaintances, rented property, or received shelter from the authorities. Initially, local, public, and volunteer agencies banded together in Miami to assist the refugees.[8] But as the numbers escalated, unease grew among the local population. And when, at the end of the missile crisis, it became clear that the Cubans were not likely to go home any time soon, politicians in South Florida took action. They requested emergency help with the "refugee crisis" from the federal government. In response, the Kennedy administration organized a large-scale program to resettle Cubans throughout the United States. It seemed to work, at first. By 1966 about 135,000 people were resettled all over the United States, with the largest concentrations in New York and California.

But in 1965 Castro agreed to the departure of large numbers of "traitors to the revolution." The "freedom flights," as they were called by the Cubans in Miami, continued until 1973 and by that time another 340,000 refugees had entered the United States, most choosing to stay in Miami. And that was not the only issue. Miami's appeal to the exiled Cubans was simply irresistible, and the resettlement scheme was a losing proposition:

All the time that the freedom flights were coming into Miami, resettlement flights were leaving it in an attempt to distribute more evenly the burden of refugee resettlement. By 1978, 469,435 Cubans had been settled away from Miami. To federal and local bureaucrats, this was ample evidence that the "problem" of refugee concentration in South Florida had been resolved. In the late 1960s, however, a discreet countertrend started that saw resettled Cuban families trek back to Miami on their own. In 1973, a survey estimated that 27 percent of the Cubans residing in the Miami metropolitan area had returned there from other US locations. A survey conducted by the Miami Herald in 1978 raised that valuation to about forty percent. As a consequence of this accelerating return migration, by 1979, on the eve of *Mariel*, close to eighty percent of Cubans in the United States were living in Miami, making it, in effect, Cuba's second-largest city and the refugees the most concentrated foreign-born minority in the country.[9]

During the first year of Castro's revolution, life in South Florida seemed to be going on as usual. For most Miamians, the Cuban revolution initially seemed another episode of a familiar story and it was mainly greeted with indifference. In the 1960s, "Miami Beach's spectacle of idleness, luxury and sex remained the predominant national and international image of the city."[10] The Beatles performed there on their first tour in the United States in February 1964, at the Deauville Hotel on Collins Avenue for a crowd of twenty-five hundred. They played in only two other American cities, New York and Washington, D.C. In 1965, Jacky Gleason moved his popular TV show from Manhattan to Miami Beach, exposing the allure of Miami to national audiences on a weekly basis.

But economically things were not going well and South Florida in the 1960s showed something of a disconnect from the rest of the country. The period from 1961 to 1969 witnessed one of the most sustained periods of economic expansion the nation had ever known, with annual growth rates near 5 percent. At the same time, South Florida's economy was lackluster. The strong performance of manufacturing in the U.S. economy as a whole was mostly irrelevant to South Florida, where manufacturing had always been insignificant. It witnessed only minimal growth in tourism and most economic indicators were flat. The real estate business cycle had turned down after the high-rolling 1950s. The financial drain on resources with the arrival of Cuban refugees did not help. Then, in the early 1970s, the United States and much of the world economy went into a prolonged recession, which kept parts of the South Florida economy down for a long time.

The stagnation of the 1960s was particularly visible in downtown Miami. Since the turn of the twentieth century, this had been the bustling center for retailing, commerce, and popular culture. Prominent hotels were just around the corner on Biscayne Boulevard, and Bayfront Park was a popular public space. Within a few years, shops closed, hotels struggled, and people stopped coming. Petty crime increased and the area turned desolate at night.

In Miami Beach, the decline was conspicuous as well. By the mid-1960s, the MiMo hype had faded, money had become scarce, and not much of anything was being built. The deco district, already passé in the 1950s, turned seedy. Lincoln Road lost its shine and upscale shopping moved north to Bal Harbor. The Fontainebleau was operating well below capacity and in the circumstances its flamboyant pretentiousness turned a shade pathetic. A number of small hotels on Ocean Boulevard were forced to open up to middle-class northern retirees whose definition of excitement was bingo night. South Beach, once the most fashionable destination for the nation's jet set, gradually became known as a slow-paced retirement resort. It acquired the cheerless nickname "God's Waiting Room."

The economic malaise was reflected in the decreasing growth rates of Dade County's resident population: from 89 percent in the 1950s it dropped to 36 percent in the 1960s, then to 28 percent in the 1970s. Between 1960 and 1980, Dade County witnessed only one new incorporation, though Islandia could hardly be regarded a real town.[11] Most significantly, net domestic in-migration for Dade County decreased in the 1960s and then, in the 1970s, it turned negative: domestic out-migration had started to exceed domestic in-migration, in no small part owing to accelerating migration from Dade to Broward by those who had little tolerance for Cuban immigrants. It was reflected in the changing numbers of non-Hispanic whites: they still grew by 29 percent in the 1950s but fell to 4 percent in the 1960s, and turned to -1 percent in the 1970s. It was a fundamental reversal of what had happened in the first half of the twentieth century. Even though Dade County continued to receive large numbers of immigrants from the rest of the United States, since the early 1970s net domestic migration has consistently been negative.

For Broward County things were different. It had never witnessed the excesses of Miami or Miami Beach and thus developed more steadily. It had lagged behind Dade County during the first half of the twentieth century but seemed to be catching up as its population quadrupled in the 1950s. The Broward economy in the 1960s did not mirror national trends of sustained expansion, but it was not as stultified as the Dade economy, and the Broward population still doubled. It did so again in the 1970s, with a growing number of migrants coming from Dade County. Broward's steady growth was reflected in numerous incorporations, including Pembroke Pines, Lauderdale Lakes, Sunrise, Coral Springs, North Lauderdale, Parkland, Tamarac, and Coconut Creek.

In the 1950s and 1960s, the civil rights movement was gathering momentum across the country. As late as the early 1960s, segregation laws discriminated against South Florida's blacks. Blacks were systematically kept from using public facilities such as beaches, swimming pools, parks, hospitals, transportation, and schools. Many private restaurants, hotels, bars, and stores refused service to them. Prior to 1945, they were not allowed on any of Miami's beaches—beginning that year, Virginia Key had the one and only beach designated for "coloreds." Because it was not connected to the mainland by bridge, people had to get there by rowing a boat.

Pervasive discrimination kept blacks from moving into white residential areas. Miami Beach was all white. The Beach police enforced a midnight curfew, and many famous black entertainers, like Ella Fitzgerald, Count Basie, and Billie Holiday, were forced to leave the island after their shows. They would usually perform again for a black audience in late night hours at the Lyric Theater or one of the other clubs on N.W. 2nd Avenue in Overtown, popularly referred to as Little Broadway. Famous blacks who visited Miami over the years, like W. E. B. DuBois and Zora Neale Hurston, too, would stay at hotels in Overtown. In 1963, when Harry Belafonte did a show at the Eden Roc on the Beach and actually spent the night there, it made local news headlines.

Overtown was the heart of South Florida's black community. It was there in the Greater Bethel AME Church in 1958, in front of an "overflow audience," that Martin Luther King campaigned to double the number of black registered voters.[12] By 1950, Overtown was home to nearly half of Dade County's black population and it had evolved into a tight-knit community. Most were working-class people, but there were many thriving small businesses and many families owned their homes.

But by the time American blacks finally won legal recognition of their constitutional rights, Overtown was heading into a sharp decline.[13] The overall slowing of South Florida's economy, and particularly the downturn in construction, had a negative impact from the early 1960s onward. As blacks started to gain access to stores outside Overtown, retail business in the district suffered. But irreversible destruction came with the building of two major highway flyovers right through the middle of Overtown. Construction of I-95 and I-395 began in the 1960s and was finished in 1976. The first split the area into western and eastern parts; the second cut through the larger eastern part and resulted in a north-south divide. The large spaces beneath the elevated expressways swallowed up a large part of the area and turned it into a wasteland. The local traffic circulation system turned dysfunctional. Total forced displacement was estimated at 12,000 people and another 4,830 decided to move out on their own initiative. In 1960, Overtown had peaked at a population of 33,000. By 1970, the community had lost more than half of its population and a third of its businesses. Home ownership dropped more than 50 percent.

Many people who left Overtown went to Liberty City, an area just to the north that consisted mainly of New Deal public housing projects from the 1930s. The creation of Liberty City had some additional, more insidious origins: Miami's business and political establishment "conceived of this project as the nucleus of a new black community that might siphon off the population of 'Colored Town' and permit downtown business expansion. The availability of federal housing funds mobilized the civic elite, who seized this opportunity to push the blacks out of the downtown area."[14] In other words, Liberty City was invented in part to allow the expansion of Miami's central business district into Overtown. With the construction of the highways and the demise of Overtown in the 1960s, Liberty City grew quickly but it never replaced the Overtown community of the past. Against the backdrop of the prolonged economic downturn of the 1960s and 1970s, it transformed into a ghetto. Opa Locka, which also experienced fast growth of its African American population during the 1970s, had a similar fate.

The achievements of the civil rights movement did not translate into economic gains for South Florida's blacks. The protracted recession played its part but so did ongoing racial discrimination. The massive arrival of the Cubans seemed to make things worse still with increased competition for jobs and affordable housing. In addition, black concerns were overshadowed by public debates on the Cuban refugee crisis.[15] Black discontent and frustration rose, as did racial tension.

The first time that things came to a boil was during the Republican National Convention in Miami Beach in August 1968—four months after the assassination of Martin Luther King. The situation became explosive when, shortly before the convention, George Wallace came to town to showcase his racist campaign for the presidency in front of an enthused crowd of white supporters. With the national media attention focused on Miami during the convention, African Americans organized a rally to protest racial policies of the Republican Party. The police went in, a confrontation ensued, and things turned violent. The Liberty City riot went on for several days, took four lives, and drew national attention.

On August 16, 1968, when things had quieted down, the black-owned *Miami Times* newspaper put it this way: "The riot last week came as no surprise to us. It should have not surprised any of you either. If you had only looked around you and seen the results of social injustice and inequality, surely you would have seen the disturbance coming."[16] Printed in a newspaper that was almost exclusively read by blacks, those words were not likely to reach the people who most needed to hear it.

The single most dramatic year in Miami's history was probably 1980. Three different stories had been underway in South Florida for some time, with distinct origins, different characters, and following separate logics. As in the plot of a fashionable drama movie, the stories would gradually converge, then intersect and reach a common climax. That climax happened in the summer of 1980.

The first story was triggered in Cuba. On April 1, several thousands of Cuban asylum seekers occupied the Peruvian embassy in Havana. The event drew international attention and caused

Figure 13. Mariel refugees arrive at Key West on board the *Lady Virgo*, 1980. State Archives of Florida.

considerable embarrassment to the Cuban regime. After two weeks of failed negotiations and threats, Castro decided to open the port of Mariel to anyone who wanted to leave. The Cuban government allowed ships and boats from Miami and elsewhere to enter the port and pick up the human cargo. But the people who were gathered at Mariel were not only the dissidents who had sought refuge in the Peruvian embassy. Castro seized the opportunity to empty his jails and, it was said, mental hospitals, mixing them with the dissidents. The Cuban leader declared, "Those that are leaving from Mariel are the scum of the country— antisocials, homosexuals, drug addicts, and gamblers, who are welcome to leave Cuba if any country will have them."[17]

About 125,000 *marielitos* entered the United States over the next six months. Eighty percent ended up in Miami.[18] The first groups of new refugees were greeted with sympathy and enthusiasm. But when the size of the stream of refugees started to register in South Florida, apprehension set in, and when it became apparent that Castro had used the event to rid himself of delinquents and mental patients, apprehension turned to panic. Even if the actual numbers of "deviants" remained a matter of speculation, there could be no doubt that the *marielitos* were very much unlike the wealthy entrepreneurial classes of the first wave of refugees. Most were poor and had little education. Criminal elements soon made their presence known. Already during the summer months of 1980, South Florida saw a spike in crime rates, particularly in Miami Beach and Little Havana, where many of the newcomers were housed.

The situation was reported on almost daily in the news. The local authorities called in vain to have the refugees diverted to Costa Rica and other destinations in Central America and the Caribbean—anywhere but Miami. Even among the Cubans who had been in Miami for some time, concern grew and some distanced themselves from the *marielitos* out of fear of seeing their reputation blemished. Their worries were understandable: according to national polls, by 1982 the large majority of the U.S. public held negative views of Cubans, more negative than of any other immigrant group in the country.[19]

The second story took off in downtown Miami about four months before the Mariel boatlift got under way. In the early morning hours of December 17, 1979, thirty-three-year-old Arthur McDuffie, a black motorcyclist, was beaten to death by an all-white group of policemen. Before the beating, McDuffie, an insurance salesman and a former U.S. marine, had been chased by the police at high speed through parts of Liberty City and Overtown. The reason for the chase was never quite clear, but police records did show that McDuffie had accumulated traffic citations and was driving with a suspended license. When McDuffie gave up and got off his motorcycle at the corner of North Miami Avenue and 38th Street, a scuffle ensued. The policemen handcuffed McDuffie, removed his helmet, and hit him savagely over the head with clubs and fists until he collapsed. It was a gruesome scene: "McDuffie lay immobile, his head split open and his brain swelling uncontrollably."[20] Subsequently, one of the police officers ran his vehicle over the motorcycle to create the impression that the injuries were the result of an accident. Four days later, McDuffie died in Jackson Hospital. The Dade County examiner would later testify that McDuffie's wounds were "the equivalent of falling from a four-story building and landing head-first . . . on concrete."[21]

The four police officers were suspended before the end of December. It turned out that they all had considerable track records of citizen complaints and internal affairs probes. Emotions ran high in Miami and the McDuffie trial was moved to Tampa. It started on March 31, 1980, a day before the Cuban dissidents in Havana headed for the Peruvian embassy. For that one day, at least, all eyes in Miami were on the trial. The four officers were indicted for manslaughter, as well as tampering with or fabricating evidence. The charge against one of them was later elevated to second-degree murder.

The trial lasted about six weeks. Then, on May 17, an all-white jury in Tampa announced the verdict: the four policemen were acquitted on all charges. The news sent shockwaves through the black community. Within hours of the verdict there were demonstrations in downtown Miami and in Liberty City. When police forces confronted the demonstrators, violence erupted, which quickly spread to the Black Grove and Overtown. The governor of Florida called in thousands of National Guard troops to restore order, but the riots still lasted a full three days. Eighteen people died, hundreds were wounded, and damages were estimated up to two hundred million dollars. They were the worst race riots in U.S. urban history, to be superseded only by the riots in Los Angeles in 1992.

This was not just about McDuffie, no matter how perverse the case or the outcome. "Many Miamians, whites as well as blacks,

Figure 14. Riots in Liberty City following the McDuffie verdict: a National Guardsman tells a motorist to keep moving, May 19, 1980. © Miami Herald Media Company, 1980.

were shocked by the acquittals. But for blacks, the trial had a significance that went beyond the McDuffie case itself. It represented the truest, most damning test of the entire legal system."[22] Frustration among Miami's blacks had been building for years in spite of, or maybe fueled by, the legal achievements of the civil rights movement. Economic advancement was wanting, relations with the Miami police had been profoundly hostile from the beginning, and it seemed that blacks could be discriminated against, maltreated, and even murdered with impunity. The six weeks of the McDuffie trial coincided with the first phase of the Mariel boatlift. The massive arrival of ever more Cubans and the media attention it demanded, precisely at this time, must have compounded a sense of isolation among many blacks, who received painfully little sympathy for their plight from other Miamians.

The third story's origins lay in Francois Duvalier's Haiti. Also known as Papa Doc, Duvalier was elected as Haiti's president in 1958. His despotic and murderous regime terrorized the population and condemned the majority of Haitians to egregious poverty. According to many measures, Haiti was the most impoverished and most repressive nation in the Western Hemisphere. By the late 1950s and early 1960s, many of the more affluent Haitians had already left the country and sought refuge in places like New York, Paris, and Montreal. Despite its similar climate and tropical environment, South Florida prior to the civil rights movements did not appeal to Haitians because of its blatant racism.

After 1977, refugee flows toward South Florida started to pick up, slowly at first, and gathered momentum. By early 1980, the so-called Haitian boat people were streaming into South Florida almost daily, crammed into small rickety boats that were barely able to make the 720-mile journey. A number of efforts to reach South Florida failed dramatically. One of the most tragic incidences was in October 1981 when a flimsy vessel named *La Nativité* sank in a storm less than a hundred yards off the coast and thirty-three dead bodies washed upon the shore near Fort Lauderdale. The migrants were probably dumped off a large smuggling ship and herded onto *La Nativité* a few miles off the coast. The going smuggling fee was said to be around $1,500 per person.[23]

When the Mariel boatlift took off in May 1980, the Haitians, too, responded to the call for freedom. Refugee numbers increased rapidly in the early summer months and peaked in August 1980, at the same time that Cuban arrivals reached their highest volume. The number of registered Haitian refugees for that month was 2,477 and the total for 1980 was 24,530.[24] That did not include those who escaped interdiction or detention—in the fall of 1980 it was estimated that every day about 200 Haitians entered South Florida illegally.

Between 1977 and 1981, approximately 60,000 Haitians sought refuge in South Florida. The local and national perception of Haitians was very negative, in part perhaps because so little was known about them. Indeed, Haitians have suffered some of the worst stereotyping in the modern history of the Americas.

Figure 15. Intercepted Haitian refugees waiting to go ashore at the Coast Guard station in Miami, April 14, 1980. © Miami Herald Media Company, 1980.

Many looked at the boat people as poor, uncivilized, voodoo-practicing peasants who were likely to carry diseases such as tuberculosis and, later, AIDS. These stereotypes fueled the resolve of local governments to lobby for stringent federal policies to curb Haitian immigration.

Haitian refugees received a different legal treatment from Cubans as most were considered economic refugees rather than

CHAPTER 3

political ones. Many were sent back and others had to endure extensive clearance procedures. Krome Detention Center in southwest Dade County, the main site for the processing of Haitian refugees, was overflowing. It was common to be detained for prolonged periods of time. By July 1982, almost two years after the number of intercepted refugees peaked, there was a backlog of 32,000 cases. Being black, poor, modestly educated, and lacking good English-language skills, most of those who were allowed to stay faced an uphill battle. They settled in concentrated areas of Dade and Broward counties such as the area northeast of Overtown that would become known as Little Haiti, the city of North Miami, and Fort Lauderdale. Haitians became the largest immigrant group in Broward County in the early 1980s.

In more than one way, then, 1980 proved to be a turning point. First, it raised anxiety among non-Hispanic whites to the level of despair.[25] In the eyes of Miami's white establishment, their city was under siege. Near the end of the year, an English-only referendum was passed as a means to resist the Cuban siege. Non-Hispanic whites feared that their city was forever lost.

For the Cubans already in Miami, the events of 1980 served as a wake-up call. On the one hand, the arrival of the *marielitos* indicated that the Cuban stay in Miami would not be as temporary as they first hoped and expected. On the other hand, the hostile and organized response of the local population to the growing Cuban presence provided a lesson to the Cubans. After 1980, Cubans set their eyes on Miami and laid claim to the city. They naturalized in large numbers to become enfranchised, and the number of Cubans in political office increased notably.

Finally, Miami's African Americans were caught in between. Instead of tasting the long awaited fruits of the victory in the civil rights movement, African Americans were crowded out of Miami's political apparatus. The sharp contrast between the harsh treatment of Haitian refugees and the federal government's pampering of Cuban immigrants provoked accusations of racism. Economically, the successes of recent Cuban immigrants intensified feelings of relative deprivation among African Americans. Relations between the two groups were cool and distant and would remain so for many years. At times they would find themselves in open conflict with each other, as when Nelson Mandela visited Miami in 1990—he was revered by African Americans but scorned by Cubans for his sympathetic relations with Fidel Castro.[26]

The multiple crises of 1980 and the subsequent surge in crime rates tarnished Miami's national image. These vexing times were perhaps best reflected in the infamous *Time* cover story in October 1981, which was titled "Paradise Lost?" It chronicled South Florida's volatile recent history and elaborated on the exploding drug trade and crime epidemic. The article featured a map of South Florida that showed main tourist sites and beaches, alternated with alarming symbols such as guns to indicate high-crime areas, boats overloaded with Haitian refugees off the Atlantic coast, and small airplanes and cigarette boats carrying cocaine. The piece had turmoil, declivity, and danger written all over it. The publication was received with indignation and a fair bit of denial by the local establishment—it was clear that the "magic city" had been transformed in ways beyond its control. The *Time* article dealt another blow to the bewildered state of mind of South Floridians.[27]

Organized crime had been a part of Miami's history since the early twentieth century and was particularly striking during the 1920s and 1950s. After Castro's revolution, a considerable part of Havana's Mafia activities shifted to Miami. The Havana connection was no more, but things only seemed to get busier in South Florida. In 1967, *Newsweek* dubbed Miami "Mob Town, USA" and referred to the "syndicated beach front" of Miami Beach.[28] More was yet to come. The surge in crime in the late 1970s and early 1980s was extraordinary, even by Miami's standards. In 1979,

Miami already had by far the highest crime rates of all major cities in the nation. Then, in 1980, violent crime rose another 82 percent and the murder rate went up 78 percent.[29] Much of it was "disorganized" organized crime, the sort of chaos to emerge in a place that actually had an impressive tradition of illicit networks but that was thrown into disarray with the sudden appearance of a range of new illicit opportunities and connections, and plenty of characters to seize the day. This was the era of the "cocaine cowboys," immortalized in Brian de Palma's remake of the movie *Scarface* in 1983.

In the late 1970s and early 1980s, the cocaine-trafficking business firmly established itself in the city, with major ties to Colombia and other offshore regions. The willing participants included old-time mobsters, ex-CIA agents, some *marielitos*, bent bankers, opportunistic lawyers, corrupt police officers, small airplane owners, petty criminals, and an ambitious new crowd of South American gangsters, mainly from Colombia. The cocaine business set off new waves of violence that made headlines around the country. The *New York Times* referred to Miami as "Murder City, USA," a place where crime had gone "berserk."[30] The following report from the *Miami Herald* describes one of the leading characters on the scene and gives an impression of Miami's outlandish criminal milieu at the time:

Griselda Blanco, the so-called "godmother of cocaine," was known in the 1980s as a psychopath who gleefully settled debts with the pull of a trigger. At the time of her arrest, she was tied to no less than forty assassinations. She was the organizer of one of the most notorious killing sprees in Miami's history in which hit men murdered two rival gang members and killed four innocent bystanders in the Dadeland shopping mall in 1979. She named her fourth son Michael Corleone, after the character in the *Godfather* movie, and brought all her sons into the trade (they were all murdered, eventually). When finally caught in 1985, she seemed destined for the electric chair, but the case was scuttled because of a scandal at the state attorney's office involving one of Blanco's former hit men having phone sex with one of the prosecutor's secretaries. In the end, she received a 20-year sentence.[31]

Miami's surreal qualities shone like never before during these years. They merged the undying attraction of beaches, balmy weather, and palm trees with a pervasive climate of fear and crime. The small area of South Beach became home to an unlikely combination of residents, including Orthodox Jews, *marielitos*, and midwestern retirees. The deco district's faded glamour and paled pastel colors formed an unlikely decor for the placid retirement communities. Seated quietly in customary rows on their hotel porches, the aging folks must have wondered what they were looking at.

In central Miami, Little Havana had become a reality while most of the suburbs still had a distinctly southern U.S. feel where Latinos were viewed as aliens. Latinos themselves dismissed the suburbs as a backcountry where you could not even get a decent *cafecito*.

The early 1980s were confusing times. It was not clear if the days of glamour were really over, how long the Cubans would stay, if the absurdly high crime rates would ever come down, if the Haitians and other refugees would keep coming, and if race relations would recover from the McDuffie riots. Northerners weren't coming to Miami in droves anymore. After Mariel, population growth rates slowed. The years 1982–83 witnessed a shrinking of Dade County's population, a rare event indeed. For many residents and outside observers, it just was not clear anymore what Miami was, or what it was turning into.

This ethnic transformation was unprecedented in major cities in the United States and it has never been repeated. In 1960, about 80 percent of Dade County's one million people were non-Hispanic whites and only 5 percent were Hispanic. By the early

1980s, in just two decades, there were more Hispanics than non-Hispanic whites and the cultural fabric of this metropolis had fundamentally changed. Hispanics formed an absolute majority and the share of non-Hispanic whites fell below 30 percent (the share of blacks slightly increased from 15 percent to about 20 percent). Places like Hialeah experienced a complete makeover: almost entirely Anglo in 1960, they were more than 90 percent Hispanic by 1990, with the bulk of the Hispanic population being Cuban.

In 1980, Miami became "Cuba's second largest city." Cubans were now the single largest ethnic group in the county, about a third of the total population. Many other immigrant groups arrived in the 1980s and 1990s in large numbers: Nicaraguans, Colombians, Haitians, Dominicans, Hondurans, Jamaicans, Peruvians, Venezuelans, Mexicans, Argentineans, Brazilians, and Ecuadorans, as well as smaller groups from other countries in the hemisphere and beyond.

The arrival of Nicaraguan exiles started in the late 1970s and in some ways it was a repeat performance of the Cuban influx, even if the numbers were not as high. A dictator with U.S. sympathies (Somoza) was removed by leftist rebels (Sandinistas), causing the rich and the entrepreneurial classes to seek refuge in Miami, the designated haven for such occasions. Anastasio Somoza himself did as deposed Cuban leaders before him: when he saw the end was nigh, he secretly bought himself a bayside estate in Miami and filled some bank accounts on Brickell Avenue. He arrived in Miami in 1979 and never left: he is buried in the same cemetery as the Cuban presidents Carlos Prio and Gerardo Machado, on Miami's Calle Ocho. About fifteen thousand Nicaraguans came in the late 1970s and more waves followed in the mid- and late 1980s. While culturally distinct, there were strong ideological sympathies between Cubans and Nicaraguans in Miami.

The population transformation was concentrated in Dade County. Broward County was quite different: it became the default destination for many non-Hispanic whites who decided they did not want to live in "Latin America." Their sentiments were expressed on bumper stickers reading: "Will the Last American to Leave Miami Please Bring the Flag." The Jewish community that had only arrived since the 1920s started moving north as well after the mid-1970s,[32] to northern Miami Beach, Broward County, and Palm Beach County. By 1980, Hispanics were still less than 4 percent of Broward's population and most of those were Puerto Ricans, not Cubans. Non-Hispanic whites were still a large majority, with about 75 percent. Most of Broward's foreign-born population at that time was from Europe. In sharp contrast to Dade County, Broward County still looked very much like the old America—it was as if the U.S. border was right there on the county line.

What was most astonishing was that the city actually found a new form by the late 1980s, that it restabilized as quickly as it did after multiple deep crises and the wholesale rearrangement of its social structure. It was never the same, of course, but the sense of crisis had lifted. When reviewing South Florida's urban history of the twentieth century, it is apparent that it was in the 1980s that Miami really earned the label "magic city" that was bestowed on it for more gratuitous reasons in the 1920s.

One of the early signs of this magical resurrection was, ironically, the wildly popular TV series *Miami Vice*, which first aired in September 1984. Instead of further damaging Miami's image as a drug-infested and crime-ridden city, the show somehow gave Miami renewed appeal. The illusory world of *Miami Vice*, with its unique visual palette and innovative musical scores, was a play on the city's surreal culture of the early 1980s, notched up to even higher levels of phantasmagoria. The secret behind its success, the producer Michael Mann once said, was "no earth tones." Carl Hiaasen commented about the series, "All the chamber of commerce types were worried about the effect it might have on tourism. Then they realized that if you show people some palm trees and a nice beach, they don't really care if they have to step over a couple of corpses to get there."[33]

The transformation was reflected in the reorientation of the *Miami Herald*. The city's largest newspaper had traditionally voiced concerns of the Anglo population. In the early stages of the transition, with stability gone and the future uncertain, the newspaper often took a negative stand against the massive influx of Hispanics. This culminated in the *Herald*'s highly critical position toward the arrival of the *marielitos* in 1980. But it soon became clear that there was no way back, and as it became apparent that Miami actually might have a rewarding future as a new kind of multicultural metropolis, the newspaper changed its tune. By 1988, when the influx of Nicaraguans peaked as a result of the termination of U.S. aid to the Contras, the *Herald*'s editorials were quite sympathetic; they shared in the welcome extended to the Nicaraguans by the Cubans, who considered them brothers-in-arms. In the same year, the newspaper introduced a brand-new Spanish language edition, *El Nuevo Herald*, independent of the English edition and with its own reporting staff and editors, most Cuban Americans. Importantly, the newspaper spoke out against the English-only campaigns by (dwindling numbers of) hard-core Anglos. It should be remembered that by this time Hispanics had become a majority. At the *Miami Herald* and in commercial circles all over, it was increasingly realized that "bilingual Miami was profitable, monolingual Miami was not."[34]

In all, it had been an amazing ethnic and cultural overhaul. Within less than twenty-five years, Miami's population had changed beyond recognition. Few would have predicted it and many had doubted that the city would overcome its crises. But it did. Miami turned itself "magically" into an entirely new kind of multicultural metropolis or, as some would have it, a "Latin city." And, as the next chapter shows, even that was only half the story.

The Miami Growth Machine

Another profound transformation took place in Miami between the early 1970s and the mid-1980s. This was not high drama that played out on the front pages of the newspapers or consumed public debate. Befitting Miami's political reputation as the "intrigue capital of the hemisphere,"[1] it was a rather stealth-like change that, in the early stages at least, occurred mostly under the surface. Unnoticed by many ordinary citizens and overshadowed by the tumultuous events just described, it would still change the city forever. Indeed, *without* it the ethnic transformation could not have been sustained. It was the remaking of Miami's economy or, better said, of its *political* economy, from a tourist town into a high-wired international trade and finance center.

In a seminal paper written in 1976, Harvey Molotch introduced the idea of the "urban growth machine." He argued that in order to understand cities better, we need to broaden our perspective beyond the usual sociological traditions and focus on the cities' political economies. The thrust of his argument was that the ways and directions in which cities develop are largely determined by the economic growth strategies of business elites: "The desire for growth provides the key operative motivation toward consensus for members of politically mobilized local elites, however split they might be on other issues. . . ." It follows, said Molotch, that "the very essence of a locality is its operation as a growth machine." Thus, the particular nature of any given urban growth machine is a matter of the consensus forged by the local elites.[2]

Miami makes a fascinating example of an urban growth machine, with the point "however split they might be on other issues" being especially significant. The key issue here is that Miami's growth machine underwent a major overhaul in the 1970s and early 1980s, well *ahead* of the massive ethnic and social transformation described in the previous chapter. And it could hardly have been different, for the growth machine was in the hands of the business elites who operated without significant public controls or interference, while local residents' cultural adjustment to the immigrant waves was a much slower and more arduous process.

This de-synchronous transformation was particularly visible when, in the wake of the upheavals of 1980, the Anglo grassroots movement Citizens of Dade United got an ordinance passed that prohibited "the expenditure of any county funds for the purpose of utilizing any language other than English or any culture other than that of the United States."[3] Eight years later, the movement was still alive and kicking: in 1988 it successfully pushed an English-only amendment to the Florida state constitution with approval by 84 percent of Florida's voters. But by that time, as we shall see, the growth machine had been fully reconditioned to rely significantly on the Spanish-language skills of Miami's work force! Indeed, already in 1980, the year of multiple social and cultural crises, Miami's economic reorientation was firmly underway, having begun in the early 1970s.

Local boosters had flirted with notions of Miami as a potential international business center already in the early 1940s, but it is important to separate this flirtation from the actual economic restructuring, which did not happen until the early 1970s. Promotional publications of the Miami Chamber of Commerce's Industrial Department in 1941 and 1943 referred to the city as the "Gateway to the Americas," declaring without hesitation, "Already all signs point to Miami as the meeting place between businesses of the two Americas after the war." It was really all hot air then, typical booster language without any substance. In the 1930s, similar claims had been made about Tampa.[4] What made such language interesting was that it reflected the gradually changing place of Miami in the geographical *imagination*. Soon, the message was wrapped in cartographic images used to suggest the self-evident truth about Miami's "incredible" location. The City of Miami celebrated its fiftieth anniversary in 1946 with a booklet that included a (rather primitive) map that put Miami right in the center of the entire hemisphere with concentric circles indicating its reach in all directions. The caption read, somewhat awkwardly: "Centering the Hemisphere: Situated virtually at the center of the Western Hemisphere, Miami is nearer more important cities than any other metropolis in the New World. Within an air-flight radius of 24 hours lies all of the capitals, ports and trade centers of North and South America."[5] The booklet even played up the Latin connections: "Miami is becoming more and more cosmopolitan . . . with a Spanish flavor." Clearly, at that time Hispanics were still viewed as exotic neighbors, not yet as guests who had overstayed their welcome—they comprised less than 3 percent of the resident population in 1946. None of this should have been taken very seriously: the booklet also solemnly claimed that "scientific studies show worker efficiency to be from 15 to 20 percent greater than in the colder sections of the country."

In 1959, Dade County's Development Department published an economic survey that included a more polished version of the "centric" map, and it would be reproduced time and again for decades to come. Even then, it was still little more than posturing. The Chamber of Commerce and local government still concentrated on old-fashioned (and futile) efforts to lure labor-intensive manufacturing (!) from the north to the region. That was the main purpose of the sales pitch.

By 1972, the University of Miami had published an atlas of metropolitan Miami that opened with a different hemispheric map. It had Miami in the middle of a network with spokes radiating outward to a range of major cities north and south. The title said, "Metropolitan Miami . . . Gateway to the Americas. Linked by air to major cities in the hemisphere."[6] While air passenger transport was increasing, South Florida's international economic connections were in fact still negligible.

Miami was on the eve of its economic transformation, but most people would not have been able to foresee it, not even the most ardent city boosters. What some of Miami's business elite had wildly fantasized for a couple of decades suddenly had real potential because of an extraordinary culmination of events. As William Jennings Bryan, a U.S. presidential candidate and a real estate orator in Coral Gables in the 1920s, once said, "Miami is the only city in the world where you can tell a lie at breakfast that will come true by evening."[7]

Economic transformation was born from the confluence of five factors. First, when the Cubans started arriving in Miami after Castro's rise to power, the city's economy was running out of steam. As noted earlier, South Florida did not enjoy the sustained high growth that characterized the overall U.S. economy during the 1960s. Miami never had a strong manufacturing base and it relied to a large degree on tourism, transportation, construction, retailing, and services. Indeed, in 1962, retailing was the largest sector of Dade's economy in terms of employment.[8] Construction had been strong through the late 1950s but was now in a cyclical downturn. Tourism had always been a fickle business and Miami's appeal faded some during the 1960s. It was a time void of excitement in South Florida's economy, with the opening in 1971 of Disney World to the north as a faint highlight. With the eruption of the oil crisis of 1973 and the onset of a nationwide recession, prospects for Miami's traditional economy looked dim.

Second, Miami did not have the kind of old-boy network that characterized many cities in the Deep South. It lacked an establishment that had been in place for generations and that was prone to intransigence. Instead, apart from a small landed elite that had been around for two or maybe three generations, Miami's capitalists, entrepreneurs, and business leaders had always come and gone, even more than most of the rest of the population. Things had become more stable in the 1950s compared to, say, the 1920s or 1930s, but most of the city's economic movers and shakers came from elsewhere in the United States and the pioneer spirit was no stranger to them. In other words, Miami's business elite was dynamic and adaptable.

The third and perhaps decisive factor was the spectacular increase in human resources in terms of business expertise and international connections. As noted, the first waves of Cuban immigration brought thousands of seasoned entrepreneurs and business people looking for ways to start over. Subsequent waves of immigrants brought many smaller business owners who sometimes simply transplanted their businesses to Miami, as well as large numbers of professionals. Some already had extensive business relations in Latin America, and many had the potential to create such networks. The impact of the arrival of these human resources in Miami is reflected in the fact that until around 1960, cities like New Orleans, Tampa, and Houston were deemed more likely candidates to become the Caribbean commercial center.[9] Miami's new immigrants were going to make a huge difference.

Fourth, during the 1960s and 1970s air travel came within

reach of the masses or at least became available to international business travelers. The number of air passengers in the United States doubled between 1950 and 1960 and then quadrupled between 1960 and 1970, reaching a total of two hundred million. Despite the oil crisis, the number grew to reach three hundred million by 1980. Air travel was (and is) crucial to Miami owing to its eccentric location, allowing it to be connected to the north, but also to the Caribbean and Latin America.

Finally, the growth process was helped along with the timely injection of massive amounts of capital in the South Florida economy from the illicit drug trade in the latter part of the 1970s and the first half of the 1980s. The drug-trafficking business played a major transformative role in the incipient stages of Miami's emerging trade and finance sectors.

All the pieces were in place for a major and swift overhaul of Miami's growth machine. It was, in the words of Maurice Ferré, then the mayor, "like the perfect storm."

Few ordinary people knew about the Non-Group. Formed in 1971, it was a sort of fraternity of a dozen white non-Hispanic business leaders—the doyens of Miami's corporate establishment. It became so powerful that Miami's mayor later called it "the shadow government of Dade County." Despite consisting of Miami's most influential businesspeople who were quite well known individually, not many locals had ever heard of the organization. It did not maintain formal records.

According to Molotch's thesis, behind-the-scenes politics form a standard ingredient of urban growth machines. This assumes a distinction between "symbolic" and "real" politics. The former is the stuff that is printed on the front pages of the local newspapers. The latter is the kind that takes place in back rooms and on golf courses, less visible but often more important.[10] The name Non-Group fits perfectly with what two other well-known scholars, in a related argument, famously termed "non-decision-making": the idea that the most important issues are often not decided upon in a formal setting but are instead kept off the agenda.[11]

One of the group's founders and its main leader was Alvah Chapman, the CEO of Knight-Ridder (the company that owned the *Miami Herald*). Chapman, a South Carolina native, came to Miami in 1960 as the general assistant manager to James Knight. Chapman was from a family well versed in the newspaper business. Before coming to Miami he had sold his own companies and apparently he was ready for a new challenge. One of the things he liked about his new post, he once said, was that it had no formal job description, allowing him considerable freedoms to make things happen. He played a big part in modernizing the company and making it more profitable. In 1976, after the merger of Knight and Ridder, he was promoted to CEO. Through the years, he showed great dedication to the common causes of South Florida, yet he seemed always to maintain something of a detached, unemotional judgment. In the local news media, Chapman has been referred to as "the linchpin in the Miami Business Machine."[12]

The Non-Group met once a month at one member's home to discuss a range of issues purportedly of public interest. The group might have initially formed in response to the "Latin invasion" and as an effort to preserve Anglo values, a knee-jerk reaction to maintain a semblance of order for business at a time of extreme turmoil. Most of the members were either bankers or developers, representing the two frontline industries that thrive and depend on urban growth.[13] There can be no question that the group was eager to explore new and more rewarding business strategies for Miami. It quickly spawned relations with influential Cubans and it came to promote a sense of common interests among various (ethnic) business factions. Already in 1973, the first Hispanics were tapped as members of the Non-Group. One of them was Armando Codina.

Codina was of the Pedro Pan generation, arriving in the United States at the age of fourteen in 1962. He lived in New York until 1970 and then moved to Miami. This was important, as it turned out, because Codina grew up outside the Cuban enclave and connected easily with non-Hispanic Americans. His first position in Miami was with the Cuban-owned Republic National Bank, where he was fired because he "got into frequent arguments with the bank's president over its policy of hiring tellers who could only speak Spanish, and of its poor treatment of English-speaking customers."[14] Codina started his own business, a medical payments company. He sold it after about five years, much to his financial betterment, and went into real estate. Codina was one the first Latinos accepted by the Anglo power groups, opening the door for many others in the Hispanic community. Shortly after joining the Non-Group, he became a member of the Downtown Development Authority and got involved in various civic projects. By 1980, he owned one of Miami's biggest real estate companies and later he became the first Hispanic to chair the Miami Chamber of Commerce. Chapman later said of Codina that "he played a huge role in bridging the gap between the Anglo and Hispanic communities."

The most significant player of all may have been Maurice Ferré, the first Hispanic mayor of Miami—and the first Hispanic mayor of any large city in the United States. He was in office from 1973 to 1985, precisely the period during which the city's political economy was reconstituted. Ferré's personal background was vitally important to his political career. He was born in Puerto Rico to a wealthy entrepreneurial and politically connected family. In the 1920s the family lived in Miami, where his father worked in real estate. The family returned briefly to Puerto Rico; Maurice was born at that time, but he grew up in Miami and could claim to be something of a homeboy. Ferré was the perfect breed for political office at that moment: Hispanic but *not* Cuban; foreign born but raised in South Florida and highly acculturated to American ways; and last but not least, very well attuned to Miami's corporate circles through his father's and his own businesses. His family was, as one observer put it, "Puerto Rican by birth, Yanqui in spirit."[15] The time was exactly right for Ferré as he facilitated the early phases of integrating the old establishment and the new Cuban elites. In the late 1990s and 2001, Ferré ran for office again but by then Cuban domination of the political scene was well established and his congenital lack of *cubanidad* cost him the elections.

Ferré had been one of the co-founders of the Non-Group, but he withdrew when he became mayor in 1973. He lacked the broad networks of informal influence of someone like Chapman, but he was probably the most forward-thinking leader of his day. He developed a clear vision of Miami as a hemispheric business center in the mid-1970s, ahead of most others. He was the only ethnic hybrid of the Non-Group's original members, all the others coming from the North American non-Hispanic white establishment. His family had business operations across the Americas long before Miami's establishment was ready for such ventures. According to Ferré, the Non-Group was important in bringing together business leaders of various ethnicities, and it was certainly interested in promoting growth and stability, but initially it did so without any vision for Miami's economic future. Beginning in the late 1970s, Ferré shuttled local business leaders to Latin America to open their eyes to the possibilities there but most, he said, were "slow learners and many conservative people here had no idea what was happening."[16] During his twelve years in office, Ferré seems to have pushed the economic transformation more than anybody else, while maintaining majority support from an ever-growing range of constituencies, including assertive Cubans, militant blacks, and reactionary whites. The latter included the Citizens for Dade United, whom he said were "clueless about the city's future."

Another (later) member of the Non-Group was Luis Botifoll. Even though he was a generation older than Codina and known for his strong support of Cuban causes, Botifoll, too, was the kind of hybrid who could easily relate to both worlds. Botifoll studied law in Havana and did graduate studies in the United States (Tulane) in the 1930s. The first time he visited Miami he was sixteen. As an adult, he came up to South Florida with his family for yearly vacations. Botifoll was part of the first wave of exiles in 1960. He was a highly experienced and established businessman with a good feel for U.S. corporate culture. Multinational corporations in the United States were quick to recognize his potential. He spent his first years in the United States supporting anti-Castro organizations, but after a few years he was approached by a group of Chicago investors to work as a consultant on the prospects of the Central American Common Market, requiring him to travel throughout Central America.[17] Soon afterward, other U.S. firms solicited his advice regarding Latin American operations. In the late 1960s, Botifoll wanted to turn his attention back to the Cuban cause but "the lure of business kept beckoning him." In 1970, he became a U.S. citizen and joined the board of directors of Republic National Bank. Four years later, he became vice chairman.

It would go too far to say that the Non-Group controlled Miami's political economy or that it was operating according to some single-minded agenda. It is better viewed as a powerful growth coalition with a hard core, but difficult to define at the edges, a network that involved a range of individuals and organizations at different times. In accordance with the original growth machine argument, the Non-Group worked to forge solidarity among the business classes and a sense of community among the broader population. In all, it was instrumental in bringing together business leaders of different cultural backgrounds, in promoting the primacy of growth through an increasingly international economy, and in generating a new discourse about what was good for Miami.[18]

In 1977 the Business School of Florida International University published a report entitled *Potential of South Florida as an International Finance Center*.[19] It reflected quite clearly that a process of economic restructuring was underway and that a new consensus had been emerging in the business community. The report, the authors said, "could not have been written without the support of many banking executives in the South Florida area." This was true enough, for it had the interests of the banking sector written all over it. The preface stated that "the last few years have overcome the basic inertia associated with new ventures and a strong tendency towards internationalization which continues to gather force and momentum is readily evident." One of the requirements for further progress, the authors noted, was a "change of attitude" across the broader business community.

More concretely, the report called for a change in banking laws: "The Florida statutes should be amended to permit the chartering and operations of foreign banks in the state." Most in the financial sector agreed that a change in the statutes would benefit all and that Miami would attract greater flows of capital. They got what they wanted within a year of the report's publication. First, Florida's laws were changed to allow foreign banks to establish limited operations in the state (none were allowed at all until 1977). Then, in 1978, along with the passing of the U.S. International Banking Act, the State of Florida changed its regulations to allow foreign-controlled Edge Act banks to accept foreign deposits. One of the key lobbyists in these efforts was Maurice Ferré, then the mayor of Miami, who, as a former representative in the Florida House of Representatives, had close ties in the state capital of Tallahassee.

It was an important step in what was already a remarkably dynamic sector of Miami's economy, which had begun with the arrival of Citizens and Southern National Bank in 1969, the first Edge Act bank in Miami. The U.S. Edge Act of 1919 allowed banks to set up branches in multiple states across the country and engage in foreign transactions—and such branches were referred to as Edge Act banks. The fact that Miami had no such activity until 1969 says a lot about its chambered domestic economy in earlier times. But things were now rapidly changing.

At the time of publication of Florida International University's report in 1977, another ten U.S. Edge Act banks had appeared on the scene and nineteen more came to Miami from 1978 to 1980. On January 1, 1981, Miami had a total of thirty-three Edge banks, more than any other city in the United States—New York had twenty-eight, Houston sixteen, Los Angeles and Chicago fourteen each, and San Francisco five.[20] All of this had happened in just eleven years.

Many foreign banks were established as well. Between 1977 and 1981, no fewer than thirty-four branches and representative offices of foreign banks started operations in Miami.[21] Some of these were Edge banks (four were set up by 1980) and others engaged mainly in trade financing. By 1984, the number of Edge banks had grown to forty-three and there were a total of forty-five foreign banks.[22] Another significant trend was the foreign acquisition of Florida commercial banks, something that escalated the international reorientation of Miami's economy: by November 1980, twenty-five acquisitions had been completed or were pending.[23]

In little over a decade, then, Miami's banking scene shifted from a small number of parochial commercial institutions into a national and international banking center with strong ties to the Caribbean and Latin America, and with a diversified cast of participants, including major banks from the United States and the world. The boom, according to a report by the City of Miami in 1982, was "spurred by the expansion of international trade in the city, low Florida taxes, changes in Florida law increasing powers of the Edge Act banks, and their increased use by foreign institutions." It added that "private deposits had become a key issue in the Miami banking community, especially from Latin American individuals."[24]

What the report did not say was that banking in Miami quickly assumed a profile that was very different from the rest of the nation: it was highly imbalanced in that it generated much more funds from abroad then it was able to place abroad. Moreover, about 80 percent of the liabilities of Miami's banks in 1980 were in the form of private deposits, compared to only 15 percent for U.S. banks in general.[25]

The explosive growth of Miami's banking sector was driven in large part by the drug-trafficking business and related money-laundering activities. Miami's international business machine, one might say, kicked in on cocaine. Mike McDonald was an agent with the Criminal Investigation Division of the IRS in the late 1970s. He worked the money side of the drug business in Miami and had a close-up view of the enormous scale of Miami's financial "imbalance":

Treasury had done an analysis of the flow of currency going into the Federal Reserve System and showed that, in 1978 and 1979, the entire currency surplus of the United States was attributed to South Florida. Billions and billions of dollars of cash was taken out of the economy, put into the [Miami] banking system, . . . and shipped back to the Federal Reserves in San Francisco, New York, Chicago . . . that's when I looked at that and said . . . "Oh, my God! This is beyond any imagination, what we're dealing with here." It was unbelievable how much money was going into these banks in cash. We had people walking in with rope-handled shopping bags and deposit slips going into banks. We had twelve individuals in Miami who were depositing $250 million or more annually into non-interest-bearing checking accounts. And no reports were being filed, or very few reports were being filed. . . . Miami very quickly became not only the import capital of the United States for marijuana and cocaine, but it became the financial center for it.[26]

The city had become the wholesale cocaine center of North America. Before the transition, in 1971, the cash surplus of the Miami banking area was $89 million. It meant that local banks received more cash from local clients than they gave out, but the numbers were still relatively modest. In 1974, it had grown tenfold to $924 million. Five years later the surplus skyrocketed to $5.5 billion, greater than the combined surpluses in the rest of the country. In 1982 the surplus peaked at $8 billion, twice the combined surplus in the rest of the entire nation, and by 1985 it was still $5.96 billion.[27] Most big cities in the country, in contrast, would run cash deficits. The Federal Reserve found one single bank in Miami that had forwarded $65 million of cash surplus, of which 63 percent or $42 million was in twenty-dollar bills.[28] South Florida was awash in a sea of money: "Miami's banks were taking in so much cash that they began to charge a fee just to accept a deposit! In one case, the bank even accepted, as a gift from a depositor, a high-powered money-counting machine. One money-changing business in Miami received $242,238,739 in $5, $10, and $20 bills in a single five-month period in 1981. Its bank counted and deposited all that cash, which was brought to the bank in paper bags and cardboard boxes."[29]

The majority of banks in South Florida were involved. A few, like Castle Bank and Miami National Bank, were actually controlled by organized crime. One non-bank institution, the World Finance Corporation, was nicknamed "Miami's Giant Drug Laundromat." Some other banks were notorious for repeated violations and they must have been highly dependent on hot money:

Great American Bank, Bank of Miami, Sunshine Bank, Northside Bank of Miami, and Popular Bank and Trust Company among them. And many others that are still operating today (sometimes under different names) were known to handle suspected drug money or systematically underreported cash transactions to the Treasury: for example, Bank of America, Capital Bank, Southeast Bank, and Republic National Bank.[30] To be sure, banking in Miami in those years was great business and most banks made miraculous profits.

The case of Republic National Bank illustrates the point. According to Costa's biography of Luis Botifoll, the bank was not doing very well in the mid-1970s, but things improved remarkably in subsequent years. Profits more than doubled in 1978, reaching $1.7 million, and by 1984 they shot up to $7.2 million. During the same time, deposits increased from $152 million to $677 million. Costa then asks the obvious question as to how these "tremendous achievements" were made possible. His answer betrays excessive sympathy for the subject of his biography: "The combined skills and talents of these two men, Luis Botifoll and Aristides Sastre, president of bank operations, led the bank to greater economic stability and community service." The author does note that a few years later "something irregular began to surface," but he never explains what the irregularities entailed other than that "an internal crisis originating in operations was developing," which led to a "scandalous situation" that was then said to be resolved by Botifoll, who dutifully dismissed the wrongdoers. There was not a word about the kinds of business that sent profits soaring or that led to the irregularities.[31]

The enormous amounts of money involved in the cocaine business explained the explosion in Miami's crime rates. As the cash surplus surged, so did the murder rate. In the early 1980s, a kilogram of cocaine in Columbia cost traffickers about $1,500. It was sold wholesale in the United States for about $35,000 and had a street value double that. Said Carlos Toro, a former cocaine traf-ficker, "We were selling cocaine at $72,000 a kilo. It cost us—each kilo—to produce it, to bring it, our final cost of production of that kilo of cocaine went down to maybe $1,500. Now, so, I mean, the profits were, I mean, in the . . . millions of dollars."[32] Such profit margins and the opportunity to make a great deal of money in a very short time proved irresistible to a lot of people. Greed and the prospect of massive instant gratification pushed the limits of crime and violence.

The vast sums of illegal cash as well as the crime took law enforcement by complete surprise. In the early 1980s, large numbers of additional police officers had to be recruited. Many had questionable credentials and quite a few ended up behind bars themselves. It was not something that could be controlled by city and county governments. In January 1982, the federal government announced the formation of the South Florida Drug Task Force. Several hundred agents from the Drug Enforcement Agency, Customs, the Coast Guard, and the Treasury Department were assigned to South Florida. Vice President George H. W. Bush headed the task force. On the occasion of its inauguration, Bush stated, "South Florida cannot be a haven for criminals, for sophisticated and organized drug traffickers and for hired assassins." This meant, of course, that it was exactly that. But the principal objective of the task force appeared to be courting Floridian votes for Republican candidates in the November elections of the House of Representatives—and the task force itself did not make a dent in the cocaine business.[33]

It is hard to overestimate the importance of the drug industry to the regional economies it bonded together—or the congeniality of political and economic interests that kept it going. In 1987 it was estimated that revenues from the cocaine trade constituted 10–20 percent of Columbia's total exports, 25–30 percent of Peru's exports, and no less than 75 percent of Bolivia's exports.[34] And the small islands of the Bahamas, much like South Florida, were overwhelmed by the cocaine business. The Bahamian prime minister made a dramatic statement in 1980, saying that cocaine trafficking "is the greatest single threat to the social, economic, fabric of the Bahamas. . . . Unchecked it will destroy us, absolutely destroy us . . . the money available is just too great." Later he was himself implicated in a scandal related to drug money.[35]

In the early 1980s, it was claimed that drug trafficking and money laundering together constituted Florida's biggest industry, with annual revenues of at least $10 billion dollars. The value of the drug trade was four times as high as the total legitimate trade between Florida and Latin America, and 80 percent of it went through Greater Miami. The drug trade in the early 1980s was also "by far, the largest single financial link between Miami and the Caribbean."[36] An economist at Florida International University estimated Greater Miami's "underground economic activity" for 1981 at about a third of the area's total output, with most of it being drug related.[37]

Banks constituted the first line of beneficiaries of these illicit circuits of capital. They took in huge amounts of money that went into non- or low-interest-bearing checking accounts and in turn they put out business and consumer loans at considerable rates—in the early 1980s, well above 10 percent. It was small wonder that so many wanted to get into the banking business. Miami was the only place in America, one banker said, where people would just walk off the street into a banking office to inquire if it was for sale. But it went far beyond banking.

Even if drug money got things rolling in the beginning, businesses soon diversified into a range of legal activities—because money laundering required it, and because it was profitable. This was particularly evident in banking but it applied across the economy. As one study concluded, this "tended to blur the boundaries

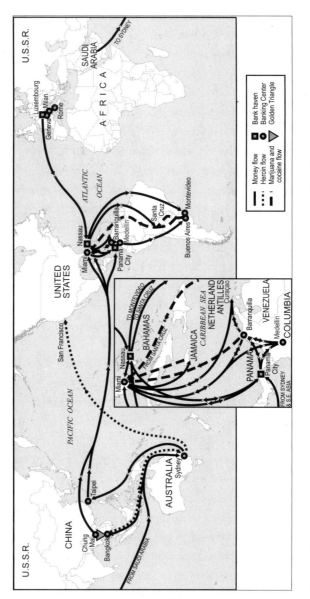

Figure 16. Miami in global networks of narcotics and money laundering, around 1979. Source: P. Lernoux, *In Banks We Trust* (New York: Anchor Press, 1984). Map redrawn by Chris Hanson.

between the legitimate and illegitimate by creating substantial gray areas in the economy."[38] The cocaine trade's "trickle down" or "multiplier effects" must have been especially pervasive because of the nature of Miami's economy: the absence of a large and relatively autonomous manufacturing sector, and the presence of highly interrelated "post-industrial" services (real estate, construction, trade, tourism and entertainment, finance, and so forth).

Much of the illegal money was recycled into real estate and construction. Interest rates were high and the national economy was down, but Miami was booming. An estimated $1.5 billion of illegal money was invested every year in the real estate sector, in turn an essential driver of the area's large construction industry. In one twelve-month period, offshore firms involved in money laundering bought more than $130 million of Florida real estate, almost all of it in Miami-Dade County.[39] And not all of it went through offshore entities: as much as 20 percent of real estate in Miami was being purchased in cash.

Illicit funds not only fueled banking, real estate, and construction, but also retailers of luxury items such as yachts, cars, airplanes, and jewelry. Many lawyers, accountants, and other professionals benefited as well. In 1989 Dexter Lehtinen, then a U.S. attorney, told the *New York Times* that from 1986 to 1989 (and this was after the peak), $220 million in cash was spent on cars in Miami, about ten times more than in other cities its size. In addition, over a four-year period in the early 1980s, lawyers in Miami did $153 million of business in cash transactions, again about ten times the normal rate.[40] Some of the law enforcement officials saw the illicit trade for what it was worth: "You know what would happen if we really did our job here? If we were 100 percent effective, we would so drastically affect the economy that *we* would become the villains."[41]

But that was in the early 1980s when the influence of the drug

Figure 17. Coast Guard cadet Will Fediw stacks a 60-pound bale of cocaine at the Miami station, part of a 10,000-pound bust in the Caribbean waters, July 2008. Photo by U.S. Coast Guard Petty Officer 3rd Class James Harless.

trade on the South Florida economy was at its peak. After about 1985, banking regulations were tightened and law enforcement became more aggressive. Part of the drug trade started to shift elsewhere and so did some of the money-laundering activities. Murder rates came down. Miami's cash surplus grew smaller, and the days of walking up to the teller with shopping bags full of $20 bills were over.

As part of the drug business and the flow of illicit money wound down in the late 1980s, most banks actually continued to do well and only a small number went out of business (for example, Sunshine Bank). Some luxury retailers and nightclubs that started up during the high times of the drug trade, and that relied on customers eager to flaunt their newfound wealth, closed down, but most are still around today. The upscale car dealership called The Collection in Coral Gables is one such example, even though its one-time owner was sentenced to eighteen years in prison in 1993. Another illustrious example of a business that is still going strong is the Cigarette Racing Team factory in North Miami Beach, whose boats were favored by the drug-running business. Its founder was gunned down by the mob in 1987.[42]

By the end of the 1980s, South Florida's economy had become more diversified, more trade oriented, and less dependent on cocaine. In a report by the City of Miami in 1984, Mayor Ferré stated, "Up until the mid-1970s, Miami's economy centered chiefly on tourism. Today it has been displaced by Miami's present number-one industry, international trade and commerce. . . . It has become the economic gateway and bridge for world trade with the Caribbean and Central and South America."[43] Between the early 1970s and the mid-1980s, Miami's economy grew rapidly. Some of this growth drew from illicit capital, but it was more than that. There was a proliferation of internationally oriented businesses that were perfectly legitimate from the start. Many of these businesses were run by recent immigrants. During the 1970s, the number of Hispanic-owned companies was estimated to have tripled to about ten thousand. Many of these were small trading companies or companies that provided international business services.[44]

The same period also witnessed, for the first time, the establishment of large numbers of multinational corporations. Between 1970 and 1977, an average of two or three were established per year, a continuation of previous patterns. Then, between 1978 and 1983 no less than seventy new multinationals arrived in the Greater Miami area. Apart from some yearly fluctuations, the trend has been up ever since. The majority were big North American (and European) companies setting up sales and marketing branches for the Caribbean and Latin America.[45] Many of these offices relied on the new Hispanic work force and especially those with bilingual skills.

Sector-wise, the fastest growth was in finance, real estate, trade, insurance, and business services—in terms of the number of establishments and income. Tourism returned to healthy growth after the dip of 1980–81, and the share of foreign tourists increased notably. The largest relative decline was in manufacturing, the sector that local government had been trying to prop up through the late 1960s. In 1973, manufacturing still held about 17 percent of the region's jobs. It was down to about 12 percent by the mid-1980s. The biggest manufacturing industry in 1973 was garment making. It involved nineteen thousand people and it was, briefly, the third biggest in the nation after New York and Los Angeles. But in the mid-1970s these jobs started leaving, mainly for the Caribbean, where labor was cheaper. Instead, Miami became an apparel services hub and fashion center.

By the end of the 1980s, Miami was the main economic gateway to Latin America and the Caribbean, outcompeting cities such as Houston, Los Angeles, New York, and New Orleans. A special acknowledgment of this impressive transformation came a few years later when *Time*—which had vilified Miami in the "Paradise Lost" feature of 1981—took a bow: "If the go-go 1980s belonged to New York City and Wall Street, the globally-minded 1990s belong to the 'Hong Kong of Latin America,' perched on the rim of the fastest-growing region in the New World."[46] A more serious endorsement followed in 1994: the Economic Intelligence Unit published a report saying that 42 percent of Latin American business executives voted Miami as the "best suited capital of an Americas-wide free trade area," by far the best score of any other city in the hemisphere.[47] A year later, the Harvard professor Rosabeth Moss Kantor identified Miami as the prime example of a world-class trading city in the United States in her book *World Class*. Kantor attributed Miami's success to its "cultural connections"—one of the essential parts of the reconstituted growth machine.[48]

From the point of view of political economy, to suggest that Miami was overwhelmed by the Latin "invasion" or that it had become a "Latin" city is to miss the point. The reconditioning of the growth machine was overseen by the city's non-Hispanic white business elite, even if they became a demographic minority in the process. It was in concert with newly arrived Cuban business leaders, to be sure, but white non-Hispanic dominance would continue for some time. A listing of the "100 most powerful" people in South Florida in 1994 by a reputable local business journal claimed that seventy-five out of a hundred were non-Hispanic whites. Only twenty-one were Hispanics and four were African Americans.[49] The same pattern applied to other indices, such as the twenty-five most highly paid executives, only two of whom were Hispanic. Of the top executives of the fifty largest employers in South Florida, only nine were Hispanic and they were predominantly with governmental, public, or semi-public institutions.[50] In the local political arena, non-Hispanic whites were even more dominant: there were more than twice as many non-Hispanic whites as Hispanics in the elected offices of Dade County's local governments, highly disproportionate to the population shares.[51] It was well *after* the transition of Miami's political economy that the Hispanic demographic majority started to translate into numeric dominance in the city's establishment.

Still, the overhaul of the growth machine was predicated on a new consensus among the different elites and it was fueled by the large and growing presence of Cuban and other Hispanic entrepreneurs and professionals. In the early 1980s, a group of (Hispanic) economists at Florida International University emphasized the positive impact of Cuban immigrants on the economy. They hinted at the emergence of the new growth consensus and its handsome rewards: "The cosmopolitan milieu now characterizing Miami has been highly instrumental in facilitating . . . the opening of new markets, especially those to the South . . . [and an] explosive market expansion in international activities."[52] They added that Miami had acquired a unique "comparative advantage in the international economic field."[53]

Local government was enthusiastically on board and functioned to enable and facilitate the new growth strategies. The City of Miami published a report in 1984 entitled "Miami's Business Community Speaks." It showcased a range of entrepreneurs from different ethnic backgrounds all articulating the new consensus in the growth machine that emphasized international trade and finance. Miami was now the "capital of the Caribbean" and the "gateway of the Americas." This new consensus grew stronger over time, as disagreeable non-Hispanic whites left and were replaced with more accommodating foreign and domestic immigrants.

Much, perhaps too much, has been made of the Cuban "enclave economy": the idea of a self-contained and more or less autonomous economy based on tight ethnic networks. Perhaps the prevalence of this idea has something to do with the fact that Miami so often draws the attention of sociologists, anthropologists, and others who are mainly interested in the city's ethnic composition. To be sure, it has at times been reinforced by Miami's chauvinistic Cubans, who like to tout their self-made success and contrast it to Castro's dismal economic performance in the mother country. From an international political-economy perspective, Hispanic (Cuban) economic activity encompassed much more than an enclave economy.[54] And at higher levels of decision making and restructuring, it was not an enclave at all—it was an integral and essential part of a realigned, international, urban growth machine.

CHAPTER 5

The Birth of a World City

Miami's economic transformation resulted from more than the internal machinations of the city's business elite. It was also part of a much bigger story. Around the world, processes of globalization had accelerated since the late 1970s and were drawing certain cities into a global orbit, linking them to worldwide financial and economic networks.[1] These included such cities as Milan, Dublin, Hong Kong, Singapore, Frankfurt, Toronto, Sydney, and Miami. Globalization also further enhanced the position of major cities with already strong international orientations, like New York and Paris.

There have, of course, been globally oriented cities earlier in history, like seventeenth-century Amsterdam or Victorian London. What is different about the emergence of world cities in the latter part of the twentieth century is that they are greater in number and that they form a large and complex urban network that underpins the world economy. Modern world cities are a by-product of globalization. And globalization itself is based on a timely combination of telecommunication and transport advances and a near worldwide turn to free markets—both ideological and in terms of government policies. The latter was especially important in allowing the free flow of capital and trade across political borders. Urban areas that actually emerged as world cities had certain qualities that other cities lacked. They had the ability to take advantage of globalization and to assume a position of international regional centrality.

Modern world cities like Miami share several features. First, global capital uses them as basing points in the geographical organization of production and markets. As such, world cities together form a global urban network with a hierarchical nature. At the apex of this hierarchy we find the leading global cities of New York, London, and Tokyo. It is not accidental that each of these three primary global cities is located in its own continental time zone, together accounting for twenty-four-hour coverage of global finance. All three are home to the world's biggest stock exchanges and financial markets, and a wide range of headquarters of the world's biggest firms.

Second, world cities are major sites for the concentration of international capital; they perform like valves in the global circulation of capital. Very large amounts of money flow in from a variety of international places and considerable flows of money leave for other destinations. This not only reflects the role of stock markets, but also flows of foreign direct investment, trade financing, and capital flight. Some of that money "sticks" around, for example in the form of high salaries to specialized professional workers, or in real estate investment.

Third, world cities have a disproportionately high degree of command and control in the international economy, often expressed by the presence of big multinational (regional) headquarters. It is also shown by the sectors that dominate the economies of world cities: finance, transport, communications, and producer services such as accounting, consulting, advertising, and legal services. These sectors typically support and coordinate international economic activities. As command and control centers, world cities form a network that functions as the spinal cord of the global economy. The higher up a city is positioned, the greater its influence on the world economy.

Finally, world cities tend to be the destination of large numbers of domestic and international migrants. They contribute to the economic growth of these cities and especially to the development of their global linkages.

It is often suggested that there are about forty or fifty world cities today, depending on the precise criteria. Even though all function together in global networks, substantial variation among them remains. In reality, very few have truly global reach and most have more regionally defined roles. The majority, even if they share certain common characteristics, tend to have specialized functions (port cities, immigration centers, stock markets, distribution centers, certain producer services, and so forth). In most studies, Miami is included as a second- or third-tier world city with an important status as a linchpin between North and South America.

Miami's birth and early growth as a world city occurred sometime in the early 1980s. Quite apart from the internal workings of the urban growth machine just discussed, there was an international logic that drove Miami's rise—and it had as much to do with the surrounding region as with the city itself.

Miami owed its emergence as a world city to its position as an oasis of peace within the region: it was the only place in Latin America and the Caribbean with a stable political economy. From the middle of the twentieth century until the late 1980s, Latin America was one of the most politically volatile regions in the world. According to most measures, liberal democracy was a rarity across the region, and free markets rarely functioned for prolonged periods of time. The infusion of migrants and capital into Miami since the late 1950s related directly to revolutions, wars, and political instability in the Caribbean and South America.

The fall of Havana in 1959 to Fidel Castro, and his subsequent reign, functioned as a catalyst in this process. Entire layers of the formerly privileged elite fled Cuba, and Miami was the haven of choice. They brought with them their connections, skills, and, in most cases, their wealth. The Cuban exiles were followed by Nicaraguans, Colombians, Panamanians, Peruvians, and other Latin Americans who were fleeing political persecution and economic insecurity.

Seen from abroad, Miami's greatest asset was (and is) its location inside the United States. It offers what no other city in the region does: a secure and stable environment for doing business. In Miami, there are no worries about military coups, leftist insurgencies, currency devaluations, land reforms, or the nationalization of banks and other industries. The city has become particularly important as a destination for private capital flows from the international region in search of security, discretion, and a stable currency.

South Florida has received large amounts of money in the form of capital flight from the Caribbean and Latin America. For example, between 1980 and 1982, as Miami's international banking sector was gearing up, an estimated $15.8 billion fled Venezuela owing to fears of depreciation of the bolivar and of restrictive government policies. More than a third of that money ended up in South Florida banks.[2] Around the same time, the Sandinistas came to power in Nicaragua and drove out a large section of the capitalist class: "Approximately 15,000 rich [Nicaraguan] exiles transferred their assets to Miami banks in the late 1970s, moved their furniture into fashionable residences in Key Biscayne and Brickell Avenue, and invested in condominiums. . . ."[3]

In the Caribbean and Latin America, Miami fulfills an important symbolic role as well.[4] The regional elites come to Miami to shop for luxury goods, send their children to attend the University of Miami, and purchase a second home in one of the city's affluent neighborhoods. One of the best-selling international newspapers in Latin America is the international edition of the *Miami Herald*. Latin Americans tend to view Miami with admiration and envy, as a Latin American success story, and as a symbol of modernity. To Latin Americans, Miami is an important point of reference on the road to a successful future.

Let us consider Miami's rise as a world city in a broader global perspective, through a comparison with two of its contemporaries, Hong Kong and Dublin. Together, the three cities were part of the same cohort of newly emerging world cities and they have occupied comparable positions in the global urban hierarchy (with Miami positioned just below Hong Kong and above Dublin, according to most measures). The comparisons are not so much about world city rankings but rather about the conditions and processes that made these three world cities. Of particular interest are Miami's similarities to Hong Kong and its differences from Dublin—with both comparisons illuminating Miami's special circumstances.

Hong Kong has a relatively long history as a (British-controlled) international trading depot, but not until after World War II was it remade into a world city, a decade or so ahead of Miami. Hong Kong and Miami both emerged as world cities at a very rapid pace and in direct relation to the establishment of communist regimes in the region. Some 345,000 refugees from mainland China entered Hong Kong from 1949 to 1951.[5] The border between Hong Kong and the mainland officially closed in 1953, but refugees continued to arrive based on the so-called "touch-base or reached-base rules,"[6] not unlike the special rules that applied to Cuban refugees who have made it to Miami since the early 1960s. With the influx of Chinese refugees from the mainland, Hong Kong grew from about 800,000 in 1949 to 3 million in 1960. The Mariel boatlift that brought over 100,000 Cubans to Miami in 1980 had its precursor in Hong Kong in 1962, the year Mao Zedong opened the border gates to allow some 70,000 people to flood into the British-controlled territory within a couple of weeks.

In both Hong Kong and Miami, the massive refugee influx was

initially considered a huge burden and an enormous challenge, but later it turned out to be a major precondition for their formation as global cities: "As the civil war between the communists and the Guomindang resolved itself in favour of the former, a flood of refugees entered Hong Kong and appeared likely to swamp the Colony out of existence. In fact, the effect was the opposite of this anticipation—the influx of labour was accompanied by capital and entrepreneurial skills. . . ."[7]

Like Miami about ten years later, Hong Kong became a symbolic place in the ideological conflict between communism and capitalism and, fundamentally, the ascent of both Miami and Hong Kong rested on geopolitical events.[8] The resulting consequences for the local political culture, nonetheless, were different. While Miami became the scene of anti-Castro activities and conspiracies, and of a deeply politicized Cuban (American) community, the people of Hong Kong were often described as politically apathetic. Many Cubans in Miami kept motivated by their desire to overthrow Castro and return to their island; most Chinese in Hong Kong counted their blessings and did little to provoke hostilities from the mighty People's Republic.

Perhaps the most pertinent aspect of the comparison between Miami and Hong Kong lies in the particular economic roles of many of the refugees and immigrants. Hong Kong is overwhelmingly Chinese, but the economy was and is capitalist and the island has a decidedly Western character. Hong Kong became "the premier meeting-place of the Chinese and foreign social networks of capital in Asia."[9] Similarly, Miami is part and parcel of the American political economy, but its population is for the most part Latin, and Cubans are the single largest ethnic group. Hong Kong's economic hinterland is China and Miami's is Latin America. Many refugees and immigrants who fled communism had entrepreneurial skills, money, and business contacts across the region. But in order for the migrants to play a central role in the globalizing economies of these cities, they had to assume a sort of double role, or hybrid identity.

The particular character and substantial success of Hong Kong's transcultural or hybrid entrepreneurial classes are well documented: "Hong Kong is depicted as a place *in between* China and the West. . . . Overseas Hong Kong Chinese capitalists can manipulate images of both the transnational, transcultural cosmopolitan and the 'ethnic Chinese,' enabling them to position themselves on the margins of the nation, but at the lucrative center of Pacific Rim business."[10] The same can be said about Miami: it is located between the United States and Latin America and Latino/American hybrids are able to manipulate images of the American cosmopolitan and the ethnic Latino, putting them at the lucrative center of Miami's business economy. Hybrids are sometimes viewed as cosmopolitans, members of a world class who "transcend the particularities of place." Harvard business guru Rosabeth Moss Kantor describes Miami's hybrids as "comfortable in many places and able to understand and bridge differences." She points to Miami as a world class trade center that depends on the skills and abilities of cosmopolitans. "The essential resource of trade centers is connections. . . . Miami thrives because of world class connections."[11]

Hong Kong is bigger than Miami and their economies differ. There are proportionately more Chinese in Hong Kong than Latinos in Miami, and their ethnic and political status across Asia is more salient than that of the Cubans in Latin America. But the new economies of both Miami and Hong Kong are built on the existence of their transcultural entrepreneurial classes. It is this presence that gives them a special character as world cities: places on the edge, connecting regions, cultures, and markets that are distinctly different. And they do it better than any other city within their realms.

The commercial advantages of Miami's multiculturalism were

recognized in good time by the city's biggest newspaper. Since the early 1980s, the *Miami Herald* has been a strong advocate of multiculturalism and an important force in the urban growth machine. A good illustration of just how far the *Herald* had come (compared to its resistance to large-scale immigration in the 1970s) was a front-page headline in 1996 that exclaimed: "Vanishing Spanish." The article deplored the fact that only a small percentage of graduating high school students in metropolitan Miami were fully fluent in Spanish, and that most second-generation Hispanic immigrants spoke an imperfect sort of "home Spanish." It was described as an alarming trend since it would erode Miami's advantage as a bilingual community and diminish its economic competitiveness.[12]

This view was echoed elsewhere in the business community. In the same year, the Greater Miami Chamber of Commerce published a report entitled *The Economic Impact of Spanish-Language Proficiency in Metropolitan Miami*, emphasizing its huge importance and the need to maintain high standards of bilingualism of the workforce in South Florida. A year later, the *South Florida Business Journal* (1997) weighed in, deploring a shortage in Spanish-speaking workers and declaring that "Spanglish doesn't cut it in Latin America."[13]

A comparison with Hong Kong, then, confirms Miami's role as an ideological refuge in the global geopolitical landscape of the second half of the twentieth century. It also attests to the central importance in both cities of the late twentieth-century phenomenon of "transcultural capitalism," that is, an internationalized urban economy that relies on the hybrid cultural identities of the key players.[14]

Dublin makes for another interesting comparison with Miami: both emerged as world cities at the same time; both were insignificant places in the international economy prior to their transformation; and both tend to be underestimated by outsiders who have not been paying attention to modern history.

In the 1970s, the Irish economy was nicknamed the "sick man of Europe." Comparisons of Ireland with third-world countries were quite common. It was a country with a large agricultural sector, backward industries, low incomes, and considerable poverty. Most educated people wanted to leave, and many headed for the United States or Britain. There were descriptions of Ireland from those days as "the island behind the island." That is, at least, how the country was perceived in continental Europe: remote and disconnected. Dublin, compared to other European capital cities, seemed little more than a provincial town: small, stagnant, and undisturbed by the forces of the world economy.

Miami, prior to its own transformation, was at least as remote to the rest of the U.S. economy as Dublin was to Europe. Until the advent of mass air conditioning in the 1950s, Miami was just a seasonal beach resort town, long overshadowed by Tampa as South Florida's leading city. Miami was not as poor as Dublin and it had a very different economic base, but with its small size and lack of connections, it simply did not matter much to the outside world until 1959.

Dublin's makeover seemed miraculous. In 1998, Andersen Consulting declared that "Dublin is the best location in Europe for doing business." In the 1990s, Ireland had the highest national growth rates of any country in the European Union (around 8 percent per annum). Foreign investment in Ireland skyrocketed and was highly concentrated in and around Dublin. Guinness is the oldest company in Dublin, and still a very successful one, but today the city houses the European headquarters for many large high-tech and IT corporations, including Intel, Microsoft, and Oracle. Dublin also became Europe's most specialized calling center with facilities of Citibank, Hertz, Dell, American Airlines, IBM, Ericsson, and others. It became a trendy city, full of European and

American yuppies and expatriates, and returning Irish from abroad. Real estate prices escalated. As if to acknowledge the city's newfound status, Dublin was declared the European Union's "cultural capital" in 1999.[15]

For both Dublin and Miami, the globalizing economy provided an essential structure for their emergence as world cities, with rapidly developing transport and communication technologies and highly mobile global capital.[16] Both could count global languages among their assets: English in Dublin (luring large numbers of U.S. multinationals to set up European branches) and Spanish in Miami (attracting firms with designs on Latin America).

But there was a fundamental difference, too: the economic transformation of Dublin, and of Ireland in general, had a very public face and was "engineered" by national and local governments with emphatically proactive policies.[17] Paul Sweeney, in his book on the Irish success story, notes that "there is a high level of state intervention in industry, which is highly subsidized with grants, tax breaks and many other state aids. Ireland pioneered tax-free industrial zones, duty-free shopping and zero tax on export profits. It also had one of the first and possibly the most successful state agencies to encourage FDI (foreign direct investment)."[18] Peadar Kirby, in his more critical *The Celtic Tiger in Distress*, refers to Ireland as a "hunter/gatherer of FDI," a strategy that was pursued with "great determination and not a little charm."[19]

Dublin's success was based on careful planning, a mix of liberalization and government-controlled public enterprise, clever competitive investment policies, and shrewd marketing. Tax incentives for foreign investors have been extremely lucrative—to the point where they were at odds with tax harmonization directives of the European Union. Corporate taxes in Ireland in the 1990s were one-sixth of those in Germany and one-third of those in Britain. Public education is very good and the work force is highly skilled, particularly in computer use and foreign languages. Foreign investors are lured with friendly service and a customer-driven corporate culture. The Irish government called it "policy determined comparative advantage" and this policy has been pursued consistently by successive governments since the mid-1970s.

Dublin played a primary role in a small national economy and the national government was sensitive to the needs of its largest urban economy. In a way, it almost functioned like a city-state. Irish policies resembled, in some ways, the strategies of small Southeast Asian countries like Taiwan or Singapore. Moreover, Dublin *had* to be ahead of the curve of regional competitors because Western Europe is itself a stable and integrated economic region with plenty of other established and emerging world cities.

This was very different from the conditions underpinning Miami's rise to world city status. To be sure, Miami figured a lot less prominently in the minds of the national policy makers in Washington, D.C., and perhaps even in Tallahassee, Florida's capital. If Dublin was world city by design, Miami clearly was not. If Miami's success was partially based on the large-scale immigration of Cubans and others, it should be remembered that none of that was planned—in fact, it met with considerable local resistance. As described earlier, the realignment of Miami's growth machine was reactive, not proactive. While the Non-Group was instrumental in forging a broad-based consensus among the various business elites, it, too, was largely reactive to events rather than pursuing a clear vision for the future. The city's mayor during those crucial years, Ferré, was an exception. He made notable efforts to push the local business community into a more international direction, and he still laments the community's "introspective and parochial" disposition.[20] Moreover, local government had its hands full with the city's social transformation and had to balance an astounding array of constituencies.

Miami owed its ascent not so much to its own designs but instead to an external circumstance beyond its control: the persistent instability that characterized the political economy across Latin America and the Caribbean. In a sense, Miami has been feeding off that regional volatility. It happened to be in the right place at the right time.

Miami went from a very peripheral place in the U.S. national economy to a highly central node in the Western Hemisphere. Yet, after the economic transition, Miami had to sell itself anew to North American audiences. For example, the *New York Times* edition of Sunday, December 15, 1995, was supplemented with a special advertising magazine devoted entirely to Miami. The glossy cover featured photographs of slick real estate developers who were the main financiers of this expensive advertising blitz. The purpose was to lure affluent northerners to Miami: "It's time for New York and the rest of America to discover what international visitors already know." It would have been an unthinkable statement in earlier times when this was a prime destination of northern snowbirds. This was the new Miami, remade in Latin America.[21] In North America, the city is promoted as a subtropical and exotic place with great access to Latin American markets; it is the perfect location of companies with sales to and marketing oriented toward Latin America, as well as for real estate investments (a second home on the "American Riviera").

In Latin America and the Caribbean, the city hardly needs to be sold at all. It is naturally seen as a haven of stability and opportunity, with its Latin culture as one of the city's greatest attractions. For Miami's Hispanic elites, one appealing aspect of the city's Latin image is that it highlights their own crucial role in Miami's rise to prominence. Cuban economic success stories have been part and parcel of the exile historiography since day one. But the idea of a Latin city is also essential to Miami's marketing image in the south, where it is viewed with admiration and pride, and as a testament to Latin ambition and creativity.

While Miami's role linking north and south is by now fairly well known, its location between east and west is almost always overlooked. The difficulty, for most people, of imagining Miami as a strategic business hub between the western and eastern Americas has something to do with their mental map of the hemisphere and of Miami's place in it. Most people, if asked to draw a map of the Western Hemisphere, would produce a drawing in which South America is pretty much straight below North America. That is to say: straight down south.

But North America is almost entirely to Miami's west and South America is entirely to its east. Indeed, Miami is positioned on the East Coast of the United States, but it is also the most "western city of South America." Given its longitudinal position of 80.16 degrees west, there are only two cities in South America that come close, both in Ecuador: Guayaquil at 79.54 degrees west, and Quito at 78.30 degrees west.

Miami's location between east and west has been crucial to its development and this is best illustrated by comparing it to Los Angeles. The latter city is, with Miami, one of the southernmost cities of the United States, but it is positioned in the extreme west. Los Angeles is strongly influenced by its location close to Mexico, to the southeast. Conversely, Miami has relatively meager ties with Mexico largely because Mexico is too far to the west—even if Miami and a large chunk of Mexico have the same latitude. More pertinently, it is an enormous distance, west to east, from Los Angeles to places such as Panama or Bogotá and even more so to cities like São Paulo or Buenos Aires. Miami is much closer, which explains the centrality of Miami, not Los Angeles, in airline traffic in the South American region.

This is about more than absolute distance. In the global economy, longitudinal position is strategically more significant than latitudinal position, due to time differences. Miami is in the same time zone as Colombia, Ecuador, and Peru; it is one hour behind Venezuela, western Brazil, Bolivia, Paraguay, and Chile; and it is two hours behind eastern Brazil, Uruguay, and Argentina. Los Angeles, in contrast, is no less than five hours behind large parts of South America. By 11 a.m. in California, offices have already closed down in major South American cities such as São Paulo and Buenos Aires. Miami has a three-hour advantage over Los Angeles and a one-hour advantage over Houston or New Orleans—all potential competitors with respect to Latin American connections. Even just one hour can make the difference between same-day and next-day communications. Old adages claim that time is money and that good timing is everything. Because of globalization, the premiums on speed and time have appreciated as never before.

The important role of Miami vis-à-vis Latin America is expressed in the size and growth of its most international economic sectors, including finance, insurance, legal services, and a variety of management services. These are all usually referred to as producer services because they support economic production that is often dispersed to places that have the lowest labor costs.[22] Between the mid-1970s and the late 1980s, the share of Miami's workforce in producer services nearly doubled to around 20 percent, and it has steadily increased since then. The relative size of producer services is comparable to that of Chicago and Los Angeles, but Miami has much less manufacturing. Miami's producer services, in comparison, are more internationally oriented and relate in large part to economic activity in the Caribbean and Latin America.[23]

Miami's strength as a world city lies not so much in the presence of corporate headquarters or of a big stock market. There *is* no stock market and there may never be one since the city is in the same time zone as—and is closely connected to—Wall Street. Further, there are very few headquarters of big transnational corporations (TNCs). Notable exceptions include Office Depot, Burger King, Ryder Systems, Del Monte, and several cruise line companies. The city also has only a small number of the nation's biggest law firms, with Greenberg Traurig as one of the most prominent. In other words, compared to a city like New York, Miami exhibits little of the usual world city "command and control" functions.[24]

Miami's importance lies in its relational capacity, its ability to connect business flows. These are flows of finance, trade, services, people, and corporate communication. This may sound abstract at first, but it refers to very real and vital functions in the global economy. First, Miami may not have many global headquarters of big TNCs, but it does have a large number of Latin American regional headquarters, and numerous headquarters of smaller TNCs. The metro area houses approximately 1,250 TNCs, most of which are in some way oriented to Latin America and the Caribbean.[25]

Detailed studies show that Miami is hooked directly into the top echelons of global economic power, as measured through corporate network analysis.[26] The most significant connections "upward" are to New York, London, Paris, and Tokyo (that is, these cities are where the TNCs active in Miami are mostly headquartered). The most important "downward" corporate connections are with major cities in the region: São Paulo, Mexico City, Buenos Aires, and Caracas (that is, these cities are where TNCs headquartered in Miami are the most active). This means that Miami takes its orders from the pinnacle of the global economy and, in turn, has a very powerful influence on Latin America. Miami serves as the premier router, so to speak, between the corporate capitals of the world and Latin America. There is no other major world region where one single city so monopolizes the transaction of flows between that region and the rest of the world. At

Figure 18. Global intercity corporate linkages, 2002: the ten cities with the most corporate influence on Miami, and the ten cities most influenced by Miami. Source: Based on data provided by WorldCity Business, Inc., 2002, and on data collected by author.

the dawn of the twenty-first century, the leading South American business magazine, *AméricaEconomía*, declared Miami "La mejor ciudad para dirigir negocios hacia América Latina," the best city for doing business with Latin America.[27]

This is not all about usual business sectors such as finance, trade, or producer services. One of the fastest growing specialized cultural industries in Miami is the music business—and it is tightly linked to the international region. A more poignant sign of the city's cultural makeover—not to be mistaken for trivia—was the rise to local, national, and international fame in 1987 of the Miami Sound Machine and its Cuban-born diva Gloria Estéfan.

TABLE 1. Miami's Global Corporate Connections

Cities with the greatest influence on Miami*	Cities most influenced by Miami†
1. New York	1. São Paulo
2. London	2. Mexico City
3. Paris	3. Buenos Aires
4. Tokyo	4. Caracas
5. Madrid	5. New York
6. Chicago	6. Bogotá
7. São Paulo	7. Santiago
8. Amsterdam	8. Hong Kong
9. Atlanta	9. London
10. Zurich	10. Dallas

*The ten cities with the largest number of headquarters of transnational companies active in South Florida.
†The ten cities with the largest number of branches of transnational companies headquartered in South Florida.

The Miami "sound" was a mix of English and Spanish and of American pop and Latin salsa. The name Miami Sound Machine was dropped in 1989 when Estéfan went solo and her continuing success reflected Miami's new multicultural makeup. At the same time, Miami was rebranded in the worlds of music, arts, and popular imagination. Miami Beach is now the Latin American headquarters of MTV and Sony-BMG. Industry insiders point out that Miami is one of three global centers in the production and distribution of Latin music. The other two are Madrid and Mexico City.

Miami also hosts the second largest concentration of foreign banks in the nation. It has fewer banks than New York, but more than prominent and older banking centers like Chicago and Los Angeles. Miami's banks, mostly clustered in the Brickell area south of downtown and in downtown Coral Gables, specialize mainly in trade financing and private banking. Some offices deal exclusively with private depositors. The president of the Florida International Bankers Association, Seno Bril, recently remarked that "Latin American high net worth individuals have a variety of reasons why they want to hold part of their nest egg offshore. . . . They come to Miami because here is where they do some of their shopping, here is where they have some of their medical treatment, . . . where their children go to college, and a lot of them have a condominium in South Florida where they come to rest and relax."[28]

But even this notable presence of foreign banks does not tell the whole story. Miami is by far the most important foreign finance center for the majority of local banks scattered throughout Latin America and the Caribbean. These are banks without any branches abroad, but which have agreements with so-called correspondent banks abroad. For example, if a local bank client in Tegucigalpa, Honduras, wants an account in Miami, that bank will set up the account with a correspondent bank, for example Bank of America, in the Miami area. A recent study on correspondent banks for the entire Central American region found that Miami is in a league of its own: it has five times as many correspondent banks as New York (which ranked second).

Yet another expression of Miami's relational capacity lies in its unparalleled centrality in inter-American air traffic. For years, Miami International Airport (MIA) has been the biggest in the nation in terms of flights, passengers, and cargo volume to and from Latin America and the Caribbean. The airport ships more total international cargo than any other airport in the hemisphere, and it has the third largest total number of international passengers in the Americas (after JFK in New York and LAX in Los Angeles). MIA also has more airlines with regularly scheduled services than any other airport in the hemisphere. The atmosphere at MIA is distinctly Latin American, invoking the typical commentary of North American passengers that they feel as if they've already departed the United States.

Miami's seaport is less significant in terms of cargo than the airport, and so does not figure prominently in any rankings. The seaport is fully containerized, being too shallow for bigger ships carrying bulk cargo. But Miami does have the biggest cruise port in the world and sends off more than two million cruise passengers every year. Most of these arrive in Miami by air, creating a huge flow of passengers between the airport and the seaports. The world's second biggest cruise port, it should be noted, lies only forty miles north in Fort Lauderdale.

Finally, there is Miami's dominance in U.S. trade with Latin America. Miami channels more trade to and from the south than any other customs district: about one quarter of all U.S. trade with South America, about 40 percent of all U.S. trade with the Caribbean, and more than 50 percent of all U.S. trade with Central America. Miami's overall international trade tripled between 1975 and 1985 and its shares of Latin American trade have steadily increased ever since.[29]

It was in the mid-1980s that Mayor Ferré first boasted of Miami as the "Capital of the Caribbean." Twenty years later, as if to officially seal Miami's world city status, the State of Florida trademarked the label "Gateway of the Americas" with the U.S. Patent and Trademark Office.

What differentiates Miami as a world city is that it assumed international status without first being domestically important. This certainly was not true for other emerging world cities: Sydney, Toronto, Zurich, and Dublin were all top-ranked cities in the national urban hierarchy before they acquired world city functions. Perceptions of Miami in the rest of the United States tend to be overshadowed by geographic remoteness, cultural eccentricity, and the politics of Cuba—the region's economic role is almost always underestimated. This was especially true in the 1980s, following the transformation. A survey in 1987 on the best U.S. cities to establish a business ranked Miami twenty-eighth out of thirty selected metropolitan areas, with only Cleveland and Detroit getting lower scores.[30] Recent studies of Miami's image in the rest of the nation show that the city is more often in the limelight than others, but that its economic functions are still rarely mentioned.[31] All of this is in sharp contrast to the city's celebrated status in Latin America and the Caribbean.

In a related vein, Miami is in some ways disassociated from the rest of the nation, and especially from the rest of Florida. We have already seen that "disconnect," as it has occasionally been manifest in Miami's divergent economic trends from the rest of the country: the city did poorly in the 1960s when national growth was strong, and Miami was booming in the early 1980s when the nation at large was in a slump. Miami's case seems extreme but it is not uncommon for world cities. They are so much a part of global networks that they become "suspended" from their traditional regional hinterland: "Some cities—New York, Tokyo, London, São Paulo, Hong Kong, Toronto, Miami, and Sydney, among others—have evolved into transnational 'spaces.' As such cities prospered, they came to have more in common with one another than with regional centers in their own nation-states."[32]

Compare Miami with Jacksonville in North Florida: they are in the same state but worlds apart. Jacksonville has been an important North American port city (naval and commercial) since the early nineteenth century—long before Miami appeared on the map. For a considerable time it was the southernmost port on the eastern seaboard, making Jacksonville the leading city in Florida. Today, Jacksonville's port still is, and probably always will be, much bigger than Miami's. It handles large amounts of bulk and containerized cargo, and it is the second busiest vehicle-handling port in the country after New York. Each year, over half a million cars (mostly Japanese) leave the port on trucks headed north, to Georgia, the Carolinas, Virginia, and other states. Jacksonville is not to be mistaken for some economic backwater.

The point is that the two cities have extremely different histories and regional orientations; that Jacksonville is much more linked to the southeastern United States; and that there is very little that ties the two places together because Miami has evolved as a *trans*national place. A Jacksonville *Visitor Guide* shows a map of Jacksonville's geographic "reach"—concentric rings across the eastern United States all the way to Canada. It is a bit overconfident perhaps, but there is no question that Jacksonville looks to the North. Not so long ago, northern Floridians used to refer to their region as "South Georgia." Culturally, it is part of the Deep South (don't expect to be able to get a *cortadito* anywhere when you visit). And if Jacksonville is the Deep South, that leaves Miami south of the South.

Finally, Miami is unusual in that its world city functions emerged very rapidly and are not (yet) strongly rooted in the area. It is thus very different from places such as New York or London, each with long histories as international business centers. Miami is in this respect more like Dublin: the global corporate presence in the two cities is recent, primarily as small branches of transnational firms with high potential mobility.[33] The result in both cases is a lack of embeddedness of world city functions: many companies come and go without making large investments in local operations, facilities, or infrastructure, and there is little to tie them to the area. For Miami, this implies long-term economic uncertainty and high volatility. It all comes with the city's defining characteristic of transience, a quality that extends well beyond the economy into the realm of culture.

CHAPTER 6

Transience and Civil Society

The 2008 obituary for Roger Sonnabend (age eighty-three) named him "a pioneer in South Florida."[1] The chairman of the board of Sonesta, he brought one of his namesake hotels to Key Biscayne in 1969. With its iconic pyramid shape, the Sonesta was one of the first modern full-service resort hotels in the area. Sonnabend was a part-time resident who maintained a winter home on the island. He was "very much a Bostonian" and is buried in Wakefield, Massachusetts. In the footsteps of Henry Flagler, and others, Sonnabend was a *part-time* pioneer whose real home was a long distance from Miami.

The news media like to celebrate their "pioneers," and sometimes this includes even ordinary folks. In 2005, Marlene Naylor was the longest continuous resident (!) of Miami Lakes, a town in Miami-Dade County with about 27,000 inhabitants. She had moved to South Florida forty-two years before, settling in the area later incorporated as Miami Lakes. Nobody in the entire town had lived there longer than she had. But at the age of seventy-two, Ms. Naylor decided it was time to return to the Northeast and rejoin some old friends, "taking a little bit of the town's history with her."[2] What made Ms. Naylor special was not that she went home after all—it was that she had stayed so long.

Few people seem intent on making Miami their eternal resting ground. Indeed, the *Miami Herald* reported in 2002 that even if you wanted to, you could not spend eternity here. The reason: "Urban planners failed to plan for sufficient cemetery space."[3] The thought of dying in Miami seems not to occur to many people passing through this city, excepting perhaps displaced and aged foreign dictators from Central America, three of whom have their resting places at Woodlawn Cemetery.

Other mortals manage to leave even *after* they die: the bodies of an estimated 20 percent of South Florida's deceased are shipped out, more than from any other region in the nation.[4] Fort Lauderdale International Airport ships more HRs (the industry's shorthand for human remains) than any other U.S. airport and its cargo is usually headed up north. Most of the HRs going abroad depart from Miami International Airport. According to the CEO of Pierson, a leader in this business since 1964, the range of foreign destinations has steadily grown to include almost all of Central and South America and a number of European countries.[5]

The cost of shipping a body is not cheap, ranging from about five hundred dollars to well over a thousand—all fares are one-way. Some small immigrant communities in South Florida have set up special foundations to finance and arrange burials in the homeland. "We believe there's a certain honor in going home, an honor in being buried at home," says Antonio Nava, the Mexican leader of such a foundation, Hispanos Unidos de America.[6]

Transience has always been Miami's *genius loci*—a constant coming and going of people dating back to the times of Ponce de Leon. It has only intensified in more recent, global times. Very few people here seem to plan a permanent stay. For most, the city is merely an interlude in their unfolding lives.

For the past quarter century or so, Miami had relatively more foreign immigrants than any other major metropolitan area in the United States. Well over half of Miami-Dade County's current residents were born abroad, compared to just over a third in New York or Los Angeles. In nearly three out of four Miami homes, a foreign language is spoken. A majority of all foreign-born people here are from the Western Hemisphere. Cubans are the largest group by far: they number over six hundred thousand. The next largest national groups are Haitians, Colombians, Jamaicans, and Nicaraguans, each with around one hundred thousand people. Venezuelans are another rapidly growing contingent, now estimated at around fifty thousand. Miami has no less than twenty-four national groups of ten thousand or more, including a sizeable number of Canadians and immigrants from six different European nations.

Transience is not the same as immigration. Several U.S. cities have a long and common history as centers of immigration and gradual assimilation. Transience, in contrast, implies that many of those who come do not (intend to) stay. In Miami's case, this constant population flux does not just apply to foreigners; U.S. citizens behave this way too. Indeed, in the first half century of Miami's history, its transient character was almost exclusively the result of domestic migrations. Today, Miami is at once a major destination of domestic and foreign in-migration, and a major origination point for domestic out-migration. It is the only metropolitan area in the United States that has combined, for most years of its history, significant overall population growth with net domestic out-migration.[7]

Power in this city is transient, too. In 2004, the *South Florida CEO*, a leading local business journal, published a list of the "100 most powerful people" in South Florida.[8] Of these one hundred "movers and shakers," only eighteen were born in South Florida, thirty were foreign born (twenty-one in Cuba), and fifty-two were born elsewhere in the United States. Ten years earlier, a similar listing was published by the journal's precursor, the *South Florida Business Journal*.[9] Of the one hundred people on the 1994 roster, only seventeen remained in 2004. A handful had died and the

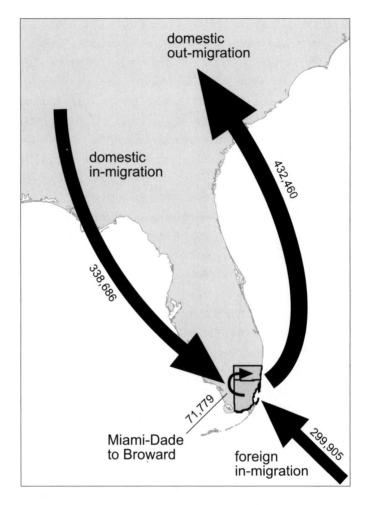

domestic
out-migration

domestic
in-migration

432,460

338,686

71,779

Miami-Dade
to Broward

299,905

foreign
in-migration

Figure 19. South Florida's migration flows, 1995–2000. The flow from Miami-Dade to Broward is the net value of migration flows between the two counties. Source: 2000 U.S. Census.

rest, nearly eight out of ten, either had moved away from South Florida or had fallen from the rankings to make place for more powerful newcomers. In 2004 the *Miami Herald* reported, "Power . . . seemed more transitory than ever in Miami-Dade County."[10]

As the table below shows, Miami is the most transient of the fifty largest U.S. metropolitan areas. The index comprises several measures of domestic and foreign transience: in- and out-migration; population living in the area five years or less; population born out of state; population with immigrant status; and foreign-born population.[11]

There is considerable variation in transience across the nation's metropolitan areas. Cities with high transience have dynamic populations and combine high in-migration with high out-migration. In contrast, metropolitan areas with low transience have more stable or stagnant demographics.

Miami leads the table, followed by Las Vegas, West Palm Beach, Orlando, and Phoenix in the top five. These are all highly dynamic metropolitan areas with very high turnover and substantial net growth. All are young cities, even by American standards. While Miami has the highest levels of foreign and overall transience, Las Vegas has very high domestic transience.

A second grouping (rankings 6–17) comprises more established cities such as San Francisco, New York, Denver, Washington, D.C., and Atlanta. These cities have longer histories but still quite dynamic populations. Then come the middle strata of America's urban landscape: Kansas City, or Minneapolis, with modest amounts of movement in and out.

The cities at the bottom of the table are the least transient and this is mainly owing to prolonged low in-migration. Places such as Cleveland, Buffalo, and Pittsburgh attracted few in-migrants for decades while out-migration was especially high in the 1970s and 1980s.

The interesting thing about transience is that at least some of it seems a good thing as it implies substantial in-migration. Indeed, one of the main challenges of the "needy" cities near the bottom of the table is to attract more people. The movement of people brings "new blood," a fresh breeze, the promise of innova-

TABLE 2. Transcience Index

Metropolitan Area	Rank	Score	Population
Miami–Fort Lauderdale, FL	1	183	3,876,380
Las Vegas, NV–AZ	2	182	1,563,282
West Palm Beach–Boca Raton, FL	3	180	1,131,184
Orlando, FL	4	176	1,644,561
Phoenix–Mesa, AZ	5	171	3,251,876
San Francisco–Oakland–San Jose, CA	6	169	7,039,362
Dallas–Fort Worth, TX	7	160	5,221,801
San Diego, CA	8	157	2,813,833
Denver–Boulder–Greeley, CO	9	155	2,581,506
Austin–San Marcos, TX	10	153	1,249,763
Los Angeles–Riverside–Orange County, CA	11	151	16,373,645
Houston–Galveston–Brazoria, TX	12	149	4,669,571
Raleigh–Durham–Chapel Hill, NC	13	148	1,187,941
Atlanta, GA	14	148	4,112,198
Seattle–Tacoma–Bremerton, WA	15	146	3,554,760
New York–Northern New Jersey–Long Island	16	142	21,199,865
Washington, DC–Baltimore, MD	17	141	7,608,070
Sacramento–Yolo, CA	18	135	1,796,857
Portland–Salem, OR–WA	19	135	2,265,223
Tampa–St. Petersburg–Clearwater, FL	20	135	2,395,997
Charlotte–Gastonia–Rock Hill, NC	21	119	1,499,293
Boston–Worcester–Lawrence, MA	22	116	5,819,101
Jacksonville, FL	23	112	1,100,491
Norfolk–Virginia Beach–Newport News, VA	24	104	1,569,541
Chicago–Gary–Kenosha, IL	25	103	9,157,540
Salt Lake City–Ogden, UT	26	103	1,333,914
San Antonio, TX	27	98	1,592,383
Hartford, CT	28	92	1,183,110
Oklahoma City, OK	29	91	1,083,346
Providence–Fall River–Warwick, RI	30	86	1,188,613
Nashville, TN	31	85	1,231,311
Greensboro–Winston-Salem–High Point, NC	32	85	1,251,509
Kansas City, KS–MO	33	78	1,776,062
Minneapolis–St. Paul, MN	34	78	2,968,806
Philadelphia, PA–Wilmington, DE–Atlantic City, NJ	35	64	6,188,463

Richmond–Petersburg, VA	36	62	996,512
Columbus, OH	37	62	1,540,157
Memphis, TN	38	59	1,135,614
Detroit–Ann Arbor–Flint, MI	39	54	5,456,428
Milwaukee–Racine, WI	40	46	1,689,572
Grand Rapids–Muskegon–Holland, MI	41	45	1,088,514
Indianapolis, IN	42	44	1,607,486
Rochester, NY	43	37	1,098,201
Louisville, KY	44	32	1,025,598
Cincinnati–Hamilton, OH	45	31	1,979,202
St. Louis, MO	46	26	2,603,607
Cleveland–Akron, OH	47	25	2,945,831
New Orleans, LA	48	25	1,337,726
Buffalo–Niagara Falls, NY	49	16	1,170,111
Pittsburgh, PA	50	6	2,358,695

tion and reinvigoration. But what if out-migration is consistently very high as well? What if most people don't stay?

We can define *social capital* as the networks, norms, and trust that facilitate coordination and cooperation for mutual benefit. In the words of the Harvard sociologist Robert Putnam: "Life is easier in a community blessed with a substantial stock of social capital. In the first place, networks of civic engagement foster sturdy norms of generalized reciprocity and encourage the emergence of social trust. . . . Finally, dense networks of interaction probably broaden the participants' sense of self, developing the 'I' into the 'we.'"[12]

Put differently, social capital allows communities to function collectively, smoothly, efficiently, and with minimal stress. It is generally understood that social capital is formed under conditions of social stability and in the context of "*durable* networks."[13] Some classic studies note that transience might erode social capital or impede its creation.[14]

Other research suggests that high levels of inequality can compound a lack of social capital.[15] Socioeconomic inequality often implies segregation and a fragmented social structure, especially where economic inequality intersects with race and ethnicity. Being one of the most unequal metropolitan areas in the United States, as well, Miami is thus doubly challenged in its capacity to generate and maintain social capital.

Social capital may be scarce in a society at large while abundant within certain smaller social enclaves. It can be balkanized, exclusionary, and used for purposes that do not benefit society as a whole.[16] That may be Miami's predicament. To be sure, the city harbors substantial social capital within certain enclaves (think of the so-called character loans made to Cubans by Cuban-American-owned banks in past years), but it is highly fragmented and exclusionary, confined to certain subcultures in the metropolitan area. As two Miami scholars observed, in-migrants' insulation within their enclaves may have positive implications for (short-term) economic adjustment, but "poorly serves interethnic communications and understanding . . . affecting even the conduct of local matters."[17] Whether the enclaves are made up of domestic or foreign migrants is effectively immaterial. Rather, the point is that neither intends to stay, both continue to identify with their original homes, and both seem little inclined to invest in social capital beyond their group.

Connections between transience, social stability, social capital, and civic culture are complex matters, likely to remain a matter of debate for some time. Meanwhile, some Miami social realities have an in-your-face quality not easily ignored. Following a series of comparative studies of U.S. metropolitan areas, two careful observers noted that "it would be hard to identify a U.S. city where civility in public dialogue seems lower."[18] In 2007, the *Miami Herald* columnist Ana Menendez, reflecting on the city's public culture, lamented that "even the most hardened optimist [would] despair at our collective rot."[19] And last year, the longtime television news commentator Michael Putney bemoaned, "I regret that you have to leave town to find the civility and common courtesy in everyday life that's expected and practiced in other places."[20]

Transience is not the only area in which Miami ranks first. The city was recently distinguished as the "most stressful"[21] metropolitan area in the nation (with New Orleans and Las Vegas coming in second and third), and Miami drivers were declared the rudest and most aggressive in the nation for three consecutive years.[22] Dave Barry once joked that in Miami "using your blinkers is a sign of weakness."

Miami's lack of civic culture is evident in the realm of ordinary life: the difficulty professional sports teams have building a loyal fan base (the Marlins have suffered the lowest attendance by far of all professional baseball teams in the nation); resistance by homeowners' associations to "historic designation" of their neighborhoods (market values are deemed more important than architectural preservation); and the lack of public support for the arts (fundraising is handicapped by the absence of a home-grown, stable, and well-endowed older generation).[23]

On September 4, 1997, Miami's citizens voted on a referendum to abolish their city—a most unusual event that attracted attention from the international news media. If approved, the referendum would have led to disincorporation: the municipality would cease to exist and Miami-Dade County would assume all local government functions. The referendum was pushed by a coalition of disaffected citizens angry over endless political corruption and mismanagement. In the end, the referendum failed owing to invested local politicians' machinations and, quite ironically, because of the political apathy of most city residents.[24]

The abolition movement was triggered by the City of Miami's

admission that it faced bankruptcy during its one hundredth anniversary. The financial mess was so glaring that there were only rough estimates of the budgetary shortfall—around $65 million—nobody seemed to know exactly.[25] Municipal bonds had been downgraded to junk. Later that year, the FBI initiated Operation Greenpalm, a sting operation that exposed widespread corruption and led to federal charges against three top city officials. The first to be indicted was the city's finance director, who was charged with "extortion, soliciting bribes, and money laundering." He agreed to be wired with a microphone, which led to the exposure of the city manager and one commissioner.[26]

Miami's bankruptcy crisis was the topic of an interesting study of 2002 in which two findings stood out.[27] First, the authors charged, the business community had more or less "written off" the city's elected officials. With "minimal involvement" of the business community, local politics lacked a basic agenda-setting force and a potential check on mismanagement. Second, Miami's electorate was "largely indifferent to the caliber of the government" that it received for its tax dollars. Taken together, this meant that local government was constrained neither by business requirements of efficiency nor by democratic demands from the voters.

Comparing Miami's fiscal crisis with New York's in the 1970s, the study noted that New York's recovery from its deep financial crisis (which had more to do with a shrinking tax base than with mismanagement) was largely attributed to the fact that the city had a "very strong constituency for good government." In Miami, in contrast, there was "simply no base for 'good government' left." Much of this, they suggested, had to do with Miami's social fabric. In Miami's urban environment, "the commons is largely defined as the self and immediate family. Professionalism and training are perceived as secondary—who you know is far more important than the knowledge that you bring to the table." That

CHAPTER 6

view is supported in a recent edition of the well-known *Handbook of Public Administration*, which commented on the bankruptcy saga: "Miami went through five years, six City Managers, two mayoral elections (one ordered by judicial fiat as a result of voting fraud) and extensive administrative turnover to overcome its fiscal woes. Miami soon came to look like a perfect candidate for anti-best practices in public management."[28]

In 2003, it was found that nearly half a million registered voters in South Florida had never cast a ballot.[29] Political apathy is not confined to local issues; it applies to national politics as well. On February 16, 2003, the *Miami Herald* ran a major front-page article entitled "A Worldwide Protest: Millions Rally Against War with Iraq." The article covered a number of huge demonstrations in a range of cities around the world, including Rome (1 million protesters), London (750,000), Berlin (500,000), Madrid (2 million), and Paris (100,000). Rallies in the United States were generally smaller. Still, New York counted 375,000 marchers, Los Angeles 50,000, and Seattle 25,000, while in Chicago and Philadelphia about 10,000 people took to the streets. Conspicuously absent from the list of major demonstrations was Miami itself, where only 700 persons joined the call for peace.

One month earlier, Miami had in fact been the scene of a huge demonstration, but this had nothing to do with the impending war in Iraq. An estimated 60,000 people marched on Calle Ocho against the leftist government of Venezuela's president, Hugo Chávez.[30] The "mega-march" was largely organized by Cuban American activists and attended by tens of thousands of Venezuelans, many Cuban Americans, Nicaraguans, and others. It was the second largest rally in Miami's history, second only to the massive protests against the repatriation in the spring of 2000 of Elián González, the child rafter from Cuba.

In Miami, political demonstrations that attract large numbers of people are virtually always aimed at *foreign* governments and are led by natives of those countries. The Cuban and Haitian governments are the usual targets, but the governments of Nicaragua, Venezuela, Colombia, Israel, and others have also been the subject of demonstrations more than once. It should be noted that there are thousands, perhaps tens of thousands, of immigrants in the metropolitan area who vote in their home countries' elections but do not participate in local politics. Voter registration drives among immigrants are often motivated to influence U.S. foreign policy with regard to their home countries. Cubans have been especially active in this regard and have led the way for many other immigrant groups.

One of the most telling events or, rather, non-events, concerned the immigration rallies in April and May 2006. There were massive demonstrations across the nation's major cities for immigration reform, demanding citizenship and a share of the American dream for new legal and illegal immigrants. For example, in Dallas and Los Angeles, about 500,000 people took to the streets, and in Chicago the crowd was estimated at 300,000. New York witnessed a series of marches throughout this period, some with an estimated attendance of 100,000. But in Miami, with the largest share of immigrants in the entire country, the biggest rally had only 4,000—even Milwaukee had three times more demonstrators. Again, on May 1, 2008, when another series of rallies was planned throughout the nation, in Miami only 75 people showed up in a small march to one of the city's INS offices.[31]

This suggests an impressive splintering of social capital even among groups that share common interests as recent immigrants. Miami's immigrant groups are highly diverse in terms of ethnicity, race, and especially class. There are many wealthy recent immigrants, and some hold powerful positions in South Florida. But there are also many who are poor and struggle to make ends meet, living their daily lives at a great distance from some of their own compatriots. There are also major differences regarding immigrants' legal status (particularly between Cubans and others), which undercut the notion of common interests in residency rights. Even among recent immigrants, therefore, solidarity seems a foreign concept.

It may be a vicious cycle. The balkanization of social capital and the lack of a common social contract push people to invest ever more in their smaller ethnic communities. An example of such exclusive or parochial social capital entails the 180 letters sent to the U.S. District Court in support of Carlos and Jorge de Céspedes, the former owners of a large Miami-based pharmaceutical company charged with "tax evasion and fraud in connection with ripping off a hospital for more than $5 million."[32] The letters came from "priests, business leaders, top supporters in the anti-Castro movement and former employees," all asking for lighter sentences in view of the brothers' "philanthropy and community involvement" (a public reputation that, according to federal prosecutors, was "carefully built").

In late 2008, federal authorities discovered a series of so-called affinity scams in South Florida. The region was a breeding ground for fraudulent financial schemes targeting members of ethnic, religious, or community-based groups.[33] Said an administrator of the Florida Office of Financial Regulation, "The frauds occur because people let their guard down around people they trust." Most of the operations worked like Ponzi schemes, where con artists persuade people in their community to invest their money and then appeal to others to commit as well. Examples of the schemes included Focus Financial Associates, which defrauded around six hundred Haitians, Unique Gems International, which targeted mainly Puerto Ricans and some other Hispanic groups, and AB Financing, which victimized some three thousand investors, most of whom hailed from Jamaica and other Caribbean islands. Some affinity scams seemed particularly geared to transnational communities.

In early 2004, the Miami-Dade County Commission on Ethics (established in 1996) declared that "in the last decade, [Miami-Dade] has . . . garnered a reputation as a hotbed of corruption. In the last six years alone, four sitting county commissioners and one School Board member were ousted from office for various abuses of the public trust. The State attorney has convened grand juries on at least four separate occasions from 1997 to 2002 to inquire into and report on problems arising out of Miami-Dade public schools, the county's contracting process and absentee-ballot voting."[34] According to a comparative study over the period 2000–2004, Miami was by far the most corrupt of a number of similarly sized U.S. cities, including Atlanta, Philadelphia, Denver, Houston, and Seattle.[35] To get a sense of this "culture of corruption" in the city's public sector, and of its occasionally surreal overtones, consider the following brief selection of a wide range of incidents reported by the *Miami Herald* since 2001:

- November 28, 2001: Gilda Oliveros, the former mayor of Hialeah Gardens, was found guilty of voter fraud and plotting to kill her husband. The heart of the prosecution's case involved "a former assistant and close friend to the mayor who claimed Oliveros tried to bully him . . . into killing her husband so she could cash in a fraudulent life insurance policy."
- February 5, 2002: Humberto Hernandez, a former Miami city commissioner, got out of jail thanks to the affair his lawyer had with his wife during his trial for voter fraud in 1998. A federal magistrate ruled that Hernandez's conviction should be nullified because his lawyer, Jose Quinon, started sleeping with Her-

nandez's wife during the trial. That romance "deprived" Hernandez of effective assistance of counsel.

- April 26, 2003: Richard Mendez, the powerful construction chief at Miami International Airport, was sentenced to four years in prison for his role in a contracts-for-bribes scheme. His wife received five months in prison for her role in the kickbacks.
- February 8, 2004: A number of public schools in Miami-Dade and Broward falsified their students FCAT scores to "make themselves look good—too good, it turned out, because the 'stunning reversal' in these schools' test performance led to probes of the School Boards."
- April 27, 2004: The Broward Sheriff's Office was caught for un-derreporting crime and falsifying "solved" crime records to inflate its performance. In subsequent months, "crime numbers rose dramatically in territories patrolled by the BSO."
- July 27, 2005: Faced with federal corruption charges and removed from office by the Florida governor, Arthur Teele, a Miami-Dade County commissioner, walked into the lobby of the *Miami Herald* building in downtown Miami and killed himself with a gunshot to the head.
- June 12, 2007: The director of the Miami-Dade Housing Agency, whose main responsibility is the provision of public housing, helped steer more than $1 million in city contracts to a company that had employed one of her ex-husbands as an executive since his release in 2004 from federal prison, where he served time for cocaine smuggling.
- September 5, 2007: Ken Jenne, the longtime Broward County sheriff, was sentenced to prison after he pleaded guilty to charges of mail fraud, tax evasion, and using his office for private gains. Among other things, he steered $1.2 million to a law firm owned by a close friend for investigating the Broward Sheriff's Office crime reports scandal (see above).
- November 4, 2009: A jury convicted Philip Davis, a former

Miami-Dade judge, on nine charges of fraud and money laundering. In the early 1990s, the judge had also been charged with bribery and he admitted to having snorted cocaine in his chambers. He was disbarred but rebounded in the late 1990s.

When Victor Monzon-Aguirre, one of the City of Miami's top administrators in 2003, announced his impending arrest on charges of forgery and grant theft, he remarked to the press, "I totally admit to these charges, but when you compare it to everything else that's happening in the rest of the county, it's nothing."[36] He had a point.

Previous chapters noted Miami's skyrocketing crime rates in the late 1970s and the early 1980s, far beyond those of any other U.S. city. The killings of nine foreign tourists within ten months in the early 1990s, too, made international headlines. These episodes were not aberrations but rather spikes in a remarkably consistent pattern of very high crime—higher than anywhere else. The reasons are not easily understood and probably reflect a combination of things. But the city's high crime rates are difficult to separate from its other civic challenges or from its flimsy social fabric.

The following numbers are reason for pause. Since 1958, when the FBI started to collect comparable crime data across the nation, Miami has had the highest annual overall crime rates of all metropolitan areas for thirty-three years.[37] That is more than two of every three years. For another ten years, Miami ranked second and it has been out of the top three only twice (Miami was fourth in 1967 and fifth in 1968). The overall runner-up, at a great distance, was Los Angeles, which clinched the top rank ten times and was second twice.

Since 1975, when the FBI expanded and specified its data-collection efforts, metropolitan Miami has also had by far the highest *violent* crime rates, ranking either first (twenty-six years) or second (eight years). Miami's consistency in this is all the more remarkable because all other "high crime" metropolitan areas (for example, Los Angeles, New York, Memphis, Las Vegas, New Orleans, San Francisco, Washington, D.C., and Detroit) have come and gone over time, and none has scored so consistently near the top for more than half a decade or so.[38]

Some of Miami's crime is violent, some is not. It covers the broad spectrum from murder to assault to embezzlement to car theft (check out the video game *Grand Theft Auto*, which is set in a Miami-like urban environment, with pastels and all). In specialized "vocations" like Medicare fraud or mortgage fraud, too, South Florida has led the nation in recent years.[39] Organized crime is still pervasive, particularly in relation to drug trafficking and money laundering. These industries peaked in the 1980s but they continue to flourish in the city's transient environment.

In 1990, the U.S. government designated South Florida as one of five High Density Drug Trafficking Areas (HIDTAs) that would receive special attention and resources from a range of federal agencies. According to the National Drug Intelligence Center in 2004, Miami ranked among the nation's top three cities for asset seizures related to money-laundering cases, together with New York and Los Angeles.[40] Miami serves as an important clearing-house for drug proceeds from other U.S. cities, mainly for Colombian dominated organizations, and this business permeates many other parts of the regular economy, continuing patterns from the late 1970s and early 1980s. A report by the U.S. Department of Justice in 2008 states that

Colombian money launderers send an estimated $5 to $15 billion in illicit drug proceeds from the United States to Colombia annually, a large percentage of which passes through South Florida. . . . Traffickers operating in the South Florida HIDTA region also launder illicit proceeds through other means, including purchasing real estate and luxury items, using money services businesses, structuring bank deposits, and commingling drug proceeds with revenue generated by cash-intensive businesses such as auto repair shops, dealerships, and hair salons. Additionally, some criminal groups and street gangs are investing in startup record labels and recording studios. To illustrate, two Miami residents were sentenced in federal court to 30 years' imprisonment in March 2008 for distributing cocaine and money laundering. These individuals used a variety of methods to launder their illicit drug proceeds, including mortgage fraud, and front businesses such as a coin laundry, a fast food franchise, and a record label.[41]

In August 2007, one of Miami's most prominent Edge Act banks, American Express Bank International, based on Brickell Avenue, was fined $65 million by federal prosecutors for "willfully failing to maintain an effective anti-money laundering program." Court documents indicated that a number of bank accounts were used to launder more than $55 million in illegal drug proceeds involving Colombian importers and "shell companies." Prosecutors said the bank "failed to know its customers or the sources of the funds." It was not that unusual. The bank, a unit of the global credit card giant American Express, became the nineteenth financial institution in South Florida to face sanctions since 2004.[42]

Miami's illicit finance is not all related to drugs. In 2003, U.S. Immigration and Customs Enforcement (ICE) established a local task force to deal with a particular type of shady character drawn to the South Florida environs: the "politically exposed person" (PEP). In bureaucratic terms, the task force was "established to address the vulnerability of relationships between private banks and corrupt foreign officials." In other words, PEPs are foreign government officials or foreign private sector business leaders who have access to foreign private or public funds, take the money, and run for Miami.[43]

Thus, when Ecuador's president, Lucio Gutierrez, visited Washington, D.C. in February 2003, he requested extradition of a number of fugitive bankers who had plundered their banks, fled Ecuador with enormous amounts of capital, and opted for "Miami and the good life, Rolls Royce convertibles and Coral Gables mansions."[44] In another example, in December 2003, ICE agents seized a 5,207-square-foot condominium in Key Biscayne that was alleged to have been bought with illegal funds by the former head of the Nicaraguan office of tax collection.[45] One of the most spectacular cases of all was revealed in a special report of the U.S. Senate in 2005: the former Chilean dictator, General Augusto Pinochet, used a baffling array of 125 accounts in banks around the world to hide an illegal money trail of 25 years, and Miami was at the center of that scheme.[46]

Miami's transient urban culture invokes the metaphor of the city as a hotel: people check in, use the facilities, and check out again.[47] They show little interest in their neighbors, they do not invest in social relations, they come with a sense of entitlement, and they have no stake in the future of the place. It would be amiss to put the blame for Miami's challenges on *foreign* immigrants or on certain ethnic groups—and not just because it smacks of xenophobia or ethnocentric bias. The point is that transience is something entirely different from immigration. The problem, if there is one, is not that people are coming; it is that most of them do not intend to stay. Besides, Miami appears exemplary in its equal opportunity environment for uncivil conduct.[48]

One may be tempted to suggest that Miami's "unruly" character is a manifestation of its youth and immaturity as a city: it is true that it has at times been reminiscent of some older large American cities in the late nineteenth century and the early twentieth. Places like Philadelphia, New York, Minneapolis, and Chicago were in their earlier days notorious for bribery, graft, mismanagement, and organized crime.[49] But that suggestion would ignore the significantly different historical contexts. Then, urban civil society and American democracy as we know it were still in the early stages of formation. In addition, people were considerably less mobile than today. The suggestion that Miami will "mature" over time ignores the fact that in this city transience and civic challenges have moved in tandem for well over a century. Miami's character is *built* on transience.

Much of the recent research on social capital in America is focused on its alleged decline, and Putnam's arguments have not gone uncontested. Miami constitutes a different case. Miami has *never* known social stability of the sort that forms and maintains social capital. When Putnam suggests that the erosion of social capital across the nation is related to "decaying institutions," he may be on to something in general—but in Miami such institutions never really matured to begin with.[50] Miami evolved in a constant state of flux. Its history represents layer upon layer of extreme transience, with social capital as elusive as the social stability it requires.

CHAPTER 7

Locals, Exiles, and Mobiles

In the past, people's identities were closely tied to place. The world was viewed as a "mosaic" of cultures and peoples, a spatial ordering where all were primarily known based on *where* they belonged. Migration happened, of course, but always in relatively small numbers and it was generally one-way and involved fundamental uprooting and full-fledged resettlement. The "natural" state of the world was seen as stable and socially coherent.

In recent years this perspective has lost ground. Writings in many academic areas have put forward a more dynamic view. The focus shifted from studying more or less stable places to intensifying and ceaseless *flows* of people, things, money, information, and ideas. If in the past human identity was viewed as fundamentally based on place, it is now sometimes defined by spatial mobility. The result is not only something akin to a restless cultural landscape but also what has been labeled a "de-territorialization of identity."[1] The question "Where are you from?" is not as revealing as it used to be—and indeed for some it may trigger existentialist ponderings.

We now understand identities to be multidimensional, naturally in flux, and less tied to place. Any individual or group is likely to have plural identities that may be complementary or even compete with each other. In Walt Whitman's poetic phrase, we all "contain multitudes." For example, one and the same Miami resident may be born in Cuba, be black, be a U.S. citizen, and have a middle-class income. How this person identifies—in Miami or elsewhere—will depend on social context and prevailing discourses.[2]

Globalization has strongly influenced this new dynamic. Traditional identities are constructed in a particular geographical context, but that construction tends to lose its integrity from exposure to globalization. For example, Caribbean migrants to the United States often face a redefinition of their racial identity because the meaning of race in the United States is different—more black and white, literally—from what it is in their home countries.

Transnational migration has superseded the simple one-way and permanent migration of the past. The literature presents conflicting ways of looking at transnational migrants. Often, they are described as a disadvantaged lot, their presence indicative of a global economy that requires the mobility of labor but that has resulted in insecure economic conditions both at home and in the adopted homeland. In this view, they have never quite left home nor have they really become full-fledged members of their new society. Their transnational status is born from necessity; their social status is precarious.[3]

Other research shows that transnational migrants are generally not the poorest in their countries of origin, or in their adopted homelands and cities.[4] They are actually privileged in a sense: they had information and financial resources and were able to undertake the move. Indeed, through remittances and transnational businesses they often play a prominent economic role and enjoy prestige in their region of origin.

Another view goes even further: it emphasizes the hybrid identity of transnational migrants and the substantial benefits this brings. In this view, people with hybrid identities have an unusual ability to relate to various cultures, to position themselves in one or the other and to communicate between them. It is a position of cultural power with potential economic rewards. A good example, of course, concerns certain groups of Miami immigrants who can present themselves alternatively as American or Latin American and who have become successful transnational business entrepreneurs.

Even in global cities, or especially in global cities, these identity shifts have not affected everybody in the same way or to the same degree. People are not equally mobile and while mobility is a choice for some, it can be a necessity for others. Global cities are the signature terrain of the "kinetic elite," but they are also home to populations with much more restrained mobility. Spatial mobility has become an essential marker of social stratification and has rearranged the social fabric of global cities. Issues of race, ethnicity, and class still matter, of course—but it is the way in which they interact with spatial mobility, that is of particular interest. It is hard to think of a more intriguing laboratory than Miami.

Miami's various population groups, and the ways they relate to the city, are best understood in the broader context of globalization, transience, and identity of place. The city's inhabitants differ fundamentally in how they identify with Miami and that, in turn, determines how they fit in. In this sense, we can think of the city's populations as composed of locals, exiles, and mobiles.[5] These categories are based on spatial mobility, or immobility, and identity of place. They have a physical dimension (being), but they also pertain to a frame of mind (belonging). Of course, not every individual in Miami may fit one of the three categories and some individuals may be situated in between, but for most the category is actually pretty clear.[6]

Locals are a minority in Miami. About 20 percent of the present-day population of Greater Miami is estimated to fall in this group.[7] These are people who consider Miami their hometown, being either born here or raised in the area from a young age. The 20 percent estimate is at the high end and includes numerous young children (including those of "non-locals" who were born in Miami) who may not remain in Miami for a lifetime. Among adults, the locally born population might be as low as 15 percent. Many of the poorest people in this city are locals. They were born and raised here, never moved, and seem to be frozen in place. Some of the wealthiest families are local, too (some of the big land developers have been here for generations), but their numbers are very small.

Exiles are those who find themselves in Miami of political or economic necessity. Over the years, their ranks have included large numbers of Cubans, Nicaraguans, Haitians, Venezuelans, and others. Exiles do not consider Miami their hometown, or the United States their home country. The future prospect of returning home, real or illusory, plays a major part in exiles' identity (at least among the first generation). This group comprises around a third of Greater Miami's population. Exiles are not very mobile: their political and economic situation usually does not allow it. Their mobility within the metropolitan area is limited too, as they tend to congregate in particular residential areas. This is particularly true for less affluent exiles.

Mobiles do not identify with Miami as their hometown and, like exiles, do not consider their stay permanent. But unlike exiles, they have come here by choice and they can leave by choice. They are at once highly mobile and relatively affluent.[8] Mobiles have always exerted a major influence on this city—its culture, its economic fortunes, and the built environment. During the first half of Miami's history, they were northerners, either vacationers or entrepreneurs. Nowadays, they are an increasingly global mix. It is important to remember that, compared to other metropolitan areas, many of Miami's foreign immigrants belong to the upper (income) classes.[9]

Today's mobiles include domestic migrants attracted to South Florida's image of sun and beaches; expatriates temporarily assigned to a post with a multinational branch in Miami; young domestic migrants drawn to Miami Beach's alternative lifestyles; wealthy Latin Americans attracted to Miami's luxuries, glamorous lifestyles, and private banking opportunities; seasonal "snowbirds" from the United States or Canada; European real estate investors; and many others. The overall number of mobiles can be estimated by proxy measures such as recent mobility and place of birth. Their share of the total metropolitan population hovers around a third, about the same as the percentage of exiles.[10]

Locals, exiles, and mobiles can be found across Greater Miami but tend to concentrate in specific residential areas, as the map shows.[11] They are not equally divided between Miami-Dade and Broward. The two counties have roughly the same proportion of locals but Miami-Dade has considerably more exiles than Broward: about 40 percent versus 25 percent.[12] In contrast, Broward has a larger proportion of mobiles: about 40 percent compared to 30 percent in Miami-Dade.

There is a series of small and large neighborhoods in Greater Miami that make up a colorful and sometimes disjointed mosaic, a punctuated residential landscape where only a few minutes by car separates disparate areas. As highlighted in the following selected "excursions" into the neighborhoods of locals, exiles, and mobiles, they inhabit different worlds, live different lives, and relate very differently to Miami.

If anybody could claim to be local in Southeast Florida it is the Miccosukee. Their numbers are small and their territory is in the Everglades, too far west to show up on any detailed urban maps. They have not played a role in the modern development of the region. The Miccosukee are at once the most native and highly

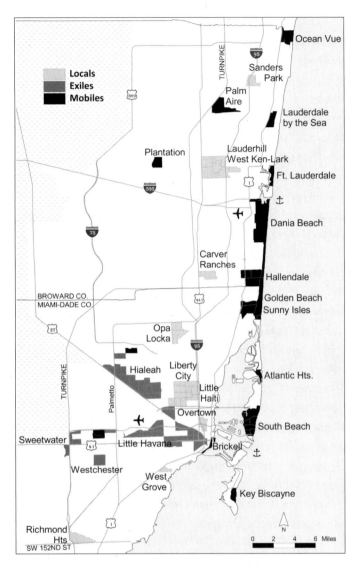

Figure 20. Residential neighborhoods in Greater Miami with high concentrations of locals, exiles, and mobiles. Based on data from the 2000 U.S. Census (see Appendix 2).

marginalized, not unlike Native Americans elsewhere in the country. They are not truly natives—they were chased down to South Florida in the second half of the nineteenth century by the U.S. cavalry and considered the Everglades the best place to hide. As the eastern parts of the Everglades were drained beginning in the 1900s to make way for agriculture and urbanization, the Miccosukee gradually moved further west.

The Miccosukee's existence was not officially acknowledged until after World War II when the use of airboats allowed detailed reconnaissance, around the time that Everglades National Park was founded. After several years of negotiation, the Miccosukee adopted their constitution in 1961 and it was approved a year later by the U.S. Department of the Interior. The Miccosukee had become a "sovereign nation" within the United States.

The reservation area occupies a large swath of northwestern Miami-Dade County and almost all of the western part of Broward County, bounded on the north by Alligator Alley (I-75). Most of these 189,000 acres are part of the South Florida Water Management District's Water Conservation Area 3A-South, but the tribe is "allowed to use the land for the purpose of hunting, fishing, frogging, subsistence agriculture and to carry on the traditional Miccosukee way of life."[13] The Miccosukee have engaged in various commercial activities such as eco-tourism, and leasing some land for cattle grazing, for gas stations along Alligator Alley, and for resorts.

The main center of Miccosukee activity is in the south of the reservation along the Tamiami Trail, just north of Everglades National Park, about forty miles west of downtown Miami. There is a police department, school, tribal administrative office, tourist attractions, stores, and several community agencies. Closer to Miami, on the corner of the Tamiami Trail and Krome Avenue, stands the Miccosukee Gaming Resort and nearby is the Miccosukee Golf and Country Club. The revenues from these "tribal enterprises" are not publicly known but are partly used to support community activity and development.

One of the most illustrious figures in the modern history of the Miccosukee is Buffalo Tiger, a former chief born in the Everglades in 1920 and who, at the time of writing, runs an "ecocultural tourism" business along the Tamiami Trail. When the U.S. government was slow to respond to demands for official recognition of the Miccosukee in the late 1950s, Buffalo Tiger sought contact and met with Fidel Castro shortly after he had taken power in Cuba. The result was that the Cuban government recognized Miccosukee nationhood, which in turn compelled the U.S. government to act.[14] This did not endear the Miccosukee to the Cuban exiles who subsequently sought refuge in Miami.

Reflecting on his early life, Buffalo Tiger celebrates the Miccosukee's former freedom and independence: "I was born out here. I thought when I was growing up we did pretty well, because we live on the reservation, we do not know white man's way too much. . . . We were taught we should live by ourself away from everybody and to live on the land. Like Glades, with plenty game, plenty food, and we not need the dollar to buy food. All we got to do is get out in the woods and hunt that is enough for us. Let me tell you, when I was younger it was a beautiful life I had."[15] But those days are gone. There are only about 650 Miccosukee tribal members left. Some live on the reservation but most are scattered across the metropolitan area. The Everglades, in Buffalo Tiger's words, "are dying" along with the old ways of subsistence. The cultural traditions of the Miccosukee are at risk and their present leaders acknowledge the accompanying dilemmas and ambiguities: "The Miccosukee Tribal leadership recognizes much remains to be done to ensure that the Miccosukee people can continue to be themselves in a constantly changing world. Values and traditions will not flourish unless they are constantly renewed and entered into whole-heartedly by the younger generations."[16]

Locals tend to be highly concentrated in certain neighborhoods and this has much to do with their inability to move, which correlates strongly with economics and with race. Areas with high concentrations of locals in Miami-Dade include Overtown, Liberty City, the West Grove, Opa Locka, Goulds, and Richmond Heights. Local areas in Broward include Carver Ranches, West Ken-Lark, and Sanders Park. These areas are overwhelmingly African American, on average 94 percent, and very poor. This does not mean that all African Americans in Miami are locals, or poor: rather it shows that those African Americans who *did* have the option to move chose to go elsewhere, leaving a more uniformly poor neighborhood behind.[17] More than 40 percent of households in the local areas live below the poverty line. The median annual household income in 2000 was only $21,000 and the per capita income was $9,900. These are also, by the way, the areas with the highest proportion of U.S. citizens, an average 95 percent. In South Florida, being there first or holding a passport does not necessarily confer any privileges.

Overtown is the best known of these local neighborhoods—though because of the primacy of race in American public discourse it is first seen as "black" and its localness is often not appreciated. It is the best known of these areas because it is the closest to downtown (and is often discussed regarding redevelopment plans for downtown Miami), because it has a long and interesting history, and because it is in some ways the most problematic local neighborhood.

From a thriving community in the 1940s and 1950s, with its own commercial center along N.W. 2nd Avenue, busy stores, high-flying nighttime entertainment, and a large proportion of home ownership, Overtown went into a deep decline and became symbolic of the inner city decay that has characterized much of urban America since the 1960s. One of the main local causes was the construction of highways I-95 and I-395: two "axes of evil" that ripped the community apart and effectively forced the majority out. Driving through Overtown today, one is struck by the wide stretches of dead space underneath the overpasses, abundant and poorly kept parking lots, the dysfunctional local road network, and a depressing human landscape featuring homelessness, despair, illicit drug use, street prostitution, and derelict housing. Overtown has one of the highest poverty rates and the worst housing in South Florida. The population is just under 8,000 and there are only 41 businesses left—compared to 389 in 1950. The recently renovated Lyric Theater, on the corner of N.W. 2nd Ave and 8th Street stands as a lonely reminder of better times—its renovation having done little to rekindle a more glorious past.

Only 2 percent of the county's African American population continues to live here.[18] Many of those who left in the 1960s moved to Liberty City, the site of one of the early (1930s) major U.S. public housing projects; it did not become a segregated black "township" until the 1960s. Liberty City has its own iconic history. Alongside the old public housing project on N.W. 12th Avenue sit the remains of a concrete wall that separated blacks from the white residential area on the east side. Nearby, the first black families in South Florida walked their kids to the newly integrated Orchard Villa Elementary School in 1959. It went from all white to all black almost overnight. Liberty City was at the center of the local civil rights movement in the 1950s and 1960s and it was here that the massive riots erupted following the McDuffie verdict in 1980. Today, the area remains an important hub for activism among the lower-income working class and the poor: it is home to several organizations such as the Miami Workers Cen-

Figure 21. Liberty City public housing, 2009. Photo by Robert Kloosterman.

ter and LIFFT (Low Income Families Fighting Together). In 2007, Liberty City formed the backdrop to a short-lived but widely publicized squatter initiative called Umoja Village.[19]

Liberty City is not a municipal town as the name would suggest. It is part of the City of Miami. Today it is the largest concentration of locals, and of African Americans, in Miami-Dade County, with about forty thousand inhabitants. The landscape is not as torn as Overtown's, but the low standard of living is clearly visible in the very modest housing. It is a strangely non-urban landscape in some ways. Mostly sparse low-rise buildings with little vegetation, some of the older projects look more like barracks than houses. The uniformly designated spaces for laundry lines in between the blocks and the overall spaciousness reflect low land values.

Another area with a high concentration of locals, but physically much smaller, is West Grove. It is an area of about sixty-five blocks, south of downtown, hemmed in between Coconut Grove

Figure 22. Bahamian-style houses in West Grove, 2009. Photo by author.

and Coral Gables. The approximately three thousand inhabitants descend from Bahamian construction workers who moved across the waters to Miami in the late nineteenth century. They have been there for about four generations now and they are some-times referred to as "South Florida's oldest living community."[20] It is a historic enclave with several remaining blocks of unique Bahamian-style small wooden houses, long protected from gen-trification by the density and stability of its population.[21] Despite the overall poverty and crime rates, the area has appeal due to its small scale, unique architecture, unmistakable local feel, and some stable residential neighborhoods.

Broward's local neighborhoods are similar to Miami-Dade's in the preponderance of African Americans and very low incomes. But they have not existed quite as long since many blacks did not move there until the middle of the twentieth century (this is also true for Opa Locka, the most northern major concentration of lo-cals in Miami-Dade). Their historical significance is less than that of places like Overtown, Liberty City, or West Grove.

The social and economic challenges for Miami's "local" neigh-borhoods are enormous. Median annual household incomes in some blocks are as low as $10,000; official unemployment is around 20 percent (probably a serious underestimation); and nearly two-thirds of families live below the poverty line.[22] Crime, too, has had a devastating effect on some areas in recent dec-ades, especially Liberty City, Overtown, and Opa Locka. This is where repeated killings of (lost) foreign tourists in the early 1990s led the city's car rental agencies to provide maps showing visitors areas to avoid, and led the county to add cautionary road signs so that oblivious visitors headed for the beach wouldn't take the wrong exit. The spatial concentration of crime in black neighbor-hoods, and the frequent indifference about crime in general, is difficult to disassociate from racial issues. During an interview with CBS television in 2007 on the topic of gun violence, John Timoney, then Miami's chief of police, remarked, "I can guarantee you . . . that if 85 percent of the people in big cities [who] were getting killed were white, there'd be a different approach to this whole thing. . . . They'd be screaming for more federal legislation. They'd be demanding it, and to hell with the NRA."[23]

African Americans have played a huge part in the creation of Miami because they made up the majority of the blue-collar work force in the first half of the city's existence—from the clearing of mangrove to the building of roads and railroads to the construc-tion of housing. They made Miami "home" early on, while the white elites maintained residency elsewhere and came to Miami to look after their investments or to vacation. Miami's African Americans, it should be noted, also served disproportionately in the U.S. military in World War II, in Vietnam, and in the Middle East: the local neighborhoods have a much greater share of veter-ans than other areas.[24]

Despite the challenges, most of these local neighborhoods have a strong sense of identity and community: the residents have often been there for two, three, or even four generations, church parishes often have long traditions, and neighbors have known each other since childhood. In Miami's wealthier areas, life unfolds inside of the homes and out of sight, and the streets are empty. In contrast, the local neighborhoods share a lively street culture where people socialize on the porch, in the yard, in front of the home, or on the sidewalk. Private and public spaces often converge on the doorstep.

Exile communities tend to cluster in space, as well. Three out of four people in the exile neighborhoods shown on the map are born abroad and nearly half are not U.S. citizens. In general, exiles are economically better off than Miami's locals.[25] The main areas are all in Miami-Dade County: Little Havana, Hialeah, and Sweetwater have large concentrations of Cubans with an added mix of Central American immigrants. Sweetwater is sometimes referred to as Little Managua but even there the Cubans outnumber the Nicaraguans. Weston, in Broward County, having experienced a rapid increase of its Venezuelan population in recent years, is now sometimes referred to as Westonzuela.[26] There are smaller pockets of select exile groups scattered across the metropolitan area.

The single most iconic residential area of current-day Miami is Little Havana. It is ground zero of the Cuban exile community: some 120 blocks strung along S.W. 8th Street, better known as Calle Ocho. The center is to the east, near downtown Miami. This is where we find anchoring institutions: Domino Park; the Bay of Pigs Monument;[27] the old headquarters of Alpha 66 (the anti-Castro paramilitary organization); the Elián González Museum; avenues and streets named for Teddy Roosevelt (who liberated Cuba from the Spanish), Ronald Reagan (who rolled back communism), and Brigade 2506 (the former recruiting outfit for Bay of Pigs fighters); the Pedro Pan memorial, which was unveiled as recently as 2009; specialty shops for cigars and *guayaberas*; and well-known *cafeterías* and restaurants like El Pub and Versailles.

Figure 23. Bay of Pigs Monument, Little Havana, 2010. The eternal flame commemorates the martyrs of the failed invasion in 1961. Photo by author.

When it comes to notions of belonging, place, and identity, it is hard to think of a more intriguing venue than Little Havana. Miami's Cubans take pride in this area and call it theirs. They have filled the area with symbols and meaning, and as such Little Havana is deeply "localized"—but the symbols and meanings always relate to the real Havana, a hundred miles away. The exile spirit and hopes are condensed in a well-known song by the

Miami-based singer Willy Chirino: "*nuestro día viene llegando*" (our day is coming).

Back in 1984, some business-minded Cuban Americans took the initiative to rename the area the "Latin Quarter." It was a slow time for tourism in the wake of the cocaine wars, there was a nationwide recession, and it was thought that "Latin Quarter" would attract tourists and be more inclusive of other Hispanics in Miami.[28] The proponents of the idea were upwardly mobile Cuban Americans who, not uncommonly, had moved out of Little Havana to wealthier areas like Coral Gables. The City of Miami approved the new name, but subsequently the local residents organized fierce protests and ultimately forced the city government to rescind the decision. The initiators of the renaming were denounced as "traitors" and "communists" out to undermine the exile cause. Xavier Suarez, the (Cuban-born) mayor at the time, was reproached for not being a "real Cuban." The attachment to Little Havana, and to Miami at large, is real and passionate—yet it always comes second. As one of the protest leaders said, "After Cuba, Little Havana is my homeland." Take out the Cuba factor, take out the exile iconography, and the place would be like a vacuum.

The exile culture is often fueled by fiercely "local" politics. Miami's Cuban politicians rally support and build their constituencies by showcasing their *cubanidad* and speaking out against Castro. The old tactic is to play "more Cuban than you" and charge that "you are no longer a real Cuban." When Alex Penelas, a second-generation Cuban, was running to be the mayor of Miami-Dade in 1996, his mother declared on a local Spanish-language radio station that it was "not his fault that he is born in this country" (that is, in the United States).[29] When the saga of Elián González ended in April 2000, Joe Carollo, the Cuban American mayor of Miami, demonstratively refused to assist the FBI in its raid of the boy's family home in Little Havana. After the raid,

Figure 24. "Un lugar sagrado" (a sacred place): Monument honoring Ernesto Izquierdo, the freedom fighter who took part in the Bay of Pigs invasion and died in 1979 fighting the Sandinistas in Nicaragua. He has been said to have been involved in the assassination of President Kennedy. The memorial was constructed in 1992, right behind the Bay of Pigs monument. Photo by author, 2010.

Figure 25. Domino Park, Little Havana, 2009. Photo by author.

he announced the firing of Miami's non-Cuban police chief for not warning the mayor about imminent FBI actions (information that the police chief was not authorized to disclose). Carollo did not, however, succeed in his bid for another mayoral term. The 2001 mayoral election went to Manny Diaz, the Cuban-born lawyer who had represented Elián González's family in Miami.[30]

Cubans are Greater Miami's largest and best-known ethnic group, and also the single largest group of exiles. Only a minority of them live in Little Havana and the area also shelters a range of other, mainly Spanish-speaking, immigrants. The largest concentration of Cuban Americans is to the northwest, in the city of Hialeah. It counts about 150,000 Cuban Americans, three out of every four residents. Hialeah has a very different feel and lacks the vibrant character of Little Havana.[31] It is mainly lower middle class in income, and it is located near some of Miami's main (light) manufacturing areas along the railroad and near one of the main drainage canals connecting the Everglades to the Miami River. If one had to identify a large and relatively homogeneous working-class residential area in Greater Miami, this would be it.

Figure 26. Elián González, seized by federal agents from his relatives' home in Little Havana, April 22, 2000. Pulitzer Prize–winning photo by Alan Diaz (© AP/Wide World Photos).

Greater Miami's six hundred thousand Cubans make this the second largest "Cuban" city after Havana. If we include second-generation "Cubans" their numbers exceed eight hundred thousand. While Cubans are not a monolithic community, the exile mind-set seems pervasive. It implies a continued focus on Cuba as homeland: an imagined future where Cuba's liberation and the possibility of return figure prominently; and a conviction that to realize this future involves a struggle. Some would argue that this struggle, *la lucha*, has been nothing less than a "holy war."[32]

It is not easy to determine how much *la lucha* has lost steam over time because of generational shifts—but it appears to be alive and well. Demographically, the first wave of Cuban arrivals (through 1964) still comprises about a third of all Cubans in Miami, and this generation has "firmly planted the banner of the exile ideology" within the Cuban community at large.[33] The majority of Cubans seem to share the exile mind-set, even many born in Miami. Fifteen years ago, David Rieff noted that Miami's Cubans have "continued to live, metaphorically at least, with their bags packed and a strong fantasy alive in their hearts of what they would do in Cuba and for Cuba when, at last, they were finally able to return."[34] Five years ago, two well-known scholars of the Cuban scene in Miami observed, "One would think that after forty years some things would have changed. But when studying Cubans in the United States and especially in Miami, one often has to explain why some things have not changed. The persistence of an exile ideology is an important part of the apparent immutability of the community."[35]

An interesting illustration of how second-generation Cuban exiles situate themselves in Miami is the local film company Kids in Exile (!), whose productions include a drama about a Cuban American family in Hialeah and documentaries on the *salsa* diva Celia Cruz and the rise and fall of Maduro Stadium. The film about the stadium is particularly interesting because it documents the role of Cubans in "bringing *beisbol* to Miami." José Aleman Sr., a wealthy Cuban exile from the Batista regime, built the stadium in 1949 at N.W. 10th Street and 23rd Avenue. Named after the Cuban baseball legend Bobby Maduro, it was home to the city's first professional baseball team, the Miami Sun Sox. It lasted only five years (owing to poor attendance and low revenues) before being disbanded, upon which Aleman sold the stadium.[36] The grounds were then used for several years by the Marlins and by the Baltimore Orioles for spring training. The film treats the demolition of the stadium in 2001 as a tragic loss to Miami's history—and the role Cubans played in it.

In his *La Lucha for Cuba* (2003), Miguel de La Torre says about these second-generation exiles: "Exilic Cubans also include those who were neither born nor raised on the island yet whose identity was forged by their parents' act of (re)membering Cuba from the social location of exile. Although exilic Cubans are not a monolithic group, they are united, no matter how loosely, by the experience of being separated from the island that defines them."[37]

While the apparent diversification of political opinions among Miami's Cubans is a popular topic in the news media, exilic "political correctness" remains very powerful and permeates debates. Institutions such as the Cuban American National Foundation (CANF) still play a powerful part in the political life of Miami's Cubans. Natalio Chediak, the Cuban American founder of the Miami International Film Festival, once remarked that "the most subversive notion that you can advance within the exile community is that this is a heterogeneous [community], that people think in a variety of ways."[38] In 2007, Ana Menendez, a columnist for the *Miami Herald*, was besieged by hate mail and threats for a column that criticized Cuban American politics. In response, she wrote another column titled "Exiles' Pain Must Include Room for Dissent."[39]

The exilic preoccupation with the homeland tends to go in tandem with a certain neglect or indifference toward Miami: "An identity as exiles has colored all aspects of the life of Cubans in the United States. It has resulted in an inordinate allocation of resources, including emotional energy, towards the primary task of reclaiming the homeland . . . ; it has reinforced a sense of exceptionalism, setting themselves apart from other immigrant and Latino groups . . . ; it has determined the nature of their participation in the political life of the new country."[40]

The apparent lack of assimilation and the insularity of Miami's Cuban community cannot be separated from the fact that never in the history of the United States has such a large number of exiles arrived in such a short time and concentrated in only one city. Presently, about 60 percent of all Cubans in the United States live in Miami. There was no need to assimilate, no need to depend on the existing social infrastructure. Cuban American business leaders prospered in Miami without joining mainstream "American" business organizations: "Rather than becoming part of the Greater Miami Chamber of Commerce, they participated in the

Cámara de Comercio Latina. Rather than petitioning for entry into the South Florida Builders' Association, they formed the Latin Builders' Association. Rather than contributing to the American Cancer Society, they supported *La Liga Contra el Cáncer*."[41]

In the wake of the Elián González affair, one non-Cuban newspaper columnist did not mince any words about the local civic disposition of exiles: "Many older Cubans view non-Cubans as irrelevant to their lives."[42]

Little Haiti is not nearly as well known. This has something to do with the Cuban community's much larger numbers and stronger voices compared to the Haitians. But it also shows that Little Haiti's character, as a place, is not as well defined or iconic as Little Havana's. Neither its center nor its boundaries are self-evident. It is located to the north of Overtown, roughly between 36th and 85th Streets and between Biscayne Boulevard (U.S. 1) and I-95. This is actually quite a large area and it is shared with various other groups, including a good number of local African Americans.

If one had to identify a center, it would be around the intersection of N.E. 54th Street and 2nd Avenue. Here is where we find the Marché au Fer, a visually striking tin-roofed shopping bazaar, a replica of the building with the same name in Port-au-Prince. It was built in 1990, functioned as an art gallery for some years, and closed down in 2002 owing to insufficient revenues. Its fate shows that Little Haiti does not figure prominently in Miamians' mental maps, and that it could not tap into the city's big tourism industry. Another ingredient of Little Haiti's iconic landscape, at some distance from the Marché, is the thirteen-foot bronze statue of Toussaint L'Ouverture (the founder of independent Haiti in 1804) at the corner of Miami Avenue and 62nd Street. The area includes ubiquitous small Catholic churches, beauty parlors, shops, and restaurants, all with French or Creole designations.

Another important Haitian concentration can be found along U.S. 1 in the city of North Miami, further to the northeast in Miami-Dade County. North Miami has an unusual mix of residents. Of the sixty thousand residents about a quarter are Haitian, a quarter are African American, a quarter are a variety of Hispanics, and a quarter are non-Hispanic white. The Haitians in North Miami are generally better off and more upwardly mobile than their compatriots in Little Haiti. They are also naturalized in greater numbers and more politically active. As a result, the Haitian Americans of North Miami were able to mobilize sufficient support to elect the first Haitian American mayor in South Florida, Josaphat "Joe" Celestin, in 2001.

Haitians are less concentrated in particular residential areas than Cubans because they have been arriving in Miami at a steadier pace.[43] They did not come in very large numbers within very short time periods, and unlike the Cubans they did not overwhelm specific areas. And, of course, their overall numbers are considerably smaller: Haitians are outnumbered by Cubans four to one. There are now about 100,000 Haitians in Miami-Dade County and around 65,000 in Broward. Given that Haitians are overwhelmingly colored and are often mistaken for African Americans, it is likely that racial discrimination and residential segregation in the housing market combined to push them to or near African American neighborhoods.[44]

Many of Miami's Haitians are exiles, even if many were not officially granted political refugee status—in contrast to Cubans. Haitians, instead, were generally considered to be *economic* refugees. This legal position was highly contested by various groups because it was obvious that many Haitians had in fact escaped political violence in their home country. At any rate, whether for political or economic reasons, many Haitians came to Miami out of necessity and they are best considered exiles, one way or the other.[45]

We can distinguish two phases of Haitian arrival in Miami.[46] The first concerned the political exiles who considered their migration temporary and who were preoccupied with the political struggle in Haiti. They viewed Miami as a place of transit, a place to organize opposition against the Haitian regime. Their politics permeated all dimensions of social life in the exile community, impeding assimilation and integration into social life in Miami.

The second phase concerned mostly working-class immigrants who were primarily motivated by economics. For them, too, making it to America was a matter of survival and they, too, shared the exile mind-set:

> All their problems revolve around work and on how to survive and create better opportunities for children and relatives in Haiti. So long as Haiti is the primary reference point, there is no need to be assimilated as Americans. . . . For the majority of Haitian immigrants, the goal is not to achieve social status [in their new country or city of residence] but to have a better economic position and more importantly to save. Therefore, it is possible to separate their position in the work place, which gives access to economic betterment, from their social and cultural life, which takes place primarily in reference to Haiti.[47]

In January 2010, in the wake of the horrendous earthquake in Haiti, there were signs that a third wave of immigrants was in the making. The U.S. government indicated it would start to process applications for "Temporary Protected Status" by illegal Haitians, possibly leading to legalization of significant numbers. There were discussions of organizing a massive airlift of orphans from the devastated island to the United States, reminiscent of the Pedro Pan operation that brought Cuban children to Miami in the early 1960s. At any rate, the disaster was consequential in Miami as it put on hold the dreams of many exiles to return in the foreseeable future and it galvanized the community's transnational character.

For many Haitians in Miami, the notion of "community" or "home" does not correspond to any particular space in the city. Many of the poor exiles find themselves trapped in inner city neighborhoods, alongside poor African Americans, with little prospect for upward mobility, but with dreams of returning to a stable Haiti. Those who have acquired more mobility maintain intense networks of communication with relatives and friends in Haiti, New York City, Miami, and Montreal. Haitian transnationals are very important to the economy back home, and their potential has not gone unnoticed by successive governments in Haiti. In 1991, the Haitian government designated the diaspora the "Tenth Department of Haiti" (the country has nine administrative territories).[48]

Yet another kind of exile is found in the southern reaches of Miami-Dade County, around Homestead and Florida City. Since the beginning of the twentieth century, when agriculture started to develop, South Florida has attracted migrant workers to provide much needed labor on the farms. Most of the work was seasonal (about eight months) and the workers were typically African Americans from the north, Puerto Ricans, and Bahamians. Today, the great majority of farm workers (sometimes still called migrant workers) come from Mexico and Central America. From the 1950s onward, many decided to stay in South Florida year-round and some were joined by their families.

The number of migrant/seasonal/farm workers in South Florida is estimated at 250,000, of whom about half are thought to have settled permanently. Clearly, definitions are inconsistent and counts are unreliable. Government agencies dealing with these workers are scattered at the local, state, and federal levels. A small number of the permanent workers have become citizens, many have temporary permits, and a good number are thought to be illegal. Surveys show that 50 percent of all migrant workers come from Mexico, 75 percent are males, their average age is thirty-two, 50 percent are married, and at least 33 percent are undocumented (other estimates are upward to 80 percent). The median completed education is sixth grade. A fair number are illiterate and most do not understand English.[49]

They are best understood as exiles because they come to Miami out of despair. Most escaped dire poverty in their homelands and try to keep their families at home afloat with remittances. Weekly wages of most farm workers are around three hundred dollars for five days of work at eight to twelve hours per day—but most are not fully employed. Some are paid hourly but many are compensated by the amount of work done (in the case of harvesting, usually by weight of produce). They have no benefits and work conditions are generally harsh. Since the majority of workers maintain families either at home or in Miami, they have among the lowest household incomes in the region. Well over half are estimated to live below the federal poverty line.

Most of the workers who are not fully employed or who are laid off resort to daily wage labor activities. They can be found hanging around some intersections or in Home Depot parking lots, hoping to be picked up for a few hours or more of work for a contractor or gardener. This is sometimes the worst work with the least pay. Their skills vary greatly as does their success in landing decent employment. In the past few decades, many found jobs in construction, a huge industry with many undocumented workers where pay is generally higher. But the construction industry ground to a halt in 2007 and many lost jobs. They now form a massive labor force of several hundred thousand, with few employment opportunities and living in precarious circumstances.[50]

Miami-Dade's farm workers live scattered across low-income neighborhoods in the southern parts of the county, on company premises, or in government-run labor camps. In the 1960s the U.S. Department of Agriculture initiated the provision of housing

Figure 27. Migrant workers' housing in south Miami-Dade, 2010. Photo by author.

for farm workers in collaboration with local governments. The first camp, adjacent to Homestead Air Force Base, was disbanded in 1972 because of a typhoid epidemic.[51] It was replaced by Everglades Labor Camp, four miles west of Florida City. That camp started out with four hundred cheap trailers and by 1992, just before it was destroyed by Hurricane Andrew, it housed about four thousand people. In the wake of that disaster, persistent rumors held that the total body count in South Florida was much higher than the official eighteen, and that authorities had quickly and secretly removed many corpses from the camp. The rumors were never confirmed but it remains unclear how many former residents ever returned.

Presently, the Miami-Dade Health Department oversees camps, providing housing to thirty-four thousand eligible workers and their families (those with family incomes below $15,000 per year).[52] Both camps, the South Dade Labor Camp and the Redlands Labor Camp, are technically run by the Homestead Housing Authority and overseen by the U.S. Department of Agriculture. The authority has been criticized in recent years for allowing the homes to deteriorate, for poor maintenance, and for an unwillingness to undertake badly needed renovations.[53]

Neighborhoods with high concentrations of *mobiles* are virtually all along the waterfront and occupy prime real estate. Notable clusters of mobiles in Miami-Dade County include Key Biscayne, Brickell, the Miami downtown waterfront, south Miami Beach, Golden Beach, and Sunny Isles. In Broward, mobiles virtually monopolize the entire coastal strip from Hallandale in the south up to Fort Lauderdale, plus some pockets further north, including Lauderdale-by-the-Sea, Ocean Vue, and Palm Aire.

Mobiles are largely drawn to Miami by the amenities—if they had to live farther inland, say next door to Hialeah or Liberty City, they probably would not be here at all. The location of many mobiles, along the coastal edges and away from the grittier scenes of common urban life, mirrors their detachment from the city. Most arrived only recently, many are part-time residents, and the majority will not stay very long.

Broward's mobile clusters have large shares of *domestic* migrants (including notable numbers of African Americans) and most are U.S. citizens. The clusters also differ from Miami-Dade's in having a large majority of homeowners, fewer renters, fewer tourists, and a much larger share of older people. Only one in five inhabitants is twenty to forty years of age and more than three in five are over fifty. Resort towns like Hallandale, Dania Beach, and even Fort Lauderdale have a much more "American" feel. It seems fair to say that this is what attracts many who live there (especially those who moved from Miami-Dade).

In Miami-Dade, the most mobile neighborhoods have far fewer African Americans, many more Hispanics, and many more *foreign*-born. Economically, mobiles are doing considerably better than either locals or exiles (their average income levels are two-and-a-half times higher), but this, too, varies from place to place. Miami-

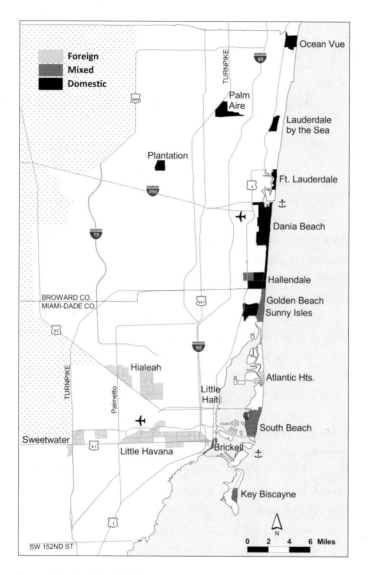

Figure 28. Residential neighborhoods in Greater Miami with high concentrations of non-locals of foreign, mixed, and domestic origins. Based on data from the 2000 U.S. Census (see Appendix 2).

Dade's mobile clusters are generally more affluent than Broward's and provide a setting where upper-income mobiles of all ethnicities, domestic and foreign, easily mix.

The most famous of these mobile areas is no doubt South Beach. It has a mix of domestic and foreign residents attracted to the beaches, nightlife, alternative lifestyles, culture, and entertainment. The area is also engulfed by an estimated ten million tourists and convention visitors per year. This is perhaps the most transient of all places in South Florida, reflected in the high proportion of rental homes (three out of four), especially in and near the deco district. More than two-thirds of the people in this area arrived within the last five years (that is, they were not living at their current addresses). Once a seasonal haven for retired northerners, South Beach has now flipped: about 50 percent of the people are between twenty and forty years old; less than 14 percent are over fifty. Nightclubs and other youth-oriented entertainment dominate the landscape. Medical care for the elderly, once one of the biggest local economic sectors, is now dwindling. Mount Sinai, the highly regarded hospital in the northwest corner of South Beach, has even run into major financial problems.[54]

The deco district went through a phase of revitalization in the late 1980s and early 1990s. It was a gentrification zone of sorts, attracting artists, a burgeoning gay population, modeling agencies, and growing numbers of tourists from the United States, Europe, and Latin America. In 1992, Gianni Versace bought a mansion on Ocean Drive, what some considered the ultimate sign that Miami Beach's comeback was complete (he was murdered, execution style, on his doorstep in 1997—suggesting that some things in Miami never changed). New hotels were built and existing ones were renovated. The Delano had a makeover in 1995 and became the new benchmark for "cool." The opening of the Loews in 1998 marked the first addition of a large major hotel in three decades.

Since 2004, Miami Beach has hosted the annual Art Basel, the

Figure 29. Ocean Drive, South Miami Beach, 2010. Photo by Soraya Nijman.

most important contemporary art fair in North America. Lincoln Road regained its luster in the 1990s and real estate prices in the area escalated upward. South Beach is now one of the largest surviving art deco districts in the world and certainly one of the most famous. It owes its survival to the slow economy of the 1960s and 1970s, which inhibited investment flows for urban re-development, and, subsequently, to the auspicious timing of a preservation movement in the mid-1970s. The area was listed as a historic landmark in the U.S. National Register in 1979.

Another striking South Beach trend is the rapid decline of the once-strong Jewish community. The city of Miami Beach witnessed a 42 percent decline of its Jewish population between 1994 and 2000, with most Jews heading to Broward, Palm Beach, or even farther north.[55] The Jewish community dominated the area for nearly half a century, in business and in politics. But by 2007 Miami Beach had elected its first Cuban mayor, and the number of Hispanic voters had well surpassed Jewish voters.[56] In historical perspective, the Jewish presence in Miami Beach was short-lived because, as we saw earlier, Jews could not establish a presence there until the 1920s owing to discrimination. It is illustrative of

South Florida's deeply transient character (and its collective lack of historical memory) that the Jews of Miami Beach were often considered one the city's most rooted communities. It was deceptive all along. Nearly two decades ago, a local Jewish demographer wrote that "to most South Florida Jews, home is elsewhere. Even people who have lived in South Florida for ten or more years will refer to their place . . . in the Northeast or Midwest as 'home.' Many Jews have not developed an overall feeling of community or a feeling that South Florida is their home. This reflects itself in a lack of support for local institutions, both Jewish and general, in comparison with levels of support shown in many northeastern Jewish communities."[57]

The presence of mobiles in the city's neighborhoods can also be seen in homestead exemptions on real estate taxes. The homestead exemption (currently $50,000) requires that a property owner live in his or her primary residence. Citizenship is not necessary but official residency in the United States is. Non-exemption usually means that owners are only part-time residents, with a primary residence elsewhere. In 2007, more than a third of all homes in Miami-Dade County were *not* primary residences. For single family homes the number was 24 percent and for condominiums it was a whopping 57 percent.[58] The figures for Broward County were somewhat lower: 32 percent of all homes were not primary residences; the numbers for single family homes and condos were, respectively, 20 percent and 52 percent.[59] But the numbers vary greatly from one neighborhood to another and non-exemptions are the highest along the waterfront.

The high-rise area east of Brickell Avenue, east Key Biscayne, and Miami's downtown waterfront area are all comparable neighborhoods in being dominated by high-rise condominiums. Condo living is ideal for part-time residents because it is easy simply to lock the door and leave. Most buildings have security and movement in and out of the premises is closely guarded. These areas

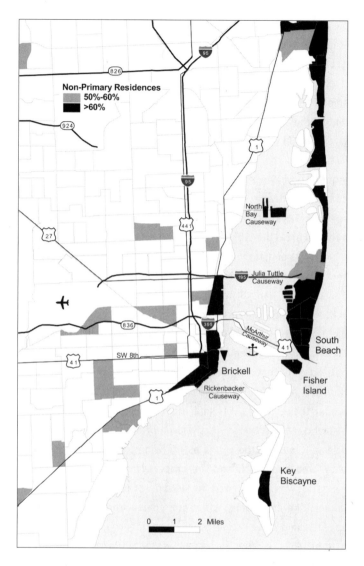

Figure 30. Neighborhoods with a high proportion of non-primary residences, 2007. Source: Miami-Dade County Office of the Property Appraiser.

have a mix of foreign and domestic transients with above average incomes. Visiting these buildings, one is struck by the emptiness—even if it is entirely sold and officially occupied (which is rare, in the present real estate downturn). It is an emptiness that sometimes lays bare the ostentatious designs of the entry and lobby areas. The proportion of condos actually occupied at any given time is relatively low, especially during the hot and humid summer months. Few people are around on the streets, in the lobbies, or in the elevators. Life takes place within the privacy of homes and people go about their own business. Public spaces are generally confined to the premises of each complex: the pool, a fitness area, the lobby.

Fisher Island, on the other side of Government Cut across from south Miami Beach, also has a very low share of primary residences: less than 38 percent. This is America's richest enclave, with an average per capita income of $236,000—more than double that of the Upper East Side of Manhattan. The real figures are higher, partly because of the difficulty gathering income data on part-time residents.[60] Home prices start at five million dollars and the fees are more than most Miamians could afford in rent. Among the residents, it is said, are Jeb Bush, the former governor of Florida, Boris Becker, and Oprah Winfrey. Fisher Island was originally built in the 1920s as the winter estate of the Vanderbilts, who had purchased the property from Carl Fisher. In the 1980s it was redesigned to accommodate about 750 luxury homes. The community has a golf course (the annual dues are $20,000 and come with a "designer golf cart"), a polo field, private beaches, a range of restaurants, a top-rated tennis center, and a deep-sea marina. The island is only accessible by water. If it is quiet that some residents seek, they are in the right place, because other inhabitants are rarely around.

Fisher Island is a long way from Little Havana, Overtown, or the migrant labor camps. The most striking thing about Miami's over-

Figure 31. Secluded Fisher Island, with downtown Miami in the background, 1999. © Miami Herald Media Company, 1999.

all transient character is that it plays out so differently for each of the city's main population groups. Here is a place where the longest established groups are also by far the most deprived; where the most iconic and symbolic areas refer to places elsewhere; and where the most coveted residential areas are monopolized by those who are least attached to the city. Miami is home to only a few and either a refuge or a playground to most others.

CHAPTER 8

Elusive Subtropical Urbanism

Imagine an American city in the subtropics, a place with abundant
nature, exotic lush vegetation, and a long shoreline on the glitter-
ing blue waters of the Caribbean Sea. It is a city on the nation's
edge, away from the gritty urban north, south of the South, and
with a brew of American and foreign influences. And imagine you
get to design it.

It is not hard to see that Miami was irresistible to the creative
spirit of planners and designers like George Merrick and others
after him. Back in the 1920s, with much of South Florida yet un-
touched, he indulged in the extraordinary opportunity to build a
subtropical town from scratch. Large parts of Coral Gables, his
legacy, have gracefully withstood nearly a century of the brutal
logic of urban redevelopment.

But the opportunities in the early 1900s were as exceptional
as George Merrick himself. In the years that followed, urban
South Florida grew fast and followed the path of least resistance.
Rapid in-migration since the 1940s and inescapable suburbanization shifted attention from designs that might have seen to basic
needs for the everyday functioning of a growing urban population.
Spurred on by the GI bill, the automobile industry, voracious developers, a federal preoccupation with highways, and the introduction of affordable air conditioning, Miami became much like

other cities in the United States: de-centered, monotonous, amorphous, and sprawling.

Urban design and planning in present-day Miami face several specific challenges. First, sustained rapid population growth and urban expansion pose questions of scale, regional differences, and integration. Second, if Miami's natural environment offers exceptional beauty and opportunities for urban design, it also sets precarious ecological limits. Third, the design of public spaces is complicated by a peculiar combination of weather and social fabric. Finally, Miami's transience tends to favor ad hoc urban projects at the expense of longer-term design and planning.

Between 1960 and 2010, the combined populations of Miami-Dade and Broward counties grew from 1.3 million people to about 4.1 million. To the north, Palm Beach County reached a population of 1.4 million, its urban area steadily creeping south to meet with Broward's sprawling suburbs. Accordingly, in 2004 the U.S. Bureau of the Census recognized a new consolidated metropolitan statistical area covering the tri-county region. With an estimated 5.5 million people, it is the nation's sixth largest metropolitan region and Florida's demographic center of gravity. Nearly another 2 million may be added by 2030.[1]

There is a specific pattern to intraregional migration: most newcomers in Broward hail from Miami-Dade while most migrants to Palm Beach County come from Broward.[2] South Florida is in some ways like a reverse-flow funnel, sucking in large numbers of foreign migrants from the south and spreading successive northbound waves of movers.

In addition to the three counties, the region now comprises more than one hundred municipalities with their own elected governments, police forces, public works, planning departments, and so on. There are also separate port authorities and school boards. To increase complexity, large planning projects often require the involvement of the state and/or federal government. Rapid massive growth combined with this kind of political fragmentation is problematic, as the growing traffic congestion shows, especially on the main regional north-south arteries (I-95 and U.S. 1). According to a recent study, the region is the thirteenth most congested in the United States. In the long run, it will need a regionally coordinated infrastructure, including expanded public transit (rail, bus), and long-term interdependent planning of air and seaports.

Large-scale planning is complicated by the region's large economic and cultural disparities. International connections and global linkages have always been highly concentrated in Miami's historic core. Here we find the main air and sea (cruise) ports, high concentrations of foreign residents, large numbers of transnational and foreign companies, skyrocketing foreign investments in real estate, and most diplomatic representations. It is where global flows of people, money, culture, commodities, corporate decision making, and ideas touch down and take off.

On the ground, one can easily identify the areas that are expressly linked to the global economy. For example, the Brickell banking district just south of downtown, with its high-rise trophy buildings, shows all the signs of a posturing international finance center. Another important international finance district is in downtown Coral Gables, mostly within a few blocks of Miracle Mile. The so-called fashion district to the north of downtown Miami offers a very different type of landscape. This was for some years the third largest manufacturing center for apparel (sweatshops) in the United States, after Los Angeles and New York, and it is closely tied to trade with the Caribbean.[3] Then there is Airport West, a large swath of urban area adjacent to Miami International Airport and along two major highways. It is filled with large numbers of storage and trucking facilities, and includes the Miami Free Trade Zone (FTZ).

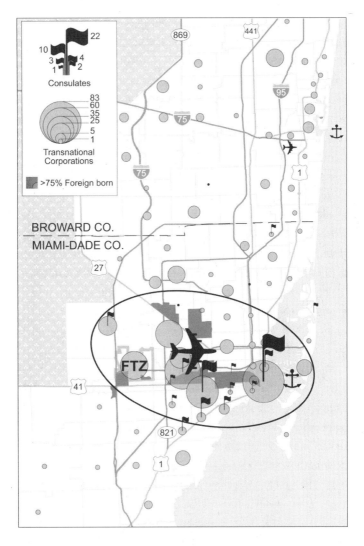

Figure 32. Global connections in Greater Miami. Sources: 2000 U.S. Census; data provided by WorldCity Business, Inc., 2002; Yellow Pages Miami-Dade County, 2009; Yellow Pages Broward County, 2009.

Miami is still the economic core of the region, as commuter patterns show. Every working day sees a net movement of 65,000 commuters from Broward to Miami-Dade.[4] But Miami's dominance is challenged. It is still by far the region's most globally connected city but other economic functions have decentralized in high tempo. A study from 2003 designated Miami the most de-centered office city in the nation, the ultimate "edgeless city."[5] Most of the regional competition comes from Fort Lauderdale.

Broward's main city is an important node with a rapidly growing airport, seaport, the second largest cruise port in the world, and a sizable cluster of international businesses. In 2002, Metro-Dade accused the Broward Commission of "corporate raiding," as it lured two major companies (Delta Air Lines and Carnival Cruises) across the county line. The event caused an uproar in South Florida politics and eventually resulted in a three-county "pact," in which the counties agreed "not to compete" for new or existing corporate investments.

In 2007, the Federal Aviation Authority declared that air traffic at Fort Lauderdale International Airport (FLIA) had grown so fast that it faced a "critical" need for expansion.[6] Meanwhile, Miami International Airport (MIA) had grown only minimally. Similarly, the past decade saw rapid business growth at Port Everglades while the Port of Miami stagnated. In 2007, container cargo at Port Everglades surpassed that of Miami for the first time, and it was expected to top the number of cruise passengers by 2011.[7] These regional shifts are often attributed to the congestion in Miami and the better and faster access to Florida's highway system on the part of Port Everglades. Fort Lauderdale's rising status was marked in 2005 when it hosted the prestigious Summit of the Organization of American States, which was held in the United States for the first time since 1974.

In recent years Hispanics have started to drift from Miami-Dade into Broward. Their share of Broward's population increased from 17 percent in 2000 to 23 percent in 2007. Broward's non-Hispanic whites no longer hold the absolute majority. But Latinos are not nearly as dominant there as in Miami-Dade. The largest foreign-born groups in Broward are, respectively, Jamaicans, Haitians, Puerto Ricans, Cubans, and Colombians.[8] The share of African Americans (21 percent) is comparable to Miami-Dade's.

Still, cultural differences between the two counties are striking, as is the intransigence of mutual perceptions. Many Miamians rarely cross the county line—when they leave Miami-Dade County it is usually via the airport. Movement in the opposition direction is generally restricted to commuters. Dave Barry's caricature description is stretched for humor, but it captures the state of mind (of Miamians, anyway):

> Like many residents of Miami-Dade County, I know very little about Broward. To be honest, I hardly ever think about Broward, except when they mention it on the evening TV news. "In Broward County today, blah blah blah."
>
> TYPICAL MIAMI-DADE HEADLINE: "City Commission Meeting Ends in Knife Fight"; TYPICAL BROWARD HEADLINE: "County to Get 147,000th Mini-Mart."
>
> There probably will never be a TV show called Broward County Vice. What kind of plots would it have? ("In tonight's episode, Crockett and Tubbs tangle with a gang of outlaws who have been ruthlessly violating their homeowners' association regulations regarding shrubbery height"). Of course, for a lot of Broward residents, dullness is part of the appeal. . . . Broward people want calm. They want order. They want Ohio, but with palm trees.[9]

From an ecological viewpoint, one must note that South Florida's recent population growth has been mainly to the west, on what were once the quiet eastern stretches of the Everglades. Gradually approaching the boundary of Everglades National Park, these were the only "empty" spaces left. Homestead, not long ago considered a remote old farming community to the southwest, was the fastest growing city in the entire state by 2007. But in recent years, as even the west seemed to run out of space, many developers shifted their gazes back downtown, and took to "infill" projects and high-rise construction along the coast.

As urbanization progressed, South Florida's precarious ecology set off alarm bells on repeated occasions, especially in Miami-Dade. This is the state's most populated county, hemmed in between two major national parks (Everglades and Biscayne), and with the highest frequency of hurricane strikes. In the past two decades, environmental debates have intensified, focusing on three big issues: the Urban Development Boundary (UDB), the Everglades Restoration Project, and hurricane insurance for home and business owners.

The Urban Development Boundary dates from 1983. It is a Miami-Dade macro-zoning instrument that separates urban/suburban development from rural/natural land uses. To the west, urban uses are prohibited; to the east they are encouraged. The result is clearly visible to anyone with a window seat on an airplane about to land at Miami International Airport: a sharp western border to a sea of monotonous red roofs signaling the residential suburbs.[10]

Suburban development does not actually abut the Everglades in most places. Also clearly visible from the air, between the suburbs and the Everglades in northern Miami-Dade (and on the west side of the UDB), are a large number of sizable rectangular bodies of water covering about eighty-nine square miles, the product of lime-stone mining. Commonly referred to as the Lake Belt Area, these quarries provide half of the limestone mining resources used in the state's construction industry every year, and about half of the area is owned by mining companies. It also contains one of the largest drinking water well fields in South Florida, serving about a million people. The industry portrays the lake belt as a protective "buffer" that keeps urban development from the Everglades, but it has been strongly criticized for emitting pollutants.[11]

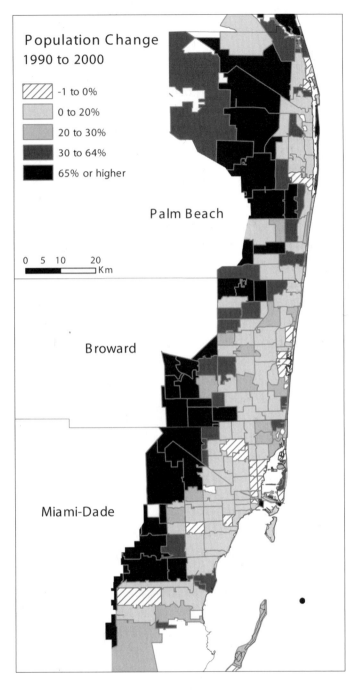

Figure 33. Western expansion of the Southeast Florida urban region, 1990–2000. Source: Based on data from the 2000 U.S. Census.

In the south, the UDB separates recent residential developments from farmlands. The boundary is more hotly disputed here
because, until recently, agricultural activities dominated both
sides. In the 1990s, landowners on the line's "urban" side made
a killing selling property to large developers, who in turn made
huge profits creating residential subdivisions. Presently, land on
the urban side of the UDB has a market value of about $800,000
per acre, ten times what it is on the other side. Predictably, perhaps, farmers on the "green" side have often lobbied for the UDB
to shift so they, too, can reap the profits.

The developers are, not surprisingly, the main forces for moving the line and every now and then consortia of developers,
builders, farmers, and financiers petition the county commission
for approval of their projects. The commission occasionally lives
up to its reputation of malleability when it concerns big business
interests: in 2009 it approved plans for the construction of a massive Lowe's home improvement store so far west (on the corner
of S.W. 163rd Avenue and Kendall Drive) that the street names did
not show up on Internet mapping search engines. That decision
was overturned by the Florida state government, sending a strong
signal to local government about its responsibilities of environmental stewardship.[12]

The second debate concerns the future of the Everglades.
Competition for water for agricultural and urban uses has put
enormous pressure on the wetland ecosystem, compounded by
ongoing pollution and the introduction of invasive species. A federal lawsuit was triggered in 1988 because the State of Florida
and the South Florida Water Management District had neglected
ongoing ecological degradation. As a result, the South Florida
Ecosystem Restoration Task Force was formed, with representation from federal and state agencies, Native American tribes, and
the counties of South Florida. The U.S. Congress demanded a plan
for environmental cleanup to be implemented by the Army Corps

of Engineers (which, skeptics would say, was responsible for "engineering" the decline of the Everglades in the first place).

In 2000, after years of negotiations, the Comprehensive Everglades Restoration Project (CERP) finally started: a $14 billion (originally), "five-year" plan to save eighteen thousand square miles of Everglades, from Lake Kissimmee in Central Florida all the way south to the coral reefs off the Keys. It is a frighteningly complex plan: sixty-eight discrete projects, including the rearrangement of levies, culverts, and canals, the digging of new wells, and the creation of new water conservation areas. The plan's goals are fourfold: to improve water storage capacity, to avoid flooding, to control salinity during dry periods, and to restore the ecology of the Everglades.[13]

It is, perhaps, the inherent impossibility of imposing such controls on a natural wetland habitat that is the most striking. For more than half a century, South Florida's settlers were preoccupied with flood control, and efforts intensified after every passing hurricane. Water levels in lakes and reservoirs had to be kept low enough to absorb the effects of coming storms. Over time, this was increasingly at odds with the urban population's growing demands for water, which requires substantial water storage.

This contradiction was expressed in an accelerating succession of water crises—either too much or too little. Typically, the dry winter and spring seasons have become times of "droughts" while the summer rains bring threats of flooding. The usual indicator is the water level in the main reservoir, Lake Okeechobee. The lake's levels have always naturally risen and fallen. But these swings have become more problematic with growing urbanization and the need for more control. One month watering restrictions are being imposed owing to a serious drought, while a few months later Lake Okeechobee has to be drained out of fear that the levies will break.[14] Whether this delicate negotiation with nature can be kept up indefinitely remains to be seen: in January

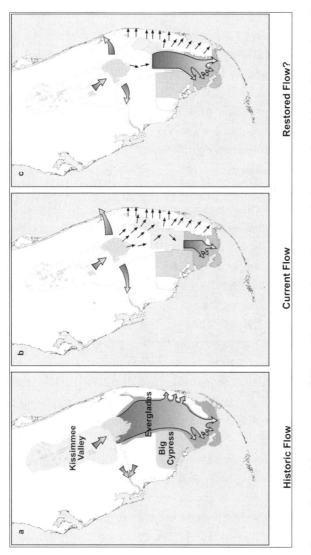

Historic Flow   **Current Flow**   **Restored Flow?**

Figure 34. The Everglades—past, current, and intended future flows. Source: *Comprehensive Everglades Restoration Plan*, U.S. Army Corps of Engineers, 2009. Map redrawn by Chris Hanson.

2006, the head of Miami-Dade's Water and Sewer Department resigned his position to protest the county's lack of planning for future water needs.[15]

The main way to secure water supply is with large water conservation areas. Lake Okeechobee used to fill that need, but by the 1980s it was no longer sufficient. Other surface reservoirs have been created, including a large one known by bureaucrats as Water Conservation Area 3A and that the Miccosukee call home. This is the area between the sugar fields to the north and Everglades National Park to the south, straddling Broward and Miami-Dade counties.

The Miccosukee have protested the "drowning" of their land north of the Tamiami Trail, pointing out that the water there is well above natural levels. Biologists, too, have noted the detrimental effect of the high water levels on various plant and animal species. But if water levels north of the trail are too high, the drying out of areas to the south, inside the park, is even more devastating. In 2009, Congress approved separate funding of $60 million for the "Everglades Skyway," the elevation of some parts of the Tamiami Trail to allow the "river of grass" to resume some its natural flow southward. This will raise the water level in Everglades National Park and lower the level in the Miccosukee reservation to the north. But the Miccosukee have emphatically opposed it, arguing it would take too long and jeopardize their existence.[16]

The Everglades restoration project has suffered almost continuous delays, partly because of litigation, and costs have escalated. By the summer of 2009 (nine years after the project began), none of the sixty-eight projects had been completed and the budget had soared to over $20 billion. Evolving budget predictions had become so arcane that a top federal engineer admitted that the budget will probably go much higher still, and that the final number was really anybody's guess.[17] It will probably take at least a decade longer than first thought—the overall project may well morph into some sort of indefinite Everglades management authority.[18]

If all of this were not enough, there are the hurricanes. Since 1888, South Florida has been hit by twenty-nine major hurricanes (that is, category 3 or higher, with wind speeds over 110 miles per hour). Hurricanes can be destructive and traumatic events with grave personal losses—they always have been. What has worsened the problem in recent decades is simply that there is so much more built environment prone to destruction. What this really means is that the problem of hurricanes has become a problem of property insurance.

These troubles began in earnest with Hurricane Andrew in 1992. The category 5 storm tore through central and southern Miami-Dade County, leaving nineteen people dead and about $25 billion in damages. More than half of all houses in the county had some damage, and 117,000 homes were destroyed. Forty thousand people left the county and did not come back, many settling in Broward.[19] Insurance claims bankrupted eleven insurance agencies and drained large amounts of money from many more. To provide insurance for many who were left without, the state was forced to create underwriting associations.

The season of 2005 exacerbated the situation with two major storms, Katrina and Wilma. Katrina first wreaked havoc in Florida, then proceeded to New Orleans, where the consequences reached catastrophic proportions. Nationwide, it left eighteen hundred people dead and estimated damages of $81 billion—the costliest natural disaster in U.S. history. More insurance companies went bankrupt. Residents and businesses in South Florida, especially, faced premium hikes for windstorm and flooding insurance of 100 percent and more. Many were scrambling to get any coverage at all.[20] Insurance premiums added to already high housing costs, and by the end of 2005 the media had begun to report on an

Figure 35. In the wake of Hurricane Andrew: Mr. Harold Keith beside his destroyed trailer park home in Florida City, August 1992. © Miami Herald Media Company, 1992.

"affordable housing crisis" facing the region's middle classes. To environmentalists, these storms just proved that if you insist on building cities in ecologically high-risk areas, nature will come back to haunt you.

The University of Miami, founded in 1925, was to feature a Mediterranean revival style. Situated in Coral Gables, it would blend

Figure 36. In the wake of Hurricane Andrew: The Country Walk area in south Miami-Dade County, August 1992. © Miami Herald Media Company, 1992.

in with Merrick's "city beautiful." The university first opened its doors to a small number of students in August 1926. Only a couple of structures were then in place—the rest would be added in coming years. But this was not to be. A month later, on September 17, a devastating hurricane swept through Coral Gables. The damages wiped out much of Merrick's fortunes and that of other financiers, and the campus designs were put in a drawer. The university's founders' hopes of resuming the plans in the following years were dashed by the ensuing economic depression. They are in the drawer still, among the special collections of the university library.

After World War II, as enrollments jumped with the GI bill and returning ex-soldiers to their sunny training grounds, the campus grew in a style that could not differ more from past visions. The university was the first in the nation to design a campus best described as "subtropical modernist." It not only vividly contrasted with the quasi-Mediterranean residential surroundings, but also differed completely from the predictable and strained

Figure 37. In the wake of Hurricane Andrew: Sister Octavia Ortega (of the order of the Missionary of Guadalupe) of Centro Tepayac, a chapel at the South Dade Migrant Labor Center, finds the cross of the razed chapel, August 1992. © Miami Herald Media Company, 1992.

emulation of "collegiate gothic" on so many American campuses. Miami was different.

The fact that modernist structures were cheaper to build than Merrick's designs no doubt played a part. But so did the general rise of modernist architecture (Bauhaus) since the 1930s, and the particular influence of architects Robert Law Reed and Marion Manley—they produced the master plan for the University of Miami campus and designed most of the buildings.[21] It was, in many ways, a splendid example of innovative design in harmony with nature. Typically, the buildings were long and narrow; classrooms had windows on opposite sides allowing air circulation and cooling. Open-air hallways on building exteriors (never on the interior) were alongside the classrooms, with minimalist steel balustrades on the upper levels. Buildings were connected by promenades with canopies offering shelter from sun and rain but otherwise open. Lush vegetation was planted to offer maximum shade. Public spaces, too, were airy, light, and optimized air circulation.

The university's new look drew attention and admiration from around the nation. In December 1948, *Life* published an article entitled "Modern College: Miami's New Buildings Set New Campus Style." *National Geographic*, too, celebrated the university's trendsetting initiative. A feature article in November 1950 spoke of "Miami's expanding horizons," praising the originality, simplicity, esthetics, and efficacy of the designs.[22]

But the following years witnessed the introduction of air conditioning—a blessing in physiological comfort but a notorious spoiler of architecture and urban design. From the late 1950s onward, new campus construction followed the dictates of efficient air conditioning: bigger buildings; fewer, deeper, and smaller windows (that cannot be opened); more concrete wall; less natural light; interior and artificially lit hallways; the virtual elimination of outdoor public spaces; and greater invisibility of people—except between classes when students walk to other buildings. These effects were compounded by the building codes of the 1960s in the wake of more hurricanes: still more concrete and even fewer windows.

These developments took shape across the region and were not confined, of course, to the University of Miami campus. In 1968, Norman Mailer described the new air-conditioned architecture of South Florida as "piles of white refrigerators six and eight and twelve stories high, twenty stories high, shaped like sugar cubes and ice cube trays on edge. . . ."[23] On the university campus, at least, remained an intriguing architectural mix. The expansive grounds are graced with such eye-pleasing vegetation that some of the newer buildings can scarcely be seen.

It is often said that urban public space serves as the city's "living room"—where different people come together and enjoy each other in an inviting environment. It seems that most Miamians reject this notion, instead valuing private spaces. The design of public spaces is challenging in all modern cities but especially so in South Florida, owing to the summer heat and humidity, combined with a collective addiction to air conditioning. Almost invariably, air conditioning demands a design that separates people from the natural environment and from each other. It closes off spaces where there could have been open exchange, stifling the creation and use of public spaces.[24]

For those who can afford it, daily life moves from air-conditioned homes, in air-conditioned cars, to air-conditioned offices or air-conditioned malls. There is something to say for that. Merely breathing in Miami in the summer, observed Normal Mailer with customary unfiltered gusto, is "not unlike being obliged to make love to a 300-pound woman who has decided to get on top."[25] For half of the year, when the heat prevails, people avoid outdoor public spaces altogether if possible—abetted by a local culture that celebrates well-dressed bodies and good looks (no sweat, please), and hair styles unfit for excess humidity. In the poor areas, bicycle riding is a common means of transport, while the affluent use their sporty two-wheelers only for weekend recreation (sweat okay). Similarly, the heat seems prohibitive for walking any distance—running for fitness is a different story. All this means that a lot of people are confined to their cars, their separation from the outside world often complete with the tinted windshields that preclude eye contact.

Miami's public transportation is used almost exclusively by the poor. At least this is so for buses (the metro rail, which runs north-south on a single line, requires a car to get to it). Get on a bus anytime, anywhere, and the odds are that *all* of the passengers are low-income Hispanic immigrants. For domestic maids—they constitute a major employment category—public transit is an absolute necessity and they seem to represent a large share of riders, along with many service workers in the tourism industry. With public transportation so clearly associated with class, those aspiring to a higher status avoid it purposely, sometimes blaming inadequate services (it is actually much better than most would know). That is quite a different picture from New York or Washington, D.C., where subway users come from all classes and backgrounds. This author, when using city buses, often finds himself under scrutiny from other passengers, presumably for his appearance as a European white middle-class male.

The second handicap in the design and functioning of Miami's public spaces, then, is extreme inequality and social polarization. Among the elites, in any case, there is a powerful urge to keep the poor and the "criminally inclined" at some distance. Miami has the second most polarized income structure of the nation's fifty biggest metro areas, second only to New Orleans.[26] The middle class here was always small and it has shrunk further in recent decades.[27] Its size has something to do with the unusual structure of the labor force. Miami is obviously an important immigration center, but it lacks economic sectors that attract highly skilled middle-class workers (as compared to, for example, San

Francisco or Vancouver or Boston). Instead, the bulk of the labor force is in tourism, consumer services, and construction, the kind of work that is typically low-skilled, low-paid, and with little opportunity for upward mobility.[28]

These inequities and the accompanying polarization, sometimes with strong ethnic or racial dimensions, are expressed in a highly segmented and divided urban space at multiple scales. Miami is said to have the highest incidence of gated communities in the nation, along with Los Angeles.[29] Most beachfront is privatized, too, with public access mainly limited to state or national parks. What is rather unusual about Miami's gated communities is the abundant use of waterways as a "natural" boundary: the renaissance of the "moat." This applies to some of the islands in the Intracoastal Waterway where access is easily controlled. For example, affluent Star Island, positioned between Miami and Miami Beach, is completely privatized and property owners installed a bridge with a checkpoint to keep out all but locals and invited guests. On Fisher Island, there is no bridge at all—the community operates a small ferry for cars with appropriate decals and people with valid identification.

At a larger scale, incorporation is the default mechanism to draw new boundaries, protect fiscal resources, and keep out the poor. Miami itself was ranked as the poorest city its size in the United States for several years, and Key Biscayne's 1991 secession did not help. Motivated by the desire to control its own abundant tax dollars, Key Biscayne formed a separate municipality, leaving Miami to fend for itself—the island already enjoyed physical separation from the mainland with the county-operated Rickenbacker toll bridge.

The third challenge to public spaces in Miami derives from the city's defining characteristic: transience. Public spaces are, in principle, for locals, much the same way that a living room is principally meant for those living in the home. Public space is owned by the public, the citizens whose taxes make it possible. But in Miami, especially along the coveted waterfront where so many transients live, it has proven difficult to establish well-functioning public spaces. It seems there are simply too few permanent residents. This is best illustrated by recent developments in downtown Miami.

The "Miami Vision for 2009" of the Downtown Development Authority aimed to turn downtown into the "business, social, and cultural center of the Americas, [capitalizing] on its unique position as a major world city in a subtropical waterfront environment."[30] Part of the idea was to "activate" the downtown waterfront, which, it should be noted, has *never* for any prolonged period of time functioned successfully as a public space. There is no doubt that better planning is needed—but a more intractable issue is *for whom* this public space is intended. As shown earlier, the majority of people here are part-time residents and highly transient. In the five waterfront census tracts from Rickenbacker Bridge in the south to Julia Tuttle Bridge up north, an astounding 70 percent of homeowners have a primary residence elsewhere.[31] Thus, the real population density is not nearly as high as the number of dwellings would suggest. It also means that many residents, when present, are only loosely connected to the urban environment and are less likely to treat it as *their* public space. It explains why the Miami riverfront and the walkways along Bayside remain desolate, especially at night.

The official suggestion that the waterfront should be a public space for *all* is rather beguiling. The nearest concentration of locals (in walking distance) is Overtown and its very proximity deters some suburbanites from coming downtown. Moreover, nearby locals would probably have different priorities, such as decent housing or jobs, if they had a say. Other Miamians, thus far, have not been attracted to the downtown waterfront. Development plans could have some effect, with improved access and designs more attuned to the environment: plenty of shade, free reign for sea breezes, and good views of the bay.[32] But it is much more difficult to address challenges arising from extreme transience and social polarization, challenges that have to do with people, not design. The built environment can be modified, at a cost, but social fabric cannot be engineered.

In the past there were other, more comprehensive, plans to turn Miami into the ideal subtropical city on the waterfront. Some were striking in terms of originality, vision, and audacity. The Interama of the early 1950s, the Magic City Plan of 1960, and the Doxiadis Plan of 1966–68 all sought to return downtown to the people, create a pedestrian-friendly environment, and make the waterfront an essential and integral part of the city, with a strong emphasis on public spaces.[33] Elements of these plans included interconnected parks and plazas, automobile-free zones, a spectacular boulevard (partially elevated) along the bay reminiscent of Havana's Malecón, and "tropical modernist" architecture that embraced the natural environment.

Interama was the most remarkable of these initiatives, its name shorthand for the Pan-American World Fair that was to open in Miami in 1968.[34] The city would be redesigned to provide the perfect backdrop to a Pan-American fair placing Miami at the center of the hemisphere. It would be a subtropical city symbolizing American-led progress—the cold war context and accompanying propaganda were hard to ignore. The planning involved a range of architects under the leadership of the eminent Louis Kahn and much of the funding was federal. Perhaps it was this very broad and political thrust that made it a mission impossible from the start. Interama produced genuine excitement but wasted lots of energy and talent over nearly two decades. Federal funds dried up and local leadership failed to generate momentum to rescue at least some parts of the plans. Some of the designs, on paper, were fantastical—none ever materialized.

One reason Miami never really benefited from long-term planning was the constant rapid turnover of local leadership, and more generally of its inhabitants. The architectural historian Jean-Francois Lejeune speaks of a "city without a memory." In the early postwar years, Miami was "the consenting victim of resort-city development patterns combined with a boom-and-bust psychology that prevented any long-term vision of productive city development and infrastructure."[35] This propensity is perhaps best illustrated in the location of Miami's city hall—which was never built as a city hall in the first place (it is a reconstructed hangar)—far away from the center along the bay in Coconut Grove. It almost underscored the city's identity at large: de-centered, detached, and with a sense of impermanence.

Much of this "resort-city" logic dissipated in the 1960s as the city's political and civic apparatus got preoccupied with the mass arrival of Cubans. That hardly increased the odds of visionary planning: with hundreds of thousands of refugees pouring in, who cared about urban design? If the years from World War II until the mid-1960s were a time of designers' fantasia, Miami turned to crisis mode in the next two decades as we have seen. At least in the early postwar years there were *plans,* even if they amounted to nothing in reality. During the 1970s and 1980s, suburbanization was all there was, gobbling up the Everglades with insatiable voracity, one subdivision after the other, not the least disturbed by planners, politicians, or activists.

Another explanation for the lack of planning and sustained visionary design lies in the real estate sector's recurrent volatility. Demand for middle-class and upscale housing, especially condominiums, is in no small measure fed from abroad. Since this demand originates in a range of different national markets in Latin America and beyond, its aggregate is highly unpredictable, depending as it does on a variety of trends and events in these nations' political economies.

Foreign demand repeatedly saved Miami real estate from a

slump, most notably in the mid-1970s, a couple of years after the oil crisis, and again in the early 1980s when the national economy was in the doldrums and real estate values were down.[36] Foreign interest continued to increase over the years (if erratically) and surpassed $1 billion in 1997.[37] By the turn of the century, real estate brokers from Bogotá, Caracas, Mexico City, Buenos Aires, and other Latin American cities were routinely traveling to Miami to seek out prospects for clients. Foreign interest in South Florida real estate was bolstered even more through federal programs that promise residency status for large investors. [38]

But once local developers and builders started counting on endless demand from abroad, the market drifted into dangerous territory, in part because foreign demand (for second homes, usually) is particularly susceptible to speculation. It is believed that foreign investors had played an important part in the region's spiraling real estate prices since the mid-1990s. By 2005, Wall Street analysts had sounded the alarm about South Florida's incredible real estate boom: up to 85 percent of all investments in downtown condominiums were estimated to come from speculators and investors.[39]

When the bubble first showed signs of deflation in 2006, then burst in 2007, Miami was at the epicenter of a nationwide meltdown. By the summer of 2009, real estate values had dropped nearly 50 percent, wiping out five years of unreal growth. Unsold inventories went sky high, especially in the downtown condominium market. In high rises built since 2003, occupancy rates averaged as low as 62 percent according to developers, and that was probably a deflated estimate. Many occupants were renters, not buyers.[40] In the early summer of 2009, 71 percent of South Florida homes purchased in the previous five years were "upside down," meaning that they had become worth less than their mortgages. An estimated one in four home loans was delinquent and Miami was among the hardest-hit cities in the nation in foreclosures.

The Miami-Dade School District reported that nearly twenty-five hundred registered students had become officially homeless—enough to fill an entire school.[41]

Market volatility impedes urban planning: one day local government is blinded with apparent prospects of endless growth, while the next day it faces a serious economic downturn. Volatility also runs interference with planning because it throws off the property tax base. In the five years leading up to the housing implosion of 2007, property taxes in Miami-Dade County increased by 32 percent, leaving local governments with plenty of funds, big dreams, and eroded fiscal discipline. Then, in 2008–9 alone, South Florida municipalities faced up to 25 percent losses in property tax revenues. Aggregate losses for Miami-Dade County in that year were nearly $24 billion.[42]

Miami intrigued Le Corbusier, one of the twentieth century's greatest designers/architects, but he considered it a far throw from the "true urban." In the late summer of 1950 he wrote in one of his sketchbooks, "Miami with the luxuries of villas, green spaces, trees budding, flowers blooming, avenues and automobiles. Enough to make one utterly sick from so much artifice."[43] Much has changed since then and Miami has certainly become a lot wider and taller. Whether it would now be considered a "real" city by the likes of Le Corbusier remains doubtful. Many parts of the metropolitan area still fit his description from six decades ago.

The downtown area did change beyond recognition, with a mature skyline and greater density. One of the best ways to see downtown Miami is to drive to Dodge Island, into the Port of Miami. Most Miamians are not likely ever to have been there. But millions of tourists have, transferring from Miami International Airport to the cruise ship terminals. The north side of Dodge Island houses eight huge terminals. From there, the view of downtown is spectacular during daytime and even more so at night.

Figure 38. Brickell and downtown Miami, seen from Biscayne Bay, 2010. Photo by author.

Figure 39. Old and new Miami, seen from the cruise port, 2010. Photo by Dewi Nijman.

The city has been home to several esteemed architecture firms, including Arquitectonica, Duany Plater-Zyberk, and Spillis Candela (the latter became part of AECOM Design in 2009). Various impressive designs were added to the downtown landscape: the extraordinary Bacardi building in 1963, the charismatic Atlantis condominiums in 1982, a series of imposing vertical structures

CHAPTER 8

including the First Union Financial Center in 1986 and I. M. Pei's Centrust building in 1987, the seventy-story Four Seasons in 2003, and more recently Cesar Pelli's long-awaited and striking twin-structured performing arts center. Most are what Richard Sennett calls "spectator architecture," the kind that is separate from the viewer, admired from a distance, and not part of the public realm.[44] Moreover, they are not part of any larger design but stand alone, dispersed and disconnected from the surrounding landscape. Miami, especially the downtown area, has become a city of projects rather than of comprehensive planning. The performing arts center was a project, as was the American Airlines Arena, as is the newly planned baseball stadium, Museum Park (in what is currently the underused Bicentennial Park on the bay, north of the arena), and the port tunnel.

The most recent noteworthy effort for an overarching plan, Miami21, was approved by the city commission in 2009. It overhauls the Miami's zoning regulations and building codes. Miami21 does not promote any particular design for the downtown area but it sets important parameters based on the principles of new urbanism. In the years to come, it should change the face of downtown with more mixed use and more pedestrian-friendly designs.[45]

By now, the downtown area is built up ever more densely and the exceptional opportunities of the past—designs from scratch on virgin lands—are history. The issue is not so much whether Miami is worse off in terms of planning than most other Sun Belt cities—it probably isn't. If not a real *city* in some regards, Miami is without doubt an exceptionally intriguing *place* with fragments of architectural beauty, a bewildering eclectic landscape, and powerful appeal—with masses of visitors to prove it. The point is that, given the natural endowments, it could have been grand.

CHAPTER 9

The First Hemispheric City

To outside observers, visitors, and even residents, Miami's unique qualities are readily apparent: the balmy weather, the scenery somewhere between ostentatious and seductive, edgy behaviors, and the occasional surreal spectacle are all hard to ignore. Miami, to be sure, can be uniquely entertaining. The city's penchant for shameless narcissism was expressed perfectly, some months ago, in the recruitment of fake paparazzi by some shrewd developers aiming to dazzle the indulging and unsuspecting crowds at sales parties of trendy upscale condos in downtown Miami.[1] As Carl Hiaasen once remarked, "Just because a place is shallow, corrupt, and infested with phonies doesn't mean it's dull."[2]

But at a deeper level, one of Miami's most intriguing qualities is, actually, that it is in some respects emblematic of America's urban future. Cities will become more global, increasingly multicultural, and more transient; urban cultures will be more fragmented and less localized; and urban elites will be increasingly footloose. Urban economies will grow more reliant on producer services, finance, and trade while manufacturing will continue to dwindle. Air travel and technology will connect cities to the wider world, foreign connections will be more prevalent, and transnationalism will be ever more common.[3]

In the past century, two other cities have marked new urban eras in the United States: Chicago in the 1930s and Los Angeles in the 1980s. Both were the subject of extensive study, large volumes of literature, and even "schools of thought." Some of this, it should be noted, reflected the presence of several major universities with an array of scholars (the University of Chicago, and UCLA and USC, respectively) who "underwrote" their cities' prominence.

Chicago, in its heyday, was considered a trailblazer of early twentieth-century urbanization. It was a time when cities and industrialization moved in tandem. The city was all about manufacturing, expressed both in the social fabric and in a fast growing middle-class working population. Urbanization at this scale and in this manner was a new phenomenon and Chicago became a laboratory of social change, urban living, human adaptation, and urban ecology. The Chicago school produced several classics of urban literature and was central to the field of urban studies for more than half a century.[4]

Similarly, in the 1980s, Los Angeles emerged as another model city or "prototopos,"[5] and it is sometimes identified as the ultimate postmodern city. The LA school gathered momentum in the 1990s and it, too, produced a large and influential literature.[6] Part of the Los Angeles phenomenon, one might say, was the speed of urban change in the newly arrived global information era.

But it was precisely that speed of change that facilitated the unprecedented rise of Miami, not Los Angeles, as the first hemispheric city. Miami has became the most centrally connected place in the Americas, routing flows of people, capital, goods, and all things imaginable back and forth between myriad origins and destinations north and south. In South and Central America and the Caribbean, there is little doubt of Miami as *the* hemispheric city, an urban forerunner, the first of a kind—a city located in the United States but belonging to the Americas at large. To the north, Miami's new role is not so readily acknowledged, in part because its emergence was so recent and in part because it has always seemed such an eccentric place, with doubtful relevance to the rest of the nation.

Cities can be characterized according to the historical context in which they emerged and first achieved prominence. In this sense, New York is a typical pre-industrial city, Chicago the emblematic early industrial city, Los Angeles a characteristic late industrial city, and Miami a typical post-industrial city. The accompanying transport technologies that facilitated the rise of these cities were, respectively, ships, trains, automobiles, and airplanes. Transport technologies are hugely important in the "natural" selection of sites that lead to the emergence of cities. In pre-industrial times, major cities were usually located at ports or at river junctions, while industrial cities often emerged near natural resources or at important railway junctions.

Miami's significance is perhaps best understood in comparison to Los Angeles because that exposes just how novel and how *different* Miami is. Los Angeles emerged as a major city during the first quarter of the twentieth century, in the late industrial stages of U.S. urban development. The city's population grew from one hundred thousand in 1900 to one million in 1920. By then, Miami counted only five thousand inhabitants, and the municipal city of Miami had been incorporated for only four years. When the Angelinos passed the one-million mark in 1920, Miami's (Dade County) population had reached only forty-two thousand. Miami was not connected to the north by rail until 1896, considerably later than most cities on the West Coast of the United States.

It is hard to think of a city that, according to traditional locational criteria for urban development, was so poorly positioned as Miami—that is, until the advent of mass air transport connecting Miami to the rest of the nation and, more importantly, to the Caribbean and Latin America. (The mass availability of air conditioning, around the same time, played a major part as well.) Miami's major growth period was in the third quarter of the twentieth century, some fifty years behind Los Angeles.

Compared to Los Angeles, Miami is to this day less connected to the U.S. national economy and urban system, and it has a more pronounced international orientation. Los Angeles's economic structure resulted from passing through various economic stages, from industrialization through de-industrialization and the rise of high-tech and information-based industries. Miami's economy, in contrast, has a more recent history and shows less layering of successive economic periods. Indeed, where Los Angeles has both old manufacturing and new high-tech industry, and shows characteristics of the Rust Belt, Miami lacks much of any of that. Its main economic sectors are trade, tourism, construction, finance, and producer services. The city's profile is decidedly post-industrial, not constrained by the remnants of earlier times.[7]

The second part of the argument is more cultural. Los Angeles is sometimes asserted to be the "first American city," that is to say the first purely U.S. city. Los Angeles is the urban culmination of a broad historical shift of the cultural center of gravity from the eastern United States to the West, a process of gradual de-Europeanization and Americanization. California at large is then considered as the terra firma of U.S. culture, and Los Angeles, in turn, as the region's symbolic capital. The urbanist Richard Weinstein observes that Los Angeles is the "first American city to separate itself from European models and to reveal the impulse to privatization embedded in the origins of the American revolution."[8] Los Angeles and more generally California (in contrast to the northeastern United States) more purely reflect an American culture in which individualization, freedom, mobility, and materialism prevail.

Miami finds itself one step further in this evolutionary scheme —as the first hemispheric city. Los Angeles was the logical end product of the U.S. cultural formation moving west. Miami, located southeast of the Deep South, is of a completely different making, only understandable in a context of the international region, the hemisphere, and globalization. That does not mean that Miami is not an "American" (U.S.) place—in some ways it is ultra-American. Rather, Miami's emergence is closely related to the globalization of the American culture and economy. Miami is in essence a product of the United States, but it is not only of the United States anymore; it has gone beyond.

In more conventional U.S. cities, immigrant assimilation follows the traditional generational trajectory in which it takes immigrants considerable time and effort to climb the socioeconomic ladder. Many recent immigrants, such as the large majority of Hispanics in Los Angeles, find themselves toiling among the underclasses. Miami, in contrast, is dominated by a foreign and highly transient upper class. "Compound Americanism" is a typical feature of the traditional history of U.S. immigration and assimilation: urban populations consisted of Irish Americans, African Americans, Arab Americans, Chinese Americans, and so forth. As a rule, however, assimilation would occur, and so far as ethnic designations continued to be used they were little more than folkloric window dressing. In the end, all became Americans. In this hemispheric city, however, even compound (or hyphenated) Americanism seems a relic: Cuban Americans (most are naturalized) are known as Cubans, Nicaraguan Americans are referred to as Nicaraguans, and so forth. There is not much in terms of a shared American identity in this city; instead there is a common realization that all are different.

The fact that Miami breaks with so many conventions is what gives the city an outspoken postmodern character. Postmodern urban landscapes are generally defined as highly eclectic and disjointed, and showcasing myriad representations in the built environment. In Miami, all this variety and disorder is crammed into a metropolitan area roughly one-fifth the size of Los Angeles. This difference in scale makes the experience of Miami's urban landscapes more *intense*: the transitions in Miami's landscape are faster, more frequent, and more punctuated.

It is sometimes said that Miami's unusual and eccentric urban culture reflects its young age, that Miami is still "growing up." Mickey Wolfson, the founder of the Wolfsonian Museum, once remarked that Miami is a city that "has not yet found its soul."[9] The suggestion is that it is a matter of time for Miami to become more established, to develop a more mature urban persona.

But Miami's urban condition is *not* a matter of immaturity or at least not entirely. Transience is Miami's *genius loci* and it is here to stay. What began with seasonal flows from the northern United States in the first half of the twentieth century has continued with ever more intense hemispheric (and global) population movements in more recent times. Present global conditions of migration and transnationalism preclude a stabilizing and permanent South Florida. In the process, Miami has become something of an urban *perpetuum mobile*, set in eternal motion because it was in the "right" place, at the "right" time.

High spatial mobility is, of course, very characteristic of the United States. According to the U.S. Bureau of the Census, about 12 percent of the total U.S. population changed addresses from 2007 to 2008. Between 1995 and 2000, some 73 million Americans moved from one state to another. The state of Florida has a mobility that is above the national average and Miami, in turn, is extreme within Florida. This is reflected in domestic and foreign in-migration, in domestic out-migration, and in mobility rates among counties in southeastern Florida (mainly from Miami-Dade to Broward and from Broward to Palm Beach). Spatial mobility, it /

seems, is an integral part of the South Florida mind-set: a poll in 2007 revealed that 37 percent of Floridians and 50 percent of Miamians considered moving.[10]

Transience continues to define Miami's character and foreign in-migration remains very high, but the pattern of domestic population movements did change in some ways. First, the early 1970s saw a major reversal from domestic net in-migration to domestic net out-migration. It signified Miami's profound reorientation from a North American beach resort to a centrally positioned hemispheric metropolis—a hemispheric metropolis, that is, with an emphatic Latino flavor that is attractive to some northerners but not to all. Second, more recent years witnessed a reversal of long established seasonal migration flows: in the old days, snow birds from the north came down to Miami during the winter to enjoy the balmy weather. Nowadays, they are more likely to land near Fort Lauderdale or even further north in Palm Beach County. At the same time, upper-income Miamians have started to leave in the summer for cooler resorts to the north, from North Carolina northward along the eastern seaboard.

Seen this way, the so-called Cuba factor is only one part of a much bigger picture. Miami is more than a haven for Cuban exiles, more than Havana's alter ego. For decades, there was a strong conviction on Miami's streets that the wished for demise of Fidel Castro would have massive repercussions in South Florida. At first, it was thought that, when that time came, many Cubans would return to the island, and Miami would somehow be restored to what it was in old times. As time went on, the realization sunk in that many Cubans had been in Miami too long, and that the second and third generations, at least, are here to stay no matter what happens in Cuba.

The prospect of radical change in Havana dissipated in the past decade or so. The Cuban economy has opened up, foreign investors (except from the United States) have flocked in, and international tourism has become a major sector and source of revenues. This is not to say that the economy or ordinary Cubans are doing well—they aren't. Nor is it to suggest that political oppression has ended. The point is rather that Cuban communism is not what it used to be. Through selective and gradual change, the regime has more or less immunized itself against an overthrow. Raúl Castro has taken the reigns, bringing an end to the personification and vilification of Cuba's dictatorship through Fidel. That personification used to play a key role in the political mobilization of Cuban exiles. Not so long ago one popular bumper sticker in South Florida read "No Castro, No Problem"—and that was meant for Fidel, not Raúl.

At any rate, by now even the most tumultuous regime change in Cuba is not likely to fundamentally alter Miami's course. It might have done so three or four decades ago, but not anymore. The main changes will occur in Cuba, not in Miami. If Cuba were to become a free society "overnight," it is estimated that about 20 percent of Miami's Cubans would return to live in Cuba, but they would almost certainly maintain some form of residency in Miami.[11] Many "returnees" would be from the entrepreneurial classes and a good number would seek to reclaim property or (re)start businesses. At the same time, it is expected that this outflow would be offset by the migration of Cubans from the island to Miami for family reunification.[12] In all, the picture might resemble what happened in East and West Germany after reunification. Many East Germans came to the West as they were finally freed from hardship and dictatorship, while West Germans (usually with East German roots) went the other way, looking for entrepreneurial opportunities and reclaiming property. It was not altogether a happy reunion and the same might be in store for Cuba.

For Miami, changes in Cuba that allow more openness and more interaction will only intensify the city's hemispheric role. Add

Havana to Miami's list of key economic intercity relationships that already span the globe, from New York to Madrid to São Paulo. The liberation of Cuba will provide new energies for what will be a reinvented transnational Cuban community for whom *both* Miami and Cuba will be considered a homeland. It could be the purest form of transnationalism yet as geographic origin and destination may become indistinguishable. Havana could, in theory, give Miami a run for its money by draining some of its resources and it could turn out to be a serious competitor for international business. But in the long run, Miami will almost certainly prevail, if only for its single biggest and proven asset vis-à-vis other Caribbean or Latin American cities: it is located inside the United States.

Here at the end of the twenty-first century's first decade, it is hard not to be blinded by the economic crisis and accompanying gloom and doom that hit South Florida particularly hard. First, an affordable housing crisis developed around 2005 as a result of spiraling home values combined with escalating home insurance rates in the wake of two major hurricanes (Wilma and Katrina). That crisis deterred people from moving to South Florida and simultaneously pushed out lower- and middle-income residents.

When the housing market bubble finally burst in 2007, Miami was at the epicenter, along with Las Vegas and a number of California cities. The drivers of this crisis were of national proportions, to be sure, but Miami was at the forefront because of hugely inflated prices combined with massive construction (especially condominiums in the downtown area) and oversupply. The ensuing credit crisis impeded market movement and made for a prolonged paralyzing standoff between buyers and sellers. The city's inventory of homes was larger than ever before, foreclosure rates were among the country's highest, condo associations went bankrupt, and even though home values dropped 40 percent from 2007 to 2009, Miami seemed frozen in a real estate lull.

In September 2007, the *Wall Street Journal* ("Is Florida Over?") published the first in a flurry of news media reports proclaiming South Florida's demise. *Time* ("The Sunset State") followed suit with what seems to have become a decadal eulogy, occasioned first by the cocaine cowboys in 1981, then by a string of tourist murders in 1992, and last by the real estate crisis in 2008. Finally, the *New York Times* repeated it all obligingly in 2009 ("On the Mat, Florida Wonders Which Side Is Up").[13] The lamentations were mainly based on the harsh economic times and Florida's rather sudden end to population growth since 2007. The state experienced a (slight) population decline from 2008 to 2009, which was unprecedented in the last half a century.[14]

There has to be something irresistible about Miami, something that compels the national media to either magnify its glory or pronounce the city dead and buried. Perhaps the city's surreal qualities invoke such exaggerated reporting. Or maybe it is because people tend either to love or hate the place, with little room for balanced judgment. To be sure, Miami has been written off before, sometimes under circumstances considerably worse than the present (for example, 1926, 1981, 1996). Once the "magic city" got back on its feet, the doom scenarios were soon forgotten and hyperbole swung the other way.

Market swings have *never* brought down any major city, and the downturn of recent years was just that, a (profound) market swing.[15] Cities emerge, grow, develop into major urban centers, or, in contrast, implode, because of broader structural conditions that relate to the wider region. Miami's economic future lies in its ability to function as the main gateway to Latin America for the United States and increasingly for the rest of the world.

Great cities, throughout history, may be defined as centers of cultural and economic innovation, places that determine the direction and speed of change of a civilization. In a classic article in 1938, the sociologist Louis Wirth proposed a deceptively simple set of social conditions for the emergence of a great city: size, density, and diversity.[16] None of these criteria is easy to quantify and it may be impossible to set any numeric threshold—but it still makes for an intuitively compelling argument. In Wirth's view, cities are like chambers of combustible change, induced by myriad intense human encounters.

Miami has met two of these conditions, size and diversity, but it still lacks density. This is why, no matter how local boosters talk up the notion of Miami being such a wonderfully diverse place, it does not tend to *feel* like one. For the most part, Miami consists of sprawling suburbs where ethnic and racial groups and income classes are highly segregated. Diversity is of little consequence if there is limited interaction. Downtown developments (more high-rise and planned according to the principles of new urbanism) are likely to push things along, but change will be slow. Miami will not be another Manhattan any time soon.

Transience complicates things. Miami is a laboratory of sorts because it represents a social experiment of major proportions and with relevance far beyond South Florida: What is the role of diversity when accompanied by extreme transience? What is the effect of rapid population turnover on the frequency, intensity, and nature of encounters among diverse populations? Could such turnover further the role of the city as a creative, dynamic, innovative milieu? Or is it just too much, taxing the social fabric and exceeding the innate needs of human beings to live in a secure, more predictable, and less stressful environment? The strains of this new kind of transient, global urbanity have at times taken a toll on this city. But if transience is here to stay, it is just possible that Miami will learn to cope with it, to benefit from the positives and to manage its dangers. In that sense the suggestion that Miami needs more time to "develop its soul" may hold some truth.

Great cities at their most influential moment in history are not the neatly ordered and pleasant environs that top the "best places to live" rankings.[17] Instead, they tend to be disorderly, combustible, tense, stressful places that harbor apparently incompatible groups and set innovative trends. They are, in many ways, free cities: free of strong government and free of domination by any one particular group. They are frontier cities.

Metropolitan Miami does not belong to the Miccosukee, not to the Cubans (despite what some may think), not to African Americans, not to the remaining Anglos, not to Jews, not to Haitians, not to U.S. citizens, and not to any particular group of domestic or foreign immigrants. When it comes to the "right to the city," it is difficult indeed to privilege any particular group. When it comes to expectations of assimilation, it is quite impossible to designate a legitimate target or purpose. Assimilate to what?

The Chinese American geographer Yi-Fu Tuan has described the importance to most human beings of both the enlightenment of the "cosmos" and the comfort of the "hearth."[18] The hearth represents the trusted and familiar environment of the home, where there is a collective attachment to place and a sense of belonging. The cosmos, in contrast, is the scale of worldliness, diversity, and individual freedom.

There is no question that globalization and mobility bring a world of excitement, cultural enrichment, and broadening horizons. To cosmopolites and the affluent, Miami is an intriguing and quite comfortable city. But if it is the scene of the expanding cosmos, Miami also displays the fraying hearth. If cities are synonymous with civilization, Miami provides a glimpse of the fate of civilization in the global era. What is at stake here and in other globalizing cities is a social order and civility that do not come naturally. Tuan describes the ideal as follows: "Bonding based on propinquity and kinship is natural to us. By contrast, kindness to strangers who may not reciprocate and civility in impersonal transactions are a watermark achievement of civilization."[19] Herein lies a challenge of immense proportions to metropolitan Miami and other cities at the forefront of globalization: making the city into a cosmopolitan hearth.

The Transience Index

The table in Chapter 6 that lists U.S. metropolitan areas according to their transience rank is based on the Transience Index. This index combines weighted statistics from the U.S. census of 2000, some of which pertain to 1995–2000. The geographical entities are the fifty Metropolitan Statistical Areas (MSAs) or, if applicable, Consolidated Metropolitan Statistical Areas (CMSAs), with the largest populations.

The index is based on this formula: $A + B + C + D$, in which

A = a score of 1–50 based on the percentage of the 2000 population that was born out of state. A score of 50 corresponds to the highest percentage.

B = a score of 1–50 based on the percentage of the 2000 population that did not live in the (C)MSA in 1995. A score of 50 corresponds to the highest percentage.

C = a score of 1–50 based on the percentage of the population that is foreign born. A score of 50 corresponds to the highest percentage.

D = a score of 1–50 based on the number of domestic and foreign in-migrants age five and older from 1995 to 2000 as a percentage of the 2000 population age five and older. A score of 50 corredponds to the highest percentage.

The various values are taken from or derived from the following tables from the U.S. census of 2000 (all for [C]MSAs):

A: Table P001001: total population; Table P021003: population born in state of residence.

B: Table 025001: total population age five and older; Table P025003: population living in the same house in 1995; Table 025006: population living in a different house but same (C)MSA in 1995.

C: Table P001001: total population; Table P021013: foreign-born population.

D: PHC-T-22, Table 2: flow from abroad to CMSA; total population age five and older.

APPENDIX 2

Mapping Locals, Exiles, and Mobiles

Two of the maps in Chapter 7 (figs. 20 and 28) are based on data from the U.S. census of 2000. Miami-Dade and Broward counties together constitute 626 census tracts. The geographical size of tracts varies considerably and is generally based on population density. The population in most tracts ranges from a few thousand to about eleven thousand people.

The most extreme tracts in terms of localness or transience (81 out of 626) are selected as follows:

- The "most local" tracts are identified as those with a minimum of 65 percent of the population born in-state *and* a minimum of 92 percent who lived in the metropolitan area five years earlier in 1995. This resulted in a selection of 24 "most local" tracts.
- The least local or "most transient" tracts (57) were compiled in two steps. The first selection pertained to tracts with at least 75 percent of the population having been born abroad (33 tracts). The second selection identified all tracts with at least 85 percent of the population born out of state *and* at least 30 percent of the population who did not live in the metropolitan area five years earlier in 1995 (24 tracts).

Figure A1 shows clusters of census tracts with extreme concentrations of locals, exiles, and mobiles based on the percentage of

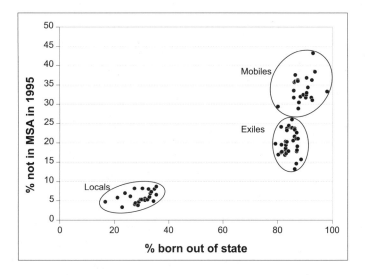

Figure A1. Census tract clusters with high concentrations of locals, exiles, and mobiles. Source: 2000 U.S. Census, Tables P001001, P021003, P025001, P025003, P025006.

the population born out of state and the percentage of the population who did not live in the metropolitan area five years earlier. Tracts identified as exiles and mobiles both have a very high proportion of people who were born out of state (over 78 percent)—the difference is that mobile tracts in recent years have shown greater mobility than exile tracts. The first map (fig. 20) in Chapter 7 is based on this scatter plot.

Figure A2 draws a different distinction among the 57 "most transient" tracts. It plots the percentage of the population that was born out of state versus the percentage born abroad. As such, it allows us to differentiate among tracts with concentrations of foreign transients, tracts with domestic transients, and tracts with a mix of foreign and domestic transients. The second map (fig. 28) in Chapter 7 is based on the clusters in this scatter plot.

APPENDIX 2

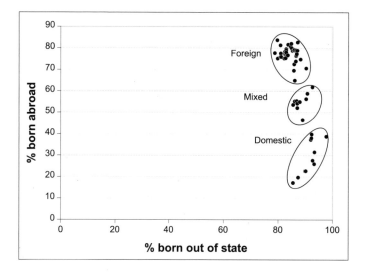

Figure A2. Census tract clusters with high concentrations of domestic transients, foreign transients, and mixed transients (both foreign and domestic). Source: 2000 U.S. Census, Tables P001001, P021003, P021013.

N O T E S

Chapter 1

1. P. Mercer, "Miamians Tangle with Developers Over Curious Tequesta Indian Ruin," *New York Times*, February 15, 1999; BBC, "The Mystery of the Miami Circle," January 25, 2001 (www.bbc.co.uk/science/horizon/2000/miamicircle_ transcript.shtm l); M. Bawaya, "The Amazing Tale of the Miami Circle," *American Archaeology* 6 (2001): 12–19; Florida Dept. of State, Bureau of Archaeology, "Miami Circle" (2007) (www.flheritage.com/archaeology/projects/miamicircle/ index.cfm); R. Wheeler, and R. S. Carr, "The Miami Circle: Fieldwork, Research and Analysis," *The Florida Anthropologist* 57 (2004): 3–10.

2. J. H. Hann, *Indians of Central and South Florida, 1513–1763* (Gainesville: University Press of Florida, 2003); W. E. McGoun, *Ancient Miamians: The Tequesta of South Florida* (Gainesville: University Press of Florida, 2002).

3. The numbers are based on data from the U.S. census. For an overview of Dade County's demographic history, see Miami-Dade County, Department of Planning and Zoning, *Miami-Dade County Facts*, July 2005. For a comparative perspective on the history of urbanization in the United States, see C. Gibson, "Population of the 100 Largest Cities and Other Urban Places in the United States, 1790 to 1990," Population Division Working Paper No. 27 (Washington, D.C.: Population Division U.S. Bureau of the Census, 1998) (www.census.gov/population/www/ documentation/twps0027.html).

4. R. Mohl, "The Settlement of Blacks in South Florida," in T. D. Boswell, ed., *South Florida: The Winds of Change*, 121 (prepared for the Annual Conference of the AAG, Miami, April 1991).

5. Dana A. Dorsey came to Miami from Georgia to work as a carpenter. He ended up a very successful developer and realtor. Dorsey was the first owner of the

southern tip of Miami Beach that would later become Fisher Island, and present-day Dorsey Park was given by him and his wife to the city of Miami in 1917 to be used as a green space for black people in the segregationist times.

6. J. C. Mills, *Highlights of Greater Miami* (Miami Shores, Fla.: Mills Publications, 1952), 3.

7. J. Sewell, *John Sewell's Memoirs and History of Miami, Florida* (1933); B. Reilly, *Tropical Surge: A History of Ambition and Disaster on the Florida Shore* (Sarasota: Pineapple Press, 2005).

8. The assassination was attempted by Guiseppe Zangara, an Italian self-declared anarchist who had arrived in Miami only a few months earlier. He later claimed to have protested the fate of poor working-class people in America (this was at the time of the Great Depression). All of the bullets missed Roosevelt but a few bystanders were wounded. The visiting mayor of Chicago died of his injuries a few days later.

9. M. Stoneman Douglas, *Everglades: The River of Grass* (New York: Rinehart, 1947).

10. Broward followed in the footsteps of his predecessor William S. Jennings, who had avowed similar goals.

11. W. W. Jenna, *Metropolitan Miami: A Demographic Overview* (Coral Gables: University of Miami Press, 1972), 24.

12. At the federal level and in local circles, there were some signs of growing awareness of the environmental impact on the Everglades, but it was not consequential in a political sense. Frank Stoneman (the father of Marjorie Stoneman Douglas), who came to Miami in 1903 to start the *Miami Evening Record* (which would become the *Miami Herald* in 1910), was known for his critical stance against the drainage projects.

13. H. Muir, *Miami, USA*, expanded ed. (Gainesville: University Press of Florida, 2000), 120.

14. P. George, "Miami: One-Hundred Years of History," *South Florida History* 24 (1996).

15. T. D. Allman, *Miami, City of the Future* (New York: Atlantic Monthly Press, 1987), 190.

Chapter 2

1. T. H. Weigall, *Boom in Paradise* (New York: A. H. King, 1932).

2. D. MacCannell, *The Tourist: A New Theory of the Leisure Class* (Berkeley: University of California Press, 1999).

3. G. Bush, "Playground USA: Miami and the Promotion of Spectacle," *Pacific Historical Review* 68 (1999): 153–72.

4. Ibid., 156.

5. J. C. Mills, *Highlights of Greater Miami* (Miami Shores, Fla.: Mills Publications, 1952), 66–67.

6. T. D. Allman, *Miami, City of the Future* (New York: Atlantic Monthly Press, 1987), 192.

7. G. E. Merrick, *Planning the Greater Miami of Tomorrow* (Miami: Miami Realty Board, 1937), 20. Also see J. F. Lejeune, "City without Memory: Planning the Spectacle of Greater Miami," in A. Shulman, ed., *Miami Modern Metropolis: Paradise and Paradox in Midcentury Architecture and Planning* (Miami Beach: Bass Museum of Art and Balcony Press, 2009), 34–59.

8. Mills, *Highlights of Greater Miami*, 52–53.

9. B. Cumming, *A Brief Florida Real Estate History* (West Coast Florida Chapter of the Appraisal Institute, 2006) (http://web.clas.ufl.edu/users/thrall/class/g3602/floridarealesta tehistory.pdf).

10. Fisher as quoted in the PBS documentary *Mr. Miami Beach*, 1998 (www.pbs.org/wgbh/amex/miami/peopleevents/pande06.html).

11. Bush, "Playground USA."

12. P. George, "Colored Town: Miami's Black Community, 1896–1930," *Florida Historical Quarterly* 16 (1978): 441; also see A. Portes and A. Stepick, *City on the Edge: The Transformation of Miami* (Berkeley: University of California Press, 1993), 77.

13. C. Taylor, *Black Religious Intellectuals: The Fight for Equality from Jim Crow to the 21st Century* (New York: Routledge, 2002), 85; M. Newton, *The Invisible Empire: The Ku Klux Klan in Florida* (Gainesville: University Press of Florida, 2001).

14. Taylor, *Black Religious Intellectuals*.

15. Miami Digital Archives (http://scholar.library.miami.edu/miamidigital/).

16. R. A. Mohl, "Leaving Overtown: Housing, Segregation, and Postwar Black Migration," in A. Shulman, ed., *Miami Modern Metropolis*, 289–93.

17. "Mystery Graveyard May Be Deemed Historic," *Miami Herald*, September 1, 2009.

18. Information provided by the Jewish Museum of Miami Beach (www.jewishmu-seum.com).

19. Blacks also had "their" newspaper: the *Miami Times* was started in 1923 by Henry E. S. Reeves.

20. H. Muir, *Miami, USA*, expanded ed. (Gainesville: University Press of Florida, 2000).

21. The PBS documentary *Mr. Miami Beach*.

22. Muir, *Miami, USA*, 221.

23. W. Wilbanks, *Murder in Miami: An Analysis of Homicide Patterns and Trends in Dade County, 1917–1983* (Lanham, Md.: University Press of America, 1984), 14. The murder rate in Dade County escalated sharply in 1926 and 1927, reaching the enormous number of 110 per 100,000, about twelve times the U.S. average (ibid., 141–43).

24. Miami's figure of 32.4 percent was exceptionally high. The statistics for other cities were Houston 26 percent, Los Angeles 24 percent, Denver 19 percent, Boston 10 percent, and New York 7 percent (see R. P. Wolff, *Miami: Economic Patterns of a Resort Area* [Coral Gables: University of Miami Press, 1945], 117).

25. Dade County purchased Pan Am Field from Pan American Airlines in 1945 and joined it with the adjacent field, which was used by the military during the war. Pan Am was established in Miami in 1928 and flew mainly between Miami, Key West, Havana, and select northern cities. In 1945 several other airlines started operations at Miami International Airport as well.

26. Lejeune, "City without Memory."

27. R. Walker and W. Solecki, "Theorizing Land-Cover and Land-Use Change: The Case of the Florida Everglades and Its Degradation," *Annals of the AAG* 94 (2004): 319.

28. David Fairchild retired from the Department of Agriculture in 1935 and moved to Miami. His friend and co-explorer Robert H. Montgomery established the Fairchild Tropical Garden in 1938. Fairchild was passionate about South Florida's natural beauty and was connected to a variety of organizations in Washington, D.C. (among his past affiliations was membership in the National Geographic's Committee for Research and Exploration).

29. National Park Service (www.nps.gov).

30. M. Stoneman Douglas, *Everglades: The River of Grass* (New York: Rinehart, 1947).

31. M. Lapidus, *Too Much Is Never Enough* (New York: Rizzoli International Publications, 1996).

32. Mills, *Highlights of Greater Miami*, 54.

33. I. Lehrman and J. Rappaport, *The Jewish Community of Miami Beach* (Philadelphia: Annenberg Research Institute, 1956), 25.

34. H. Messick, *Lansky* (New York: Berkley Medallion Books, 1971).

35. P. Frank and L. Voltz, "Florida's Struggle with the Hoodlums," *Colliers*, March 25, 1950, 20.

36. Ibid., 21.

37. E. Kefauver, *Crime in America* (New York: Doubleday, 1951), 60; P. G. Ashdown, "WTVJ's Miami Crime War: A Television Crusade," *Florida's Historical Quarterly* 58 (1980): 427.

38. Messick, *Lansky*.

39. "Plotters' Playground," *Time*, September 22, 1958, 32.

40. Quoted in Ashdown, "WTVJ's Miami Crime War," 430.

Chapter 3

1. "Plotters' Playground," *Time*, September 22, 1958.

2. O. A. Westad, *The Global Cold War* (Cambridge: Cambridge University Press, 2005), 171.

3. A. Portes and A. Stepick, *City on the Edge: The Transformation of Miami* (Berkeley: University of California Press, 1993), 102.

4. During 1959 and 1960 the dictatorial turn of the Castro regime became evident: hundreds of Batista collaborators were executed and many more thrown in prison; large farms were expropriated and U.S. companies nationalized; diplomatic and economic relations with the Soviet Union intensified; "neighborhood committees" were created across Cuba to keep an eye on "enemies of the revolution"; and former revolutionaries who started to dissent from Castro were purged, then executed or jailed.

5. The figures on Cuban refugees are from J. Thomas, "Cuban Refugees in the United States," *International Migration Review* 1 (1967): 46–57; A. Portes and

R. L. Bach, *Latin Journey: Cuban and Mexican Immigrants in the United States* (Berkeley: University of California Press, 1985).

6. The Cuban missile crisis of 1962 brought the world to the brink of nuclear war. Its resolution meant that the Soviets could not deploy nuclear weaponry in Cuba and that the United States would not intervene in Cuban affairs—although the United States did keep control of Guantánamo Bay. All commercial flights between the United States and Cuba ceased, creating more difficulties for those who wanted to leave the island.

7. Thomas, "Cuban Refugees in the United States," 54.

8. Ibid., 47.

9. Portes and Stepick, *City on the Edge*, 104.

10. J. F. Lejeune, "City without Memory: Planning the Spectacle of Greater Miami," in A. Shulman, ed., *Miami Modern Metropolis: Paradise and Paradox in Midcentury Architecture and Planning* (Miami Beach: Bass Museum of Art and Balcony Press, 2009), 57.

11. Islandia is a South Florida oddity. When it incorporated in 1960 it had a population of about thirty, currently reduced to six. It is not clear if they are all related. News reporters have a difficult time finding them and if they do, Islandians tend to be tight-lipped about matters of governance. Islandia is a string of several dozens of small islands eight miles east of Homestead in Biscayne Bay and just north of Elliott Key. With the creation of Biscayne National Park in 1966, the townspeople found themselves in the middle of a protected area, which precluded any further development.

12. The King Center, Stanford University (http://mlk-kpp01.stanford.edu/).

13. Figures in this paragraph are from the Overtown Collaborative (www.florida cdc.org/members/overtown/expressway.htm).

14. R. Mohl, "The Settlement of Blacks in South Florida," in T. D. Boswell, ed., *South Florida: The Winds of Change* (prepared for the annual conference of the AAG, Miami, April 1991), 123.

15. There is some disagreement in the literature about the extent of actual displacement of African Americans by Cubans in the 1960s and 1970s. For example, see Mohl, "The Settlement of Blacks in South Florida"; Portes and Stepick, *City on the Edge*; S. L. Croucher, *Imagining Miami: Ethnic Politics in a Postmodern World*

(Charlottesville: University Press of Virginia, 1997); N. C. Vaca, *The Presumed Alliance: The Unspoken Conflict between Latinos and Blacks and What It Means for America* (New York: Rayo, 2004).

16. *Miami Times*, August 16, 1968, quoted by Mohl, "The Settlement of Blacks in South Florida," 133.

17. Reports from Cuba, the reliability of which is questionable, suggested that 42 percent of the *marielitos* had criminal records. Upon arrival in the United States, the numbers were impossible to determine (Portes and Stepick, *City on the Edge*, 21).

18. Ibid., 105.

19. Ibid., 31.

20. *Miami Herald*, December 27, 1979, quoted by B. Porter and M. Dunn, *The Miami Riot of 1980: Crossing the Bounds* (Lexington, Mass.: Lexington Books, 1984), 34.

21. Porter and Dunn, *The Miami Riot of 1980*, 38.

22. Ibid., 47.

23. "Death in the Morning," *Time*, November 9, 1981.

24. The figures for Haitian refugees are from "Illegal Flow of Haitian Immigrants into Florida Is Reported to Increase," *New York Times*, October 30, 1980. A. Stepick, "Haitian Boat People: A Study in the Conflicting Forces Shaping U.S. Immigration Policy," *Law and Contemporary Problems* 63 (1982): 163–96; "Waiting for INS to Let Them Become Legal Residents," *Miami Herald*, July 1, 1982; "Haitian Flood Now a Trickle," *Miami Herald*, October 26, 1982; A. Stepick and A. Portes, "Flight into Despair: A Profile of Recent Haitian Refugees in South Florida," *International Migration Review* 20 (1986): 329–50.

25. "Non-Hispanic whites" is an awkward label. The local discourse and the literature sometimes use the alternative term "Anglos," which is even more vague and imprecise.

26. For a detailed description of the Mandela issue, see Vaca, *The Presumed Alliance*.

27. The negative national and international publicity dealt many local businesses and institutions a severe blow, including the University of Miami. Tad Foote arrived as the university's new president in March 1981, at a time of crisis. Twenty years later he recalled, "Between the time I was hired and the time I welcomed

my first freshman class, more than 1,000 students withdrew and studied else-where because of Miami's troubles." (*Miami* magazine, 2001 [www6.miami.edu/miami-magazine/springo1/footnotes.html]).

28. "Miami Beach—Mob Town, USA," *Newsweek*, February 13, 1967.

29. FBI, *Uniform Crime Reports*, 1979 and 1980.

30. "Crime Termed 'Berserk' in Miami: Refugees and Drugs Blamed in Part," *New York Times*, December 23, 1980.

31. "Drug 'Godmother' Will Be Deported to Colombia," *Miami Herald,* June 6, 2004.

32. The number of Jews in Dade County peaked in 1975 at 289,000, nearly 20 per-cent of the total population (M. Shaw, *The Jews of Greater Miami: A Historical Perspective* [Boca Raton: Florida Atlantic University], 1992). The arrival of *marie-litos* in Miami Beach caused an escalation in Jewish departures.

33. B. Sokol, "Perception Is Reality: Drugs, Guns, Violence, Beauty, Style, and the Illusory World of Miami Vice," *New Times*, October 6, 2005 (www.miaminew-times.com/2005–10–06/news/perception-is-reality).

34. Portes and Stepick, *City on the Edge.*

Chapter 4

1. J. Garreau, *The Nine Nations of America* (Boston: Houghton Mifflin, 1981), 74. Referring to Miami's obscure power structures, Garreau notes, "A reporter at-tempting to get at a description of the internal workings of the place is tempted to throw up his hands."

2. H. Molotch, "The City as a Growth Machine: Toward a Political Economy of Place," *American Journal of Sociology* 82 (1976): 309–31. Molotch's article was followed by a more elaborate argument in a book written with John Logan: *Urban Fortunes: The Political Economy of Place* (Berkeley: University of California Press, 1987).

3. "Anti-Bilingual Backers Celebrate Early," *Miami Herald*, November 5, 1980. The ordinance was supported by 59 percent of all voters in Dade County and by 71 percent of all non-Hispanic whites. Of the Hispanics, 85 percent voted against, and blacks were split on the issue. The Chamber of Commerce embarked on an advertizing campaign against the ordinance in the *Miami Herald*. See M. Castro,

M. Haun, and A. Roca, "The Official English Movement in Florida," in K. L. Adams and T. L. Brink, eds., *Perspectives on Official English: The Campaign for English as the Official Language of the USA* (New York: Mouton-De Gruyter, 1990), 153.

4. *Tampa, Metropolis of South Florida: Gateway to the Panama Canal* (Milwaukee: E. C. Kropp, 1920).

5. City of Miami, *Golden Anniversary 1896–1946: Reviewing the Past, Forecasting the Future*, 1946.

6. W. W. Jenna, *Metropolitan Miami: A Demographic Overview* (Coral Gables: University of Miami Press, 1972), 4.

7. George B. Tindall, "The Bubble in the Sun," *American Heritage* (August 1965) (www.americanheritage.com/articles/magazine/ah/1965/5/1965_5_76.shtml).

8. Dade County Development Department, *Economic Survey of Metropolitan Miami* (Miami, 1962).

9. S. Sassen and A. Portes, "Miami: A New Global City?" *Contemporary Sociology* 22/4 (1993): 472.

10. This distinction was introduced in the literature by M. Edelman, *The Symbolic Uses of Politics* (Urbana: University of Illinois Press, 1964).

11. P. Bachrach and M. Baratz, "Two Faces of Power," *American Political Science Review* 56 (1962): 947–52.

12. Mr. Chapman kindly agreed to an interview with the author in the summer of 2008; he passed away six months later, on December 25.

13. In Molotch's argument, banking, development, and real estate are the key industries in the typical urban growth machine. Early members of the Non-Group included Harry Hood Bassett (Southeast Bank), Louis Hector (First National Bank), Bill Graham (of the famous Florida lineage of developers and politicians), David Blumberg (a developer and the one-time chairman of the Chamber of Commerce), Bill Colson (the founder of a prominent Miami law firm), and Hank Meyer (whose PR firm represented mainly banks and development corporations).

14. J. P. Faber, "Chairman of the Board," *South Florida CEO* (January 2004) (find articles.com/p/articles/mi_moOQD/is_1_7/ai_113071138 /pg_4).

15. S. Bishop, "The Ferre Family: Puerto Rican by Birth, Yanqui in Spirit," NACLA Digital Archives 6/6, July 1972.

16. Mr. Ferré kindly agreed to an interview with the author on February 18, 2008.

17. O. R. Costa, *Luis J. Botifoll: Exemplary Cuban* (Coral Gables: University of Miami North South Center, 1992), 86.

18. In the late 1990s, the Non-Group was renamed the Miami Business Forum and became a considerably larger and more open institution—by then, the city's multicultural character and its international orientation were no longer matters of controversy.

19. J. F. Rosado, G. R. Cepero, and J. B. Luytjes, *Potential of South Florida as an International Finance Center* (Miami: School of Business, Florida International University, 1977).

20. D. A. Baer, "Behind the Surge in Miami's International Banking," *Economic Review* (Federal Reserve Bank of Atlanta) 66 (April 1981): 12.

21. City of Miami, *Miami Business Report* (Department of Economic Development, 1982), 116.

22. City of Miami, *Miami Business Report* (Department of Economic Development, 1984).

23. Baer, "Behind the Surge in Miami's International Banking," 11.

24. City of Miami, *Miami Business Report* (1982), 116.

25. Baer, "Behind the Surge in Miami's International Banking," 10.

26. Quoted in the PBS documentary *Drug Wars* (transcript available at www.pbs. org/wgbh/pages/frontline/shows/drugs/etc/script.html).

27. G. Guliotta and J. Leen, *Kings of Cocaine* (New York: Simon and Schuster, 1989); A. P. Maingot, "Laundering the Gains of the Drug Trade: Miami and Caribbean Tax Havens," *Journal of Interamerican Studies and World Affairs* 30 (1988): 177; U.S. Senate, Organized Crime in America, Hearings before the Committee on the Judiciary, 98th Congress, 1st Session, 1983, 60; P. Lernoux, *In Banks We Trust* (New York: Anchor Press, 1984), 122; D. McClintick, *Swordfish: A True Story of Ambition, Savagery, and Betrayal* (New York: Pantheon Books, 1993).

28. McClintick, *Swordfish.*

29. Maingot, "Laundering the Gains of the Drug Trade," 181.

30. U.S. Senate, Organized Crime and Use of Violence, Hearings before the Permanent Subcommittee on Investigations of the Committee on Government Opera-

tions, 96th Congress, 2nd Session, April/May 1980, 219–20; Lernoux, *In Banks We Trust*, 133; Maingot, "Laundering the Gains of the Drug Trade," 174.

31. Costa, *Luis J. Botifoll*, 93–96. There was no evidence of any improprieties by Botifoll himself.

32. Quoted in the PBS documentary *Drug Wars*.

33. Lernoux, *In Banks We Trust*, 108; M. Massing, "The War on Cocaine," *New York Review of Books*, December 22, 1988.

34. R. Lee, "Dimensions of the South American Cocaine Industry," *Journal of Interamerican Studies and World Affairs* 30 (1988): 89.

35. Maingot, "Laundering the Gains of the Drug Trade," 171.

36. Lernoux, In Banks We Trust, 108–10; Maingot, "Laundering the Gains of the Drug Trade," 174.

37. R. Wakefield, "Awash in a Sea of Money: Billions in Cash Generated by the Cocaine Trade Fueled Miami's Economy," *New Times*, October 6, 2005 (www.miami newtimes.com/2005–10–06/news/awash-in-a-sea-of-money/).

38. Maingot, "Laundering the Gains of the Drug Trade," 176.

39. Lernoux, *In Banks We Trust*, 85, 110.

40. Wakefield, "Awash in a Sea of Money"; D. G. Cartano, "The Drug Industry in South Florida," in T. D. Boswell, ed., *South Florida: The Winds of Change* (prepared for the annual conference of the AAG, Miami, April 1991), 105–11.

41. Lernoux, *In Banks We Trust*, 85, 110, quoting a U.S. Customs officer in 1981.

42. See F. Alvarado, "Miami: See It Like a Drug Dealer," *New Times*, October 13, 2005 (www.miaminewtimes.com/2005–10–13/news/miami-see-it-like-a-drug-dealer/). The website of the Cigarette Racing company states that "Don Aronow's untimely and unfortunate death in 1987 was a sign of the turbulent times and questionable customers on Thunder Boat Row—188th Street in North Miami where he built his powerboat fame and met his demise. Aronow may have been gunned down by an assassin, but after a series of financial dealings, his name, business and legend lived on" (www.cigaretteracing.com/index.cfm).

43. City of Miami, *Miami Business Report* (1984), 3.

44. A. Jorge and R. Moncarz, *The Future of the Hispanic Market: The Cuban Entrepreneur and the Economic Development of the Miami Standard Metropolitan Statis-*

tical Area (Miami: International Banking Center and Department of Economics, Florida International University, 1982).

45. Untitled and undated document, prepared by Mr. Jaap Donath, Beacon Council, Miami.

46. "Miami!" *Time*, September 6, 1993.

47. "Free Trade in the Americas: Strategies for a Transformed Market," Economist Intelligence Unit, June 1994.

48. R.M. Kantor, *World Class: Thriving Locally in the Global Economy*. New York: Simon & Schuster, 1995, 283.

49. "Who's Who: 100 People Who Make Things Happen in South Florida," *South Florida Business Journal*, April 29, 1994.

50. "The Book of Lists," *South Florida Business Journal*, December 22, 1995.

51. Elected offices include the mayor, vice-mayor, commissioners or council members, clerk, manager, attorney, and chief of police. Of all twenty-seven municipalities in Dade County in 1996, only five had a majority of Hispanics in their elected offices, and of the six largest cities there was only one with a majority of Hispanics (Hialeah). Data provided by the Dade County Department of Elections, April 18, 1996.

52. A. Jorge, R. D. Cruz, R. Moncarz, and J. Salazar-Carillo, *A Development Model for a Modern Society: New Cross Cultural Patterns and Socio-Economic Change (The Cuban Experience in South Florida)* (Miami: International Banking Center and Department of Economics, Florida International University, 1981), 5–6.

53. Jorge and Moncarz, *The Future of the Hispanic Market*, 5.

54. Sassen and Portes ("Miami") were the first to address, tentatively, the issue of the connections between the Cuban enclave economy and Miami's transformation into a world city.

Chapter 5

1. Precisely around the time that Miami completed the overhaul of its growth machine, in the mid-1980s, a new academic literature emerged on the topic of "world cities." The most important publication was perhaps John Friedmann's "The World City Hypothesis" in 1986 (*Development and Change*, vol. 17, 69–83),

but it did not stand on its own. Other ground-breaking work in the 1970s and early 1980s was by scholars such as Alejandro Portes, John Walton, Richard Cohen, and Saskia Sassen.

2. J. Cuddington, *Capital Flight: Estimates, Issues, and Explanations* (Princeton, N.J.: Princeton University Press, 1986), 28; A. P. Maingot, "Laundering the Gains of the Drug Trade: Miami and Caribbean Tax Havens," *Journal of Interamerican Studies and World Affairs* 30 (1988): 177.

3. A. Portes and A. Stepick, *City on the Edge: The Transformation of Miami* (Berkeley: University of California Press, 1993), 152.

4. R. Grosfoguel, "Global Logics in the Caribbean City System: The Case of Miami," in P. L. Knox and P. J. Taylor, eds., *World Cities in a World-System* (Cambridge: Cambridge University Press, 1995), 156–70.

5. D. R. Meyer, *Hong Kong as a Global Metropolis* (Cambridge: Cambridge University Press, 2000), 143.

6. G. Lin, "Identity, Mobility, and the Making of the Chinese Diasporic Landscape in Hong Kong," in L. J. C. Ma and C. Carter, eds., *Space, Place, Mobility, and Identity* (New York: Rowman and Littlefield, 2003), 157.

7. I. Kelly, *Hong Kong: A Political-Geographic Analysis* (Honolulu: University of Hawaii Press, 1986), 56–57; also see Meyer, *Hong Kong as a Global Metropolis*, 179, which emphasizes capital flight from mainland China into Hong Kong during these years.

8. Meyer, *Hong Kong as a Global Metropolis*, 219; Grosfoguel, "Global Logics in the Caribbean City System"; Portes and Stepick, *City on the Edge.*

9. Meyer, *Hong Kong as a Global Metropolis*, 242.

10. K. Mitchell, "Different Diasporas and the Hype of Hybridity," *Environment and Planning D: Society and Space* 15/5 (1997): 543. Also see Lin, "Identity, Mobility"; A. Ong, *Flexible Citizenship: The Cultural Logics of Transnationality* (Durham, N.C.: Duke University Press, 1999).

11. R. M. Kantor, *World Class: Thriving Locally in the Global Economy* (New York: Simon and Schuster, 1995), 283.

12. "Vanishing Spanish," *Miami Herald*, June 14, 1996.

13. "Spanish-Speaking Workers in Short Supply," *South Florida Business Journal*,

December 12, 1997; S. H. Fradd, *The Economic Impact of Spanish-Language Proficiency in Metropolitan Miami* (Miami: Greater Miami Chamber of Commerce, 1996).

14. There are some obvious differences, of course. Hong Kong has always been much more orderly than Miami and much more tightly controlled by a central (colonial) government. Miami, in contrast, has for much of its history been "up for grabs" to those who were willing to take a gamble on the frontier. In Miami, it appears, the power of the state and the rule of law were distant matters. In this respect, it was more reminiscent of Shanghai in the late nineteenth century, when that city earned itself the epithet "Whore of the Orient." Miami's international banking district, along Brickell Avenue, is reminiscent of the architectural prowess and trophy buildings on the Bund in Shanghai. The drug trade and massive amounts of money that moved through these cities left their mark on their economies and their architecture. See J. Nijman, "Place-Particularity and Deep Analogies: A Comparative Historical Essay about Miami's Emergence as a World City," *Urban Geography* 28 (2007): 92–107.

15. Like other world cities, Dublin has also become a much more polarized society with a distinct bimodal income distribution and, according to some, increasing poverty. Some have argued that its "economic success" was accompanied by "social failure" (P. Kirby, *The Celtic Tiger in Distress: Growth with Inequality in Ireland* [New York: Palgrave, 2002], 5).

16. It should be noted that economic development funds from the European Union constituted another important external factor in the development of Dublin, a testament to active and successful lobbying on the part of the Irish government.

17. Claims about Ireland's "engineered" success sometimes have boosterist overtones. When the Irish "miracle" took off in the late 1980s, reference was made to the "Celtic Tiger," in comparison to the rapid developments of small East Asian countries such as Singapore and Taiwan. At the time of the Asian meltdown in the late 1990s, the Irish preferred another name for their success: the "fox economy"—but the Irish economy and Dublin in particular took a serious beating in the global recession that started in 2007.

18. P. Sweeney, *The Celtic Tiger: Ireland's Economic Miracle Explained*. Taylorville, Ill.: Oak Tree Press, 1998, 9.

19. Kirby, *The Celtic Tiger in Distress*, 34.

20. Interview with Mr. Ferré, February 18, 2008.

21. *New York Times*, advertising supplement, December 15, 1995, 43.

22. It is one of the arguments of world city theory that decentralization of manufacturing goes hand in hand with centralization of producer services that reflect command functions. See S. Sassen, *The Global City: New York, London, Tokyo* (Princeton, N.J.: Princeton University Press, 1991).

23. J. Nijman, "Breaking the Rules: Miami in the Urban Hierarchy," *Urban Geography* 17 (1996): 5–22; S. Sassen, *Cities in a World Economy* (Thousand Oaks, Calif.: Pine Forge Press, 2000), 64–65.

24. In 2004, Miami housed the global headquarters of only 1 Forbes 500 company; 2 Fortune 500 companies; and 9 of the nation's 500 biggest law firms. In comparison, the numbers for New York were, respectively, 78, 43, and 45.

25. WorldCity Business, *Global Economic Impact Study* (Coral Gables: WorldCity Business, 2008).

26. The TNC database of WorldCity Business (previous note) was expanded with primary data collected by this author on the geography of foreign activities of TNCs that are headquartered in Greater Miami.

27. This information is based on a survey of Latin American business leaders who were asked to name the best cities in the world for doing business with Latin America. Miami was named by 74 percent of respondents, New York by 20 percent; and Madrid by 15 percent (*AméricaEconomía*, April 25, 2003, 22).

28. *Miami Herald*, January 23, 2006: "Banking in Miami is all about location, location, location."

29. Beacon Council, *Miami/Dade County Profile* (Miami: Beacon Council, 1990), 54; U.S. Bureau of the Census, Foreign Trade Division, U.S. Trade Online (www.statusa.gov/usatrade.nsf).

30. "Can Miami Save Itself? A City Beset by Drugs and Violence," *New York Times*, July 19, 1987. A study in 1993 found that Miami International Airport ranked only twenty-fourth in the nation in terms of "national connectivity" while at the same time it had established itself as the most central air traffic node in the international region (R. L. Ivy, "Assessing Changes in Air Service Connectivity in the U.S. Southeast, 1978–1992," *Southeastern Geographer* 33 [1993]: 148–58).

31. According to a study in 2001, Miami has the "highest visibility" of U.S. cities its size; it is often portrayed in a negative light, and economic issues are rarely discussed (J. Nijman, "The Image of Greater Miami," unpublished report, Department of Geography and Regional Studies, University of Miami, 2001). A nationwide survey by Zogby International in 2008 produced similar results.

32. S. Sassen, *Cities in a World Economy*, 3rd ed. (Thousand Oaks, Calif.: Pine Forge Press, 2006), xiv.

33. On balance, though, Dublin has more large branches than Miami and Miami has more small ones. This may a reflection of the different regional markets in the European Union and Latin America (the latter being smaller and more fragmented). See Kirby, *The Celtic Tiger in Distress*, 36; M. White, "Inward Investment, Firm Embeddedness, and Place: An Assessment of Ireland's Multinational Software Sector," *European Urban and Regional Studies* 11 (2004): 243–60.

Chapter 6

1. "Head of Sonesta Chain a Pioneer in South Florida," *Miami Herald*, December 11, 2008.

2. "Pioneer City Resident Moving Back up North," *Miami Herald*, May 2, 2004.

3. "A Place for the Living, but Not for the Dead," *Miami Herald*, October 6, 2002.

4. "Body Shipping a Booming Business in South Florida," *Palm Beach Post*, June 16, 2008.

5. Personal communication, June 10, 2008.

6. "When Death Comes, Many Residents Take Next Flight Out," *Miami Herald*, August 17, 2003; "Beginnings and Endings," *Miami Herald*, July 22, 2007.

7. W. H. Frey, "Metropolitan Magnets for International and Domestic Migrants," *The Living Cities Census Series* (Washington, D.C.: Brookings Institution, 2003); J. P. Schachter et al., "Migration and Geographic Mobility in Metropolitan and Nonmetropolitan America: 1995–2000," *Census 2000 Special Reports CENSR-9* (Washington, D.C.: U.S. Bureau of the Census, 2003).

8. *South Florida Business Journal*: "Who's Who: 100 People who make things happen in South Florida." April 29, 1994. The methods used to compile this list of South Florida's most powerful people were described as follows:

We measure power in many ways: corporate, personal, social, financial. Some yield the power of their organizations, some influence through the power of their personal wealth, some through their network of connections and others through the "bully pulpit" of their elected offices. The following were winnowed from a huge list with the help of more than two dozen corporate and political leaders in Miami-Dade, Broward and Palm Beach Counties. Not all the people on this list are beloved, and not all are feared. But all share the patina of power, the exclusive mantel of prestige, authority, command and control. These are the people who can make things happen, and change the course of entire communities for better or worse.

9. *South Florida CEO*: "The 100 Most Powerful People in South Florida," January 2004.

10. "Powerful People Had a Wild Year," *Miami Herald,* January 1, 2004.

11. The index is based on selected data from the census of 2000. See Appendix 1 for a more detailed explanation.

12. R. Putnam, *Bowling Alone: The Collapse and Revival of American Community* (New York: Simon and Schuster, 2000), 67.

13. Pierre Bourdieu observed that social capital is formed in the context of a "durable network and provides each of its members with the backing of the collectivity-owned capital, a "credential" that entitles them to credit in the various senses of the word . . ." (P. Bourdieu, "The Forms of Capital," in J. Richardson, ed., *Handbook of Theory and Research for the Sociology of Education* [New York: Greenwood Press, 1985], 55).

14. See, for example, James S. Coleman, *Foundations of Social Theory* (Cambridge, Mass.: Harvard University Press, 1990): "Individual mobility constitutes a potential action that will be destructive of the structure itself and thus of the social capital dependent on it" (320). This line of thinking is not entirely new, even if the theoretical argumentation is more sophisticated and more convincing than in more dated writings. In the older literature that predates the meta-narratives of globalization and social capital, spatial mobility and transience were sometimes considered as fundamental threats to local communities. Vance Packard in his *Nation of Strangers* (New York: David McKay, Inc., 1972) lamented the growing mobility and rootlessness of the American people and he blamed it for much that was wrong with urban America: "A great many people are disturbed

by the feeling that . . . they are living in a continually changing environment where there is little sense of community" (xi). Near the end of the book he poignantly observes that "transients create fissures in a community" (257).

15. S. Verba, K. L. Schlozman, and H. E. Brady, *Voice and Equality: Civic Voluntarism in American Politics* (Cambridge, Mass.: Harvard University Press, 1995).

16. Putnam (*Bowling Alone*) refers to the overarching type of social capital as "the bridging sort." See also C. Sirianni and L. Friedland, *The Civic Renewal Movement: Community Building and Democracy in the U.S.* (Dayton: Kettering Foundation Press, 2005); J. Abu-Lughod, "Civil/Uncivil Society: Confusing Form with Content," in J. Friedmann and M. Douglass, eds., *Cities for Citizens* (New York: John Wiley and Sons, 1998), 227–37.

17. G. J. Grenier and L. Perez, *The Legacy of Exile: Cubans in the United States* (Boston: Allyn and Bacon, 2003), 12. The lack of social capital at the wider urban scale seems apparent, for example, in the meager support for the arts: "Confronted with a transient population and different expectations, South Florida cultural philanthropy faces unique obstacles. . . . Foundations of financial support, community commitment and artistic tradition have yet to be created" ("Between the Arts and a Hard Place," *Miami Herald*, July 6, 2006).

18. N. Peirce and C. Johnson, "Three Counties' Destinies Linked," *Sun Sentinel*, November 19, 2000.

19. A. Menendez, "A Cruel Irony: Cronyism Can Trump Integrity," *Miami Herald*, July 8, 2007.

20. M. Putney, "Dread, Lassitude—and Civility," *Miami Herald*, July 16, 2008.

21. Sperling's Best Places 2004. Miami ranked the highest of the fifty largest U.S. cities (www.bestplaces.net/docs/studies/stress1.aspx).

22. Autovantage Poll, 2006, 2007, 2008 (www.automotive.einnews.com/article.php ?nid = 18694).

23. "Marlins Seek a Place in the Sun," *Financial Times*, April 20, 2001; "Residents Reject 'Historic' Label," *Miami Herald*, January 23, 2005; "Between the Arts and a Hard Place," *Miami Herald*, July 6, 2006; "Marlins Win, but Fans Fail to Fill Seats," *Miami Herald*, July 18, 2008.

24. A. Steinacker, "Prospects for Regional Governance: Lessons from the Miami Abolition Vote," *Urban Affairs Review* 37 (2001): 100–118.

25. "State Financial Oversight Looms for a Miami in Dire Money Straits," *New York Times*, November 28, 1996; "Corruption, Mismanagement Edge City Towards Bankruptcy," *Financial Times*, December 13, 1996.

26. "Gloom over Miami," *Time*, June 24, 2001.

27. M. J. Dluhy and H. A. Frank, *The Miami Fiscal Crisis: Can a Poor City Regain Prosperity?* (Westport, Conn.: Praeger, 2002), xiii, 6, 111–12, 117.

28. J. Rabin, W. B. Hildredth, and G. J. Miller, *Handbook of Public Administration* (Boca Raton Fla.: CRC Press, 2006), 241. It is not apparent that things have changed much. A comparative study of the civic and political cultures of various U.S. cities, published in the *Journal of Urban Affairs* in 2008, characterizes Miami as follows: "The city appears to lack a coherent power system or regime. . . . Low levels of individual citizen and group participation do not challenge business elite dominance. . . . Local governmental leadership is generally weak due to a lack of professionalism, an overabundance of cronyism and corruption, and institutional fragmentation. . . . Local decision making tends to be reactive to immediate political and economic crises, also inhibiting an active, sustained development agenda" (L. A. Reese and R. A. Rosenfeld, "Introduction: Comparative civic culture," *Journal of Urban Affairs* 30 [2008]: 367; see also J. F. Gainsborough, "A Tale of Two Cities: Civic Culture and Public Policy in Miami," *Journal of Urban Affairs* 30 [2008]: 419–35).

29. "Rolls Swollen with Voters Who Haven't Cast a Ballot," *Miami Herald*, August 10, 2003.

30. "60,000 Unite in Miami March against Chavez," *Miami Herald*, January 19, 2003.

31. "Across the U.S., Growing Rallies for Immigration," *New York Times*, April 10, 2006; "Thousands March for Immigration Rights," CNN.com, May 1, 2006; "Thousands Rally in May Day Effort for Immigration Reform," *USA Today*, May 2, 2008; "In Miami, Across U.S., Marchers Hit the Streets," *Miami Herald*, April 10, 2006.

32. "Letters Support Pharmed Pair," *Miami Herald*, January 3, 2009.

33. "South Florida Fraud: 'Affinity' Scams Built on Trust, Familiarity," *Miami Herald*, December 31, 2008.

34. Commission on Ethics, Miami-Dade County, 2004. Corruption in Miami has a long history. Jim Smith, Florida's attorney general in the early 1980s, once pro-

fessed, "Frankly, I lie in bed sometimes at night and it . . . just scares me, the level of corruption we may have in Florida" (quoted in P. Lernoux, *In Banks We Trust* [New York: Anchor Press, 1984], 116). The impact of the Ethics Commission over the next fifteen years or so was marginal at best. An editorial in the *Miami Herald* of September 9, 2009 described it as "the sly foxes at the Miami-Dade Commission guarding the ethics hen house."

35. Unpublished research by this author, 2004. The study was based on a content analysis of the leading newspapers in these cities that selected incidents of corruption, fraud, and bribery. During the period 2001–4, Miami counted a total of 472 corruption incidents compared to 370 in Atlanta, 245 in Philadelphia, 151 in Denver, 97 in Houston, and 32 in Seattle.

36. "Former City Official Arrested," *Miami Herald*, May 21, 2003.

37. FBI Uniform Crime Reports, 1958–2007. Data pertain to metropolitan statistical areas (MSAs) with a population greater than five hundred thousand through 1961 and greater than one million since 1962. The figures pertain to the Miami MSA (Miami-Dade County).

38. Miami-Dade County government and law enforcement agencies have in recent years released figures that suggest that crime has come down (for example, "Crime Plunges in Dade, Florida," *Miami Herald*, April 24, 2001). One reason for this decline was the steady incorporation of new municipalities in the county, reducing the population residing in unincorporated Miami-Dade County. The entire nation witnessed dropping crime figures in those years, but in relative terms South Florida continued to have the highest rates among U.S. metropolitan areas.

39. On Medicare fraud, see "Feds Fight Rampant Medicare Fraud in South Florida," NPR.org, November 6, 2007 (www.npr.org/templates/story/story.php?storyId= 16045685). Inspectors from the federal Justice Department found that of nearly sixteen hundred businesses in Miami that bill for Medicare services, about one-third turned out not to exist. Total annual fraud charges amounted to half a billion U.S. dollars. On mortgage fraud, see "Mortgage Fraud Still Soaring," CNN.com, August 26, 2008 (http://money.cnn.com/2008/08/25/real_estate/soaring_mortgage_fraud/index.htm?postversion=2008082606. In 2008, Florida had the highest mortgage fraud rates in the nation, and Miami-Dade County accounted for half of all cases in the state.

40. U.S. Treasury Department, *Money Laundering Threat Assessment* (2005), 57 (www
   .treas.gov/press/releases/reports/js3077_01112005_MLTA.pdf).

41. National Drug Intelligence Center, U.S. Department of Justice, *Drug Market Analysis 2008: South Florida High Intensity Drug Trafficking Area* (Washington, D.C.,
   2008).

42. "Money Laundering: Bank Ordered to Pay $65M in Fines," *Miami Herald*, August
   7, 2007; "In Florida, Dirty Money Is Big Business," *Miami Herald*, August 8,
   2007.

43. U.S. Treasury Department, *Money Laundering Threat Assessment*.

44. "Ecuadorian President to Seek Refuge," *Miami Herald*, February 9, 2003.

45. "A Sunny State Draws Shady Deals," *Financial Times*, May 28, 2004.

46. "Pinochet's Web of Bank Accounts Exposed," *The Guardian*, June 16, 2005.

47. J. Friedmann, "The Common Good: Assessing the Performance of Cities," in H.
   Dandekar, ed., *City, Space, and Globalisation: An International Perspective* (Ann
   Arbor: College of Architecture and Urban Planning, University of Michigan,
   1998), 15–22.

48. As the local scholar and commentator Max Castro put it in one of his columns in
   the *Miami Herald* in 2001: "There's one thing you can say about the local officials
   who have been in serious trouble with the law over the last decade or two. They
   are as multicultural a bunch as you will ever find: Joe Gersten, Alex Daoud, Cesar
   Odio, Al Gutman, Carmen Lunetta, Miller Dawkins, Humberto Hernandez, James
   Burke, Pedro Reboredo, Warshaw, Perez. Sure can't blame our seemingly bottom-
   less cesspool of corruption on the political culture of any one ethnic group."

49. See L. Steffens, *The Shame of Cities* (New York: McClure, Philips and Co., 1904);
   D. P. Gaonkar and C. Kamrath, "Genealogy: Lincoln Steffens on New York," in J.
   Holston, ed., *Cities and Citizenship* (Durham, N.C.: Duke University Press, 1999),
   139–54.

50. An example of such institutions that are virtually absent in Miami are labor
   unions, reflective of the city's postindustrial origins.

Chapter 7

1. A. Appadurai, "Disjuncture and Difference in the Global Cultural Economy," *Public Culture* 2 (1990): 1–24. Also see Lin, who speaks of new identities "embedded

in mobility" (G. Lin, "Identity, Mobility, and the Making of the Chinese Diasporic Landscape in Hong Kong," in L. J. C. Ma and C. Carter, eds., *Space, Place, Mobility, and Identity* [New York: Rowman and Littlefield, 2003]).

2. S. Hall, "Old and New Identities, Old and New Ethnicities," in A. D. King, ed., *Culture, Globalization and the World-System: Contemporary Conditions for the Representation of Identity* (Binghamton: Department of Art and Art History, State University of New York, 1991), 47, 62–63. Also see M. Castells, *The Power of Identity*, 2nd ed. (Oxford: Blackwell, 2004).

3. See, for example, N. Glick Schiller, L. Basch, and C. Szanton Blanc, "From Immigrant to Transmigrant: Theorizing Transnational Migration," *Anthropological Quarterly* 68/1 (1996): 48–64. For an explanation of transnational migration as reflecting the structural needs of late capitalism, see D. Harvey, *The Condition of Postmodernity* (Oxford: Blackwell, 1989).

4. A. Portes, "Globalization from Below: The Rise of Transnational Communities," in W. P. Smith and R. P. Korczenwicz, eds., *Latin America in the World Economy* (Westport, Conn.: Greenwood Press, 1996), 151–68.

5. In the existing literature, Miami's population is often divided in the traditional triad of Hispanics, non-Hispanic whites (or Anglos), and blacks. It may seem self-evident at first but it is in fact a curious device. First, it forms an incongruous combination of race and ethnicity (Hispanics can be black or white and blacks can be Hispanic or non-Hispanic). Second, the triad is based exclusively on race or ethnicity and strictly speaking it ignores migration and mobility. Third, ethnic and racial identities do matter, of course, but they generally operate at a much finer and differentiated scale. For example 64 percent of Miami-Dade's population is identified as "Hispanic" but in reality few think of themselves (or others) as Hispanic and most would prefer national descriptors. The diversity among Latin Americans is in some ways better compared to the diversity among various European immigrant groups in American cities in earlier historical times such as the Irish, Italians, English, or East European Jews. From Cubans to Peruvians or Dominicans, Miami's immigrants experience their new city and homeland through different cultural, economic, and political lenses and there is little to suggest that they are coalescing in some sort of Hispanic melting pot—despite common or similar languages. For examples from the literature using the ethnic-

racial triad, see A. Portes and A. Stepick, *City on the Edge: The Transformation of Miami* (Berkeley: University of California Press, 1993); M. C. Garcia, *Havana USA: Cuban Exiles and Cuban Americans in South Florida, 1959–1994* (Berkeley: University of California Press, 1996); S. L. Croucher, *Imagining Miami: Ethnic Politics in a Postmodern World* (Charlottesville: University Press of Virginia, 1997).

6. There is nothing self-evidently positive or negative about localness or mobility: "Place attachment may, on the one hand, imply roots, security, and sense of place, but it may also, on the other hand, represent imprisonment and narrow-mindedness. Similarly, mobility may signify freedom, opportunities, and new experiences as well as uprootedness and loss" (P. Gustafson, "Roots and Routes: Exploring the Relationship between Place Attachment and Mobility," *Environment and Behavior* 33 [2001]: 680). Also see Z. Bauman, *Globalization: The Human Consequences* (Cambridge: Polity Press, 1998); H. DeBlij, *The Power of Place* (New York: Oxford University Press, 2007).

7. The U.S. census does not recognize categories of locals, exiles, and mobiles so this number is an approximation. According to the census of 2000, only 28 percent of Greater Miami's population was born in Florida (the lowest percentage of residents born in-state of all major metropolitan areas in the nation).

8. For a classic argument about the correlation between spatial and social mobility, see W. Zelinsky, "The Hypothesis of the Mobility Transition," *Geographical Review* 61 (1971): the "increasing freedom of spatial movement is both cause and effect of other forms of enhanced mobility. On still another level, it is also true that the two dynamic processes, magnification of power and of mobility, though distinct at their cores, are also vigorously interactional, one feeding heartily on the other" (225). Zelinsky speaks of "mobility of the mind."

9. According to the census of 2000, "only" 14 percent of Miami's Hispanic families lived in poverty compared to 23 percent in New York. The percentage of Hispanic households in metropolitan Miami with incomes above $100,000 is greater than in any other metro in the United States. When Mike Davis wrote his *Magical Urbanism: Latinos Reinvent the US City* (London: Verso, 2000) on the role of Hispanic working classes in America's cities, Miami was conspicuously absent from that book—it would not have made a good fit.

10. The notion of cosmopolitanism has been part of the social science vocabulary for a long time and has received renewed attention in debates on globalization. It needs to be mentioned here because it tends to be closely associated with questions of identity: "cosmopolitans" are often distinguished from "locals" and "exiles." But cosmopolitanism is best understood as a *mind-set* and it does not necessarily correlate with spatial mobility or the lack thereof. For more elaborate theoretical arguments, see, for example, F. Meinecke, *Weltbürgertum und Nationalstaat* (Munich: Oldenbourg, 1907); R. K. Merton, *Social Theory and Social Structure: Toward the Codification of Theory and Research* (Glencoe, Ill.: Free Press, 1949); C. Breckenridge et al., eds., *Cosmopolitanism* (Durham, N.C.: Duke University Press, 2002); U. Hannerz, "Cosmopolitans and Locals in World Culture," *Theory, Culture, and Society* 7 (1990): 237–51; J. Nijman, "Locals, Exiles, and Cosmopolitans: A Theoretical Argument about Identity and Place in Miami," *TESG* 98 (2007): 167–78; K. A. Appiah, *Cosmopolitanism: Ethics in a World of Strangers* (New York: W. W. Norton, 2006).

11. In order to allow for more detail on the map shown, it is cut off just below S.W. 152nd Street. It should be noted that there are some interesting areas further south, including concentrations of locals in Florida City and of exiles around Homestead (mainly poor migrant workers who are agriculturally employed).

12. In 2008, the foreign-born population of Miami-Dade was 51 percent compared to 31 percent in Broward. The proportion of Hispanics in Miami-Dade and Broward was, respectively, 63 percent and 24 percent. Of course, not all people who are foreign born are exiles, nor are all Hispanics. Even among traditional exile communities such as Cubans, the exile mind-set is not shared by everyone. Finally, there are non-Hispanic groups such as Haitians who are here considered as exiles.

13. See the official Miccosukee website: www.miccosukee.com/tribe_reservations .htm#.

14. Buffalo Tiger and Harry A. Kersey Jr., *Buffalo Tiger: A Life in the Everglades* (Lincoln: University of Nebraska Press, 2002).

15. Interview with Buffalo Tiger on May 3, 1984, Department of History, University of Florida (http://ufdcweb1.uflib.ufl.edu/ufdc/UFDC.aspx?a=oral&n=ufspoh p& ts=%22buffalo+tiger%22&b=UF00008050&v=00001).

16. See the official website: www.miccosukee.com/tribe.htm.

17. In recent times, the exodus of middle-class African Americans from the area's poor neighborhoods has only increased. See "Study: Blacks Fleeing Miami," *Miami Herald*, July 28, 2007.

18. See the Overtown Collaborative: www.floridacdc.org/members/overtown/expressway.htm.

19. Umoja is the Swahili word for unity. The Umoja Village was organized on a parcel of public land by a group of activists under the banner Take Back the Land in response to persistent failures by the City of Miami to provide affordable housing to low-income groups. The squatter settlement was partially destroyed by a fire and the city intervened on grounds of public safety.

20. A. M. Parks, "History of West Coconut Grove in the Context of Miami," in S. Quraeshi et al., *The Living Traditions of Coconut Grove* (Coral Gables: University of Miami School of Architecture and INUSE, 2002), 40.

21. S. Quraeshi, "The Spirit of Place," in S. Quraeshi et al., *The Living Traditions of Coconut Grove*, 17.

22. The tract with the lowest median household income in the two-county area in the census of 2000 was in Liberty City ($10,017), followed by the second lowest in Overtown ($11,402). Overtown also recorded some of the highest male unemployment at 21 percent. Some parts of Liberty City have a staggering 65 percent of households living below the official poverty line; Overtown comes in around 60 percent.

23. Police Chief John Timoney in an interview on the *CBS Evening News*, July 24, 2007.

24. According to the census of 2000, local tracts had more than one-and-a-half times the number of veterans as mobile tracts and four times as many veterans as exile tracts.

25. Twenty-three percent of exile households live below the poverty line. Median household income in 2000 was $25,000; per capita income was $11,850. Greater Miami is different from other metropolitan areas in the nation in terms of the relative position of Hispanic immigrants and native blacks (for a more elaborate discussion, see J. Nijman, "Ethnicity, Class, and the Economic Internationalization of Miami," in J. O'Loughlin and J. Friedrichs, eds., *Social Polariza-*

tion in Post-Industrial Metropolises [Berlin and Chicago: Gruyter-Aldine 1996], 283–300). For example, in Miami more blacks than Hispanics live in poverty while the opposite is true in Los Angeles and New York. Similarly, in Miami there are relatively more Hispanics than blacks with incomes over $100,000 while it is the reverse for Los Angeles and New York. Contrary to Los Angeles and New York, Miami's Hispanics hold more professional and managerial jobs than do blacks and are more employed in internationally oriented producer services than are blacks. New York and Los Angeles have had African American mayors while Miami has not—in Miami (city and county) it has become virtually imperative to be Cuban American to reach that office. Even if blacks have made real gains in the public arena since the late 1960s, those gains have been overshadowed by the social mobility of Hispanic immigrants. In all, it appears that Miami's African Americans have found themselves on the sidelines of Miami's transformation, unable to take part in the internationalization of Miami's economy.

26. "Rise of Chavez Sends Venezuelans to Florida," *New York Times*, January 23, 2008; "Venezuelan Activists Keep Up Long-Distance Battle," *Miami Herald*, February 14, 2009.

27. The plans for the Bay of Pigs invasion started under President Eisenhower and were handed down to President Kennedy, who failed to bring it to a successful end. Cuban American rebels landed in the Bay of Pigs but did not get the expected air support and were easily defeated by Castro's military force. Among Cuban Americans, the "betrayal" by the Kennedy administration led to a major shift of political support to the Republican Party. All fifteen hundred troops involved in the landing were exiled Cubans while the operation was largely paid for by the CIA. Three hundred men died. The twelve hundred survivors spent almost two years in jails in Cuba and were eventually released in return for U.S. donations of foods and goods to Cuba. They were welcomed back as heroes in Miami.

28. "The Big Uproar over Little Havana," *New York Times*, October 23, 1990.

29. G. J. Grenier and L. Perez, *The Legacy of Exile: Cubans in the United States* (Boston: Allyn and Bacon, 2003), 96.

30. Elián González was the young boy who lost his mother at sea while fleeing Cuba in November 1999. A heated dispute arose between the boy's Cuban American

family in Miami and his father in Cuba. The affair ignited a passionate response from Miami's Cuban community. In April 2000, U.S. federal authorities determined that the boy had to return to Cuba because of his father's legal claims. The FBI seized the boy from the family's house in Little Havana and subsequently returned him to Cuba. The family's house was subsequently turned into the Elián González Museum.

31. Hialeah was listed by *Forbes* as one of "America's Ten Most Boring Cities": "Hialeah among 'Most Boring Cities' on Forbes List," *Miami Herald*, January 13, 2009.

32. M. De La Torre, *La Lucha for Cuba: Religion and Politics on the Streets of Miami* (Berkeley: University of California Press, 2003), xviii.

33. Grenier and Perez, *The Legacy of Exile*, 119.

34. D. Rieff, *The Exile: Cuba in the Heart of Miami* (New York: Simon and Schuster, 1993), 27.

35. Grenier and Perez, *The Legacy of Exile*, 87. Also see D. Rieff, "Will Little Havana Go Blue?" *New York Times Magazine*, July 13, 2008.

36. "Park and Politics," *New Times* (Miami), May 10, 2007 (www.miaminewtimes .com/2007–05–10/news/park-and-politics/print).

37. De La Torre, *La Lucha for Cuba: Religion and Politics on the Streets of Miami*, 141.

38. Quoted from the film *Calle Ocho: Cuban Exiles Look at Themselves (directed by Miguel González-Pando, produced by WTVJ-Miami and Florida International University's Living History Project, 1994).*

39. A. Menendez, "Exiles' Pain Must Include Room for Dissent," *Miami Herald*, May 27, 2007.

40. Grenier and Perez, *The Legacy of Exile*, 117–18.

41. Ibid., 72.

42. R. Steinback, "Ethnic Groups Talk in Post-Elian Year," *Miami Herald*, March 11, 2001.

43. According to figures from the Migration Policy Institute, the U.S. Coast Guard interdicted between one thousand and three thousand Haitians per year in the past decade (www.migrationinformation.org/USFocus/display.cfm?ID = 214).

44. This explains why Little Havana and North Miami do not stand out as areas with the highest concentrations of exiles. Haitian exiles do not generally identify with

African Americans in the United States, despite common racial ancestry. In Haiti and other Caribbean societies, the construction of racial categories tends to be much more complex than in the United States. Race and color are "not constructed into mutually exclusive bipolar categories of black/white. Rather there is a continuum, conceptualized as a gradation along the lines of color" (C. Charles, "Transnationalism in the Construct of Haitian Migrants' Racial Categories of Identity in New York City," in N. Glick Schiller et al., eds., *Towards a Transnational Perspective on Migration: Race, Class, Ethnicity, and Nationalism Reconsidered* [New York: New York Academy of Sciences, 1992], 107).

45. As is the case with Cubans, not all can be considered exiles. Some, especially in the second generation, have gone local. There are also those who left Haiti not so much out of despair but to protect what they already had—they were better off to begin with—and there are those who have been able to work their ways up the economic ladder since they arrived in Miami. These Haitians are much more mobile and have considerably more choice about their places of residence. They are not exiles (anymore) and instead have often assumed transnational identities. They travel frequently between Miami and Haiti, they often run their own businesses, and they own property in different places.

46. Charles, "Transnationalism," 112 passim.

47. Ibid., 114–15.

48. N. L. Glick Schiller, L. Basch, and C. Szanton Blanc, "From Immigrant to Transmigrant: Theorizing Transnational Migration," *Anthropological Quarterly* 68/1 (1995): 48–64.

49. U.S. Department of Labor, National Agricultural Workers Surveys (www.florida legal.org/facts.htm).

50. The precarious working and living conditions of the migrant workers are unknown to many people in South Florida, but over the years they have provoked a growing number of activist, grass-roots, and volunteering agencies such as Centro Campesino, the Project Esperanza, the Miami Workers Center, and a range of church organizations.

51. According to the Dade County Department of Public Health, it was the first typhoid epidemic in the United States since 1939, with 210 recorded cases but no deaths (www.ajph.org/cgi/reprint/65/11/1184.pdf).

52. See the web site of the Miami-Dade Health Department: www.dadehealth.org/ enviro/ENVIROtrailer.asp.

53. See, for example, a presentation by the Society for St. Vincent of Paul, October 15, 2006: www.voiceofthepoor.org/Presentations/MIGRANT%20FARM%20WORK ERS.pdf.

54. "Mount Sinai Expects Operating Losses to Double," *Miami Herald*, December 4, 2008.

55. I. Sheskin, "Jewish Demographics in The Beaches," *Report for the Miami Beach Jewish Community Center*, 2001.

56. "Miami Beach Elects First Cuban Woman Mayor," *Miami Herald*, November 21, 2007.

57. I. Sheskin, "The Jews of South Florida," in T. D. Boswell, ed., *South Florida: The Winds of Change* (Coral Gables, Fla.: University of Miami, 1991), 174.

58. This includes single-unit residential properties (single family, condos, co-ops, townhouses) but not multi-family rental properties (duplexes, small apartment buildings, large apartment complexes, hotels, and so forth). A slight underesti- mation of primary residence may be owing to the fact that people are eligible but do not apply because they are not aware of the exemption. At the same time, the numbers could slightly overestimate primary residence owing to illegal claims. Data were provided by the Miami-Dade County Office of the Property Appraiser, July 12, 2007.

59. In 2007, Broward County had 369,922 single family homes, of which 295,594 had exemptions; 258,887 condos, of which 125,571 had exemptions. Data pro- vided by the Broward County Property Appraiser's Office, July 18, 2007.

60. "An Island of Moguls Is Latest Front in Union Battle," *New York Times*, February 1, 2007.

Chapter 8

1. Broward County, Office of Urban Planning and Redevelopment, "The Southeast Florida MSA," *Broward-by-the-Numbers* 20 (March 2004).

2. Broward County, Office of Urban Planning and Redevelopment, "Domestic Migra- tion Patterns," *Broward-by-the-Numbers* 27 (October 2004).

3. For many years apparel has been Miami's leading import, most of it coming from

the Caribbean. Fabrics are imported in Miami and cut according to design, then exported back to the Caribbean for finishing, with the bulk re-imported into the United States.

4. See "The Road to Change," *South Florida CEO*, June 2004. In the 1990s, the number of Broward County residents commuting daily to Miami-Dade climbed from 77,000 to 115,000, while the number of Miami-Dade residents commuting the other way increased from 31,500 to 60,000. At the same time, Broward commuters to Palm Beach County grew from 32,000 to 52,500, and in the other direction from 25,500 to almost 38,000.

5. See R. E. Lang, *Beyond Edge City: Office Sprawl in South Florida* (Washington, D.C.: Brookings Institution, 2003). Based on the percentage of office space in a traditional downtown versus in an edgeless city, this study classifies thirteen top metropolitan office markets as "core dominated" (New York, Chicago), "balanced" (Boston, Washington, D.C., Denver, Los Angeles, and San Francisco), "dispersed" (Dallas, Houston, Atlanta, and Detroit), or "edgeless" (Philadelphia and, especially, Miami).

6. But FLIA has a considerably smaller share of international passengers than MIA. "Expansion Critical, FAA Tells Broward," *Miami Herald*, May 16, 2007.

7. "Port Everglades' Profit Soars," *Miami Herald*, December 15, 2007; "Port Everglades: Steaming Ahead," *Miami Herald*, February 4, 2008.

8. U.S. census figures for Broward in 2000 were Jamaicans 72,000; Haitians 62,000; Puerto Ricans 55,000; Cubans 51,000; and Colombians 30,000.

9. D. Barry, "Face Off," *Miami Herald*, August 2, 1998 (www.davebarry.com/misc-col/browarddadecoverstory.htm).

10. In southern Miami-Dade County, the Urban Development Boundary curls east and then north, abutting Biscayne National Park.

11. On July 13, 2007, a federal judge in Miami halted the activities of three large mining companies because of concerns over chemical and bacterial contamination of the well field ("U.S. Judge: Halt Rock Mining to Protect Water," *Miami Herald*, July 13, 2007).

12. "Developers Line Up Again to Test Boundary in Dade," *Miami Herald*, November 27, 2007; "Contentious Lowe's Development a Step Closer," *Miami Herald*, No-

vember 28, 2007; "Miami-Dade Commission OK's Westward Expansion," *Miami Herald*, May 7, 2008; "UDB Upheld," *Miami Herald*, July 31, 2009.

13. Committee on Independent Scientific Review of Everglades Restoration Progress, National Research Council, *Progress toward Restoring the Everglades: The Second Biennial Review, 2008* (New York: National Academies Press, 2008). For an elaborate discussion of the state of the Everglades and the restoration plan, see W. Hodding Carter, *Stolen Water: Saving the Everglades from Its Friends, Foes, and Florida* (New York: Atria Books, 2004).

14. "Lake O Is So Full, It Must Be Drained," *Miami Herald*, August 28, 2008; "What Lake Okeechobee Roller-Coaster Levels Mean for You," *Miami Herald*, September 7, 2009.

15. "Water Chief Resigns," *Miami Herald*, January 28, 2006.

16. "Money, White House Pick, Revive Everglades Restoration Hopes," *Miami Herald*, February 26, 2009. For the Miccosukee position on the "Everglades Skyway," see www.miccosukee.com/tribe_environment.htm.

17. "The $15 Billion Restoration Plan Is Running Behind Schedule and Costs Are Escalating," *Miami Herald*, July 3, 2007; "Rising Costs Put Glades Project in Doubt," *Miami Herald*, November 22, 2007.

18. A fourth issue of growing concern is a rise in the sea level due to global warming—some forecast that parts of low-lying South Florida could be "under water" within the next half century. For an animation of the impact on Miami of a rise in the sea level of 0.6 meters, see www.net.org/globalwarming/sea_level/.

19. S. K. Smith and C. McCarty, "Demographic Effects of Natural Disasters: A Case-Study of Hurricane Andrew," *Demography* 33 (1996): 265–75.

20. This author included: he was forced to seek a new insurer twice in an eighteen-month period. South Florida has been at the forefront of an overhaul of the disaster insurance industry in which the buying and selling of risk of natural catastrophes (so-called "cat" bonds) has become a highly specialized and multi-billion dollar business. See "In Nature's Casino," *New York Times Magazine*, August 26, 2007.

21. C. Lynn and C. Penabad, *Marion Manley, Miami's First Woman Architect* (Athens: University of Georgia Press, 2010).

22. "Modern College: Miami's New Buildings Set New Campus Style," *Life* 25/26 (December 1948): 72–73; W. H. Nicholas, with photographs by J. Locke, "Miami's Expanding Horizons," *National Geographic* 98/5 (November 1950): 561–94.

23. N. Mailer, *Miami and the Siege of Chicago* (New York: World Press Company, 1968), 12.

24. H. Dick and P. Rimmer, "Privatising Climate: First World Cities in South East Asia," in J. Brotchie et al., eds., *East-West Perspectives on Twenty-First Century Urban Development* (Aldershot, U.K.: Ashgate, 1999), 322.

25. Mailer, *Miami and the Siege of Chicago.*.

26. This is defined as the share of households earning less than $15,000 or more than $200,000 per year (U.S. census of 2000).

27. Brookings Institution, *Miami in Focus, a Profile from Census 2000* (Washington, D.C., 2003).

28. The service sector comprises about 33 percent of employment in Greater Miami but renders only about 20 percent of economic output. Finance and real estate comprise about 9 percent of all jobs yet produce 20 percent of output. South Florida is extreme but the patterns hold across the entire state: in 2002 Florida ranked thirty-seventh of fifty in terms of median income, forty-first in terms of workers with health insurance, and fiftieth (last) in terms of workers with pensions. See R. Waldinger, "Conclusion: Immigration and the Remaking of Urban America," in R. Waldinger, ed., *Strangers at the Gates: New Immigrants in Urban America* (Berkeley: University of California Press, 2000), 308–30; B. Nissen, "*The State of Working Florida 2004*," A research report on the trends in employment, unemployment, wages, and other indices of worker welfare in the state of Florida (Miami: Center for Labor Research and Studies, Florida International University, September 2004) (www.risep-fiu.org/reports/STATE%20OF%20WOR KING%20FLORIDA.pdf).

29. D. Luymes, "The Fortification of Suburbia: Investigating the Rise of Enclave Communities," *Landscape and Urban Planning* 39 (1997): 187–203.

30. Greater Miami Chamber of Commerce, "Miami Vision for 2009," Report prepared for the Miami Downtown Development Authority, February 2009.

31. In the census tracts 27.01, 27.02, 37.01, 37.02, and 67.01, the percentages of

homeowners without homestead exemption in 2007 were 66 percent, 82 percent, 80 percent, 88 percent, and 69 percent respectively (data from the Miami-Dade County Office of the Property Appraiser, July 12, 2007). See Chapter 7 for a more general discussion.

32. Another factor is more basic still: full use of public space would demand razing Bayside Market Place, which occupies a large swath of central waterfront (all too often, shopping malls are construed as public space).

33. J. F. Lejeune, "City without Memory: Planning the Spectacle of Greater Miami," in A. Shulman, ed., *Miami Modern Metropolis: Paradise and Paradox in Midcentury Architecture and Planning* (Miami Beach: Bass Museum of Art and Balcony Press, 2009).

34. M. Hoover, "Before Disney Arrived: Florida's Ill-Fated Attempt to Build Interama," *Florida Historical Quarterly* (2008); R. A. Gonzalez, "The Fair City of Interama: Flash in the Pan or Unbuilt Utopia?" *Journal of Architectural Education* (2008): 27–40.

35. Lejeune, "City without Memory," 36.

36. In the mid-1970s, it was mainly investments from Venezuela ("Industry Outlook 2005—Residential Real Estate," *Florida Trend*, January 1, 2005). The 1980s witnessed the beginning of a trend in which many Latin American tourists in Miami turned into part-time residents. In the first two quarters of 1982, foreigners, mostly Latin Americans, accounted for 80 percent of purchases of luxury condominiums in the Miami area (A. P. Maingot, "Laundering the Gains of the Drug Trade: Miami and Caribbean Tax Havens," *Journal of Interamerican Studies and World Affairs* 30 [1988]: 176).

37. "A Billion Dollars, Three Years Running," *World City Business*, December 21, 1999.

38. "South Florida Condos Hot in Latin Capitals," *Miami Herald*, April 11, 2004; "Visas Drawing Foreign Investors to Florida," *Miami Herald*, August 11, 2009.

39. "Condo Boom Worries Wall Street," *Miami Herald*, March 11, 2005.

40. Miami Downtown Development Authority, "Residential Closings and Occupancy Status," June 2009.

41. "Students without a Home," *Miami Herald*, February 13, 2009; "In South Florida,

Most Boom-Era Home Buyers Are Under Water," *Miami Herald*, May 6, 2009; "1 in 5 Home Loans in Florida Delinquent," *Miami Herald*, March 6, 2009.

42. Miami-Dade County Property Appraiser, "2009 Preliminary Roll Confirms Significant Decline in Values," press release, July 1, 2009.

43. Le Corbusier, *Sketchbooks* (1950–54) (New York and Cambridge, Mass.: Architectural Foundation/MIT Press, 1981), 2: D16, 217, quoted in Lejeune, "City without Memory."

44. R. Sennett, "The Public Realm," *Quant* (2009) (www.richardsennett.com).

45. For example, the new codes would impose height restrictions in some places, not allow out-of-scale building or big-box stores, and require active ground use. See www.miami21.org; "Miami Revives Major Plan to Reshape City," *Miami Herald*, September 5, 2009.

Chapter 9

1. Information provided to the author by a Miami real estate insider, January 2010.

2. Carl Hiaasen, "On the Beach," *New York Times Book Review*, February 22, 2009. Also see S. Gaines, *Fool's Paradise: Players, Posers, and the Culture of Excess* (New York: Crown Publishers, 2009).

3. This is not to say that any other city in the United States is likely to turn into a metropolis with a majority of Hispanic immigrants and a highly globalized economy any time soon. The idea of an "emblematic" or "paradigmatic" city is about general directions of change across the urban system, rather than about idiosyncratic local outcomes. Many cities in the United States are likely to be affected fundamentally by trends that are found in extreme form in present-day Miami. For example, on the matter of social fragmentation and segregation, see Bill Bishop, *The Big Sort: Why the Clustering of Like-Minded America Is Tearing Us Apart* (New York: Houghton Mifflin Company, 2008).

4. For example: R. E. Park, E. Burgess, and R. McKenzie, *The City* (Chicago: University of Chicago Press, 1925).

5. E. Soja, *Postmodern Geographies: The Reassertion of Space in Critical Social Theory* (London: Verso, 1989), 191.

6. For example, Soja, *Postmodern Geographies*; M. Davis, *City of Quartz: Excavating the Future of Los Angeles* (London: Verso, 1990); M. Dear and S. Flusty, "Post-

modern Urbanism," *Annals of the AAG* 88 (1998): 50–72; J. Garreau, *Edge City: Life on the New Frontier* (New York: Doubleday, 1991); M. Cenzatti, *Los Angeles and the L.A. School: Postmodernism and Urban Studies* (Los Angeles: Los Angeles Forum for Architecture and Urban Design, 1993); G. Dymski and J. Veitch, "Financing the Future in Los Angeles: From Depression to 21st Century," in M. J. Dear, H. E. Schockman, and G. Hise, eds., *Rethinking Los Angeles* (Thousand Oaks, Calif.: Sage, 1996), 35–55; A. J. Scott and E. Soja, eds., *The City: Los Angeles and Urban Theory at the End of the Twentieth Century* (Berkeley: University of California Press, 1996).

7. For example, while Los Angeles exhibits the struggling remnants of unionized labor, this is for all practical purposes absent in Miami. The literature is not always very accurate when using the term "post-industrial." Often, and confusingly so, the term is used to refer to a past history of industrialization. What is really meant is *ex*-industrial, not *post*-industrial.

8. R. Weinstein, "The First American City," in Scott and Soja, *The City*, 22.

9. Quoted in H. Muir, *Miami, USA*, expanded ed. (Gainesville: University Press of Florida, 2000), 300. Mitchell (Mickey) Wolfson, of the Wolfsonian Museum on Miami Beach, contributed a splendid and rare cultural institution to South Florida. He is often identified as a South Florida "native," but he spent most of his youth in northeastern boarding schools and universities. During the past four decades he has been maintaining a residence in Italy.

10. Zogby International Poll, June 2007. See "South Floridians Uneasy Over Living Costs," *Miami Herald*, June 10, 2007.

11. G. J. Grenier and L. Perez, *The Legacy of Exile: Cubans in the United States* (Boston: Allyn and Bacon, 2003), 120.

12. According to a report from the University of Miami's Institute for Cuban and Cuban-American Studies (ICCAS), Cuban flight to Miami continued and even accelerated in the past decade. In 2006 and 2007, 77,000 Cubans entered Miami, record numbers since the early 1970s. Most of these refugees were said to be motivated primarily by the lack of economic opportunities in Cuba. Also see "The Top 10 Stories You Missed in 2007," *Foreign Policy* (2008) (www.foreignpolicy.com/top10-2007/index5.html).

13. "Is Florida Over?" *Wall Street Journal*, September 29, 2007; "The Sunset State,"

Time, July 10, 2008; "On the Mat, Florida Wonders Which Side Is Up," *New York Times*, August 16, 2009.

14. Population growth for the state had gone down from 1.8 percent in 2006 to 1.1 percent in 2007. It was estimated that the state would lose about fifty thousand residents in the year ending April 2009. See "Population Slide Seen for S. Fla.," *Miami Herald*, March 24, 2009; "Florida Is Losing Some of Its Luster," *Miami Herald*, January 7, 2008.

15. In the spring of 2010, there were signs that the real estate market had bottomed out and that a slow recovery was underway. Occupancy rates in the new high rises had gone up in one year from 62 to 70 percent—still low, but at least things were moving. Once again, demand from abroad played a significant part: an estimated 30 percent of all real estate buyers in the preceding year were said to be from abroad, mainly Latin America and Europe ("South Florida Home, Condo Sales Crawl Upward." *Miami Herald*, March 24, 2010).

16. L. Wirth, "Urbanism as a Way of Life: The City and Contemporary Civilization," *American Journal of Sociology* 44 (1938): 1–24.

17. J. Kotkin, "Why the 'Liveable Cities' Rankings Are Wrong," *Forbes*, August 11, 2009.

18. Y. Tuan, *Cosmos and Hearth: A Cosmopolite's View* (Minneapolis: University of Minnesota Press, 1996).

19. Ibid., 177.

INDEX

Page numbers in italics indicate figures.

public schools, Miami-Dade, 130, 131

public transportation, 175, 191

Putnam, Robert, 123, 136, 238n16

Putney, Michael, 125

Quinon, Jose, 130–31

railway, Flagler's, 11–12

Reagan, Ronald, 150

real estate sector: and Everglades drainage projects, 21; and drug-trafficking, 87; foreign investment in, 195–96, 253n36; and housing crisis, 209–10, 256n15; volatility, 195–97

Redlands Labor Camp, 163

Reed, Robert Law, 189

refugee influxes: first wave of Cuban refugees, 46–49, 97–98; Haitian boat people (1980), 58–61, 60; Haitian economic refugees, 60–61, 159–60; Mariel boatlift and Cuban asylum seekers, 54–56, 55, 61, 67, 227n17; and Miami-Hong Kong comparison, 99–100; Nicaraguan, 65, 67; Venezuelan, 119, 150

Republican National Convention and race riots (August 1968), 54

Republic National Bank, 76, 78, 83

retailing, 72–73

Rieff, David, 155–56

Rockefeller, John D., 11, 12

Roosevelt, Franklin D., 17, 222n8

Roosevelt, Theodore, 150

Royal Palm Hotel, 12, 13, 14, 29, 34

San Francisco, 121

Sassen, Saskia, 232n54, 232–33n1

Sastre, Aristides, 83

Scarface (film), 63

Second Seminole War (1835–42), 6, 19

Seminole Indians, 6–7, 38

Seminole Wars, 6–9, 19

Sennett, Richard, 199

Sewell, John, 16–17

Singapore Hotel, 42

Smith, Jim, 239–40n34

"snowbirds," 28, 41, 141, 207

social capital: and "durable networks," 123, 237n13; and enclaves, 124; and immigrant groups, 128–30; and socioeconomic inequality, 124; and transience, 123–25, 128–29, 136, 237n14, 238n17

Somoza, Anastasio, 65

Sonesta Hotel, 117

Sonnabend, Roger, 117

South Beach: deco district, 35, 40, 50, 64, 166–67, 167; in the 1950s, 40–41; in the 1960s, 50; in the 1980s, 64; revitalization, 166; upper-income mobile population, 166–68. See also Miami Beach

South Dade Labor Camp, 163

Southeast Bank, 83

South Florida Business Journal, 102, 119–20, 236–37n8

South Florida CEO, 119

South Florida Drug Task Force, 84

South Florida Ecosystem Restoration Task Force, 181

South Florida Water Management District's Water Conservation Area 3A, 143, 181, 184

Spanish-American War, 18–19

Spanish Empire in Florida, 5–7

Spanish language: bilingualism, 102; and English-only campaigns, 61–62, 67, 70, 228n3; proficiency, 102, 104 spatial mobility and identities of place, 137–71, 243n6; and affluence, 164–66; and assimilation, 155–58, 160; Broward County, 141, *142*, 148–50, 164, *165*, 168, 244n12, 249n59; and cosmopolitanism, 244n10; Cuban exile community, 150–58, 207–9; exiles, 140, 150–61; and globalization, 138–39, 212; Haitian exile community, 61, 158–61, 247nn43–44, 248n45; and hybrid identities, 100–102, 138–39; locals, 139–40, 141–50; Miami-Dade County, 141, *142*, 145–48, 150, 161–66, *165*, 244n12; migrant farm workers, 161–64, 248n50; mobiles, 140–41, 161–70, *165*; and non-primary residences, 168–70, *169*, 193, 249nn58–59, 252–53n31; poor African American local neighborhoods, 51–54, 145–50; poverty rates and household incomes, 145, 146, 149, 162, 245n22, 245n25; spatial mobility and social mobility, 140, 243nn8–9; and traditional triad based on race and ethnicity, 242n5; and transience, 206–7, 237n14; U.S. Census tract data and Greater Miami residential neighborhoods, 141, *142*, *165*, 217–19, 243n7, 243n9; and world cities, 100–102, 139. *See also* transience and civil society

"spectator architecture," 199

Spillis Candela (architecture firm), 198

sports teams, 125, 156

Star Island, 192

St. Augustine, Florida, 4, 5

Stepick, A., 227n17

Stoneman, Frank, 222n12

Stover, Russell, 25

Suarez, Xavier, 152

Summit of the Organization of American States (2005), 177

Sunshine Bank, 83, 89

Sunshine State (film), 38

Sweeney, Paul, 104

Sweetwater, Florida, 150

Tamiami Trail, 37–38, *38*, 143–44, 184

Teele, Arthur, 131

Tequesta tribe, 1–3, 5, 18

Tides Hotel, 35

Time magazine, 45, 62, 91, 210

Timoney, John, 149

TNCs. *See* transnational corporations

Toro, Carlos, 84

"transcultural capitalism," 102

transience and civil society, 117–36, 206–7, 211–12; and bankruptcy crisis and mismanagement by city government, 125–27, 239n28; business leaders, 119–20, 236–37n8; civic culture and the arts, 124–25, 238n17; condominium living, 170; crime, 132–35, 240n38; culture of corruption, 126, 130–32, 239–40n34, 240n35, 241n48; and design of public spaces, 192–94, 195; and diversity, 211–12; domestic and foreign in-migration and domestic out-migration, 50–51, 119, *120*, 206–7; early twentieth-century railroad workers and soldiers, 18–19; and foreign-born immigrants, 118–19, 128–30; immigration versus transience, 119, 135; and Miami as hemispheric "world city," 206–7, 211–12; and Miami as "most stress-

ful" metropolitan area, 125; and Miami's "pioneers," 12, 17, 117; the
1920s, 34–35; political apathy,
127–28; political demonstrations
against foreign governments,
127–28; residents buried elsewhere,
118; snowbirds and winter visitors,
28, 41, 141, 207; and social capital,
123–25, 128–30, 136, 237n14,
238n17; South Beach residents, 166;
and spatial mobility, 206–7, 237n14;
Transience Index and variations
across metropolitan areas, 121–23,
122–23, 215–16. *See also* spatial mobility and identities of place
transnational corporations (TNCs), 90,
109, 115, *176*, 235n24
transportation, public, 175, 191
Treaty of Paris (1783), 5
Tropical Everglades Park Association, 39
Tuan, Yi-Fu, 212, 213
Tuttle, Julia, 9–11

Umoja Village, 147, 245n19
Unique Gems International, 129
University of Miami: architectural design, 186–90; hemispheric map of
Miami (1972), 72; and Merrick, 26,
187; and Miami's tarnished national
image, 227n27
urban design and planning, 173–99; architecture and public places, 186–95,
197–99; commuter patterns, 175,
250n4; downtown waterfront development plans, 193–94, 253n32; early
planning initiatives and visions,
194–95; ecological threats and environmental debate, 178–85, 251n18;

and economic and cultural disparities, 174–78; and economic decentralization, 177; the Everglades, 181–85;
fashion district, 175; international finance districts, 175; Miami21 plan for
downtown, 199, 254n45; and political
fragmentation, 174–75; and population growth, 174; public transportation, 175, 191; and real estate sector
volatility, 195–97; "resort-city" logic,
195; skyline and "spectator architecture," 198–99; social inequalities and
polarized income structure, 191–92;
spatial mobility and intraregional migration, 174, 177–78, 206–7; subtropical modernism, 187–89, 194;
University of Miami, 186–90; Urban
Development Boundary (UDB),
179–81; western expansion of the
urban region (1990–2000), *180*
Urban Development Boundary (UDB),
179–81
"urban growth machine" thesis, 69–70,
74, 229n13
urbanization: nineteenth-century, 9;
twentieth-century, 20, 202
U.S. Department of Agriculture, 163
U.S. Edge Act (1919), 80
U.S. Immigration and Customs Enforcement (ICE), 134
U.S. Post Office building, 35

Vanderbilts, 12, 170
Venetian Causeway, 21, *26*
Venetian Pool (Coral Gables), 26
Venezuela: flows of private capital to
Miami banks, 98; immigrants to
Miami, 119, 150; investment in Miami